Sportswriters' Choice

edited by
Richard P. Goldman

SPORTSWRITERS'
CHOICE

Their Best Stories
...as Selected by
the Authors

A. S. Barnes and Company   •   New York

Printed in the United States of America
American Book–Stratford Press, Inc., New York

Foreword

One day at prep school my sophomore English teacher, a man whom I greatly admired, strode into class, held up a column by Red Smith and said, "This, gentlemen, is English." I can remember being enormously pleased by that remark. The teacher had said what I secretly believed but hadn't wanted to say out loud in that academic atmosphere; my judgment was supported by authority, my opinion backed up by critical insight.

Today I feel more strongly than ever that the Hotchkiss instructor was right. Red Smith and the other top-drawer sportswriters—Jimmy Cannon, John Lardner, W. C. Heinz, to name three—regularly turn out some of the finest nonfiction prose to be published each year. That this fine prose accounts for a very small percentage of the millions of words written on sport every year is unfortunately true. This book is not an attempt to defend American sportswriting as a whole, but to present the American sportswriter at his best.

Actually the term *sportswriter* encompasses three different kinds of writer: the reporter, the columnist and the magazine staff and free-lance writer.

The sports reporter seldom has the opportunity to compose finished prose, for he faces two major problems. He frequently must rattle out a story and turn it in paragraph by paragraph to meet a deadline, and he must describe today a ball game or race or fight that often is not appreciably different from the game or race he described yesterday or the fight he wrote about last week. Because of the limitations of his job and often of his talent, the sports reporter rarely is able to produce the fresh word or trenchant phrase that might make his stories come alive.

The sports columnist is a former reporter who, because of his writing skill, has graduated to the more lucrative job of columning. He writes on the average a thousand words a day, five or six days a week, or somewhere between two hundred fifty and three hundred thousand words a year. In the case of the best of the columnists, a surprisingly high percentage of this is good prose. The columnist is not restricted to the who-what-where-when-why pattern, nor is he handicapped by the reporter's extreme limitations of time and subject matter. His field is the entire sports world; his major requirement is to be consistently interesting. Sometimes he is the best writer in the newspaper, and often he is the most widely read.

The writer working on a sports magazine piece has more time to polish his story and more space to develop a story in depth. Consequently, as the contents of this anthology suggest, much of the best sportswriting appears in magazines. These publications cover a wide range; from *The New Yorker*, for example, to *Man's Day*; from *Harper's* to *Sport*.

The contributors to this book are, with a few exceptions, columnists, former columnists (who no longer write on sport), and magazine staff and free-lance writers, for, as I have indicated, this anthology is not concerned with events and personalities so much as it is with good writing. I have asked the men I considered to be the best sports*writers* to select their own favorite work.

The most striking aspect of the book is the variety of types of writing represented. You will find here several examples of excellent straight reporting, a historical essay, a poem, biography, several analytical articles, a piece that could be termed fact-fiction, some exposé stories, humor, anger, nostalgia, whimsey, sorrow, bitterness. They are all part of the broad field of sportswriting.

In a few cases a writer begged off selecting a favorite piece, saying he was unable to make a choice, and in those instances I have selected an article which I thought representative of his work. In each case this is printed with the author's consent. Often a writer was kind enough to send me a few words pertaining to his story—why he selected it, how he happened to write it, the background of the story or something of that nature—and I have used these explanations, when received, as introductory notes to the articles.

I want to express my sincere appreciation to the writers represented in this book, who graciously contributed articles, even though—and this is true in every case—they had never met me personally. I am indebted also, more than I can say, to Reid Johnson, whose help and advice during the time this book was assembled proved invaluable. I hope I have been able to repay him by introducing him to a body of writing with which he was not previously familiar, the incisive, imaginative writing that is turned out by the best of America's sportswriters.

RICHARD P. GOLDMAN

Contents

Sportswriters' Choice

The Sportswriter

This article first appeared in the Washington *Post and Times Herald,* August 13, 1957, and is reprinted by permission of that newspaper.

At the time I wrote "The Sportswriter," I liked the idea myself—and this isn't conceit because every writer puts out material which he himself dislikes when it comes up in print. I guess I was thinking of Bobby Burns' phrase: "I wish I had the gift to give you, to see yourself as others see you." I was just trying to make a composite picture of a sportswriter (including myself) with all his foibles and his eternally juvenile heart.

I guess the reason I selected this piece was because I was overwhelmed by the response. People seldom write to pat you on the back. They generally write when they're angry at something you said. But first of all "The Sportswriter" was printed in the Congressional Record and then followed requests from colleges, high schools and other publications. I figured if this were something the public liked, you'd like it too. After all, the public is the best judge.

I was surprised to see my own judgment vindicated. It seldom is. Columns I think are great never cause a ripple. This isn't great by any means—this sportswriter's column. Whatever it had, it hit home.

BOB ADDIE

He affects sports shirts, sports jackets, sports overcoats, and sports shoes. He would like to affect a sports car, but he can only afford the sports cap. But, as you can see, he is a sport all the way.

He usually has had very little sports experience on the playing field. In high school and college, he was the official scorer, the waterboy, the equipment man, the team manager. When anyone asks him if he played college football, he says: "I was too light."

He's a frustrated foreign correspondent (who is a frustrated sportswriter). He would like to wear a trenchcoat, smoke a pipe, wear a fuzzy hat with a feather in it, speak nine foreign languages, and escort mysterious Swedish beauties out of the country a step ahead of the Russian spy ring which is trying to steal the secret on how to wear seersucker suits without wrinkling the cloth.

He's also a political seer and thinks he never misses picking a presidential race. After all, he figures, he picks sixteen teams in the major leagues in baseball and then picks the No. One football team in the country out of hundreds of aspirants; so how hard can it be to pick between two candidates?

He can never leave his work because people won't let him. After all, he's in sports and sports to most people are recreation and relaxation. People like to relax talking about sports.

If he marries—and he usually does to pick up a reader—his wife generally knows nothing about sports and couldn't care less. If he has any kids they must be in the mold of the champions he has admired.

If people look down their nose at his occupation, the sportswriter is quick to remind you that some of our most respected pundits were once sportswriters—people like Westbrook Pegler, Paul Gallico, the late Heywood Broun, Scotty Reston, Drew Middleton, Eddy Gilmore, George Dixon, and

Winston Churchill. (Churchill covered cricket during the Boer War.)

He's proud of his profession and points to such giants in his business as the late Damon Runyon, the late Ring Lardner, the late W. O. McGeehan, the late Grantland Rice, and the late O. B. Keeler. The reason he admires all the late sportswriters is that our hero will never admit anyone alive is better than he is. But still he's proud of his integrity and points to the famous line of W. O. McGeehan, who was once offered a sum of money for a story. "If it's a bribe, it's not enough," W. O. said. "If it's a gift, it's too much."

He always brings up the story of John Kieran, the erudite, onetime sportswriter of the New York *Times*. John was asked to speak at Yale but some students objected to the compromise with intellectualism in allowing a sportswriter to address a group of old Eli's sons. So Kieran made his entire address in Latin.

He's proud, too, of the "characters" in his business—fellows who have become legends with their flights of whimsey. There was the old sportswriter, for instance, who was asked by a cub: "Is that the west where the sun is setting?" And the veteran replied: "If it isn't you have one helluva story, son." Then there were the two New York sportswriters in Texas covering the Giants spring training years ago. They got homesick while "tapping the tea" and decided to take a taxi all the way back to New York. As they got in the cab, one said: "You'd better get in first because I'm getting out on 34th Street."

He is, after all, a newspaperman so he's proud of his scoops. But the day he writes a story which beats everybody else, people will forget where they read about it.

He is quick to defend and slow to offend. He can count on the fingers of one hand the number of athletes who have ever thanked him for a story but if he had a dime for every guy who threatened him when he wrote a critical story, he'd be too rich to write sports.

He can pontificate on the strategy of a football coach who has something like one hundred intricate plays at his command and usually has them executed with the precision of a machine. But that doesn't awe the sportswriter, who figures all coaches are managing editors with their brains knocked out. (Or maybe it's the other way around.)

He lives in a beautiful world where it's always game time and yesterday's tragedies fade like the ripples on a lake. He's the eternal juvenile who would not change places with a king. He's Pagliacci, the Pied Piper, Walter Mitty, Peter Pan, and Jack Armstrong, the All-American Boy.

A Scholarship for Jackie

This article first appeared in *SPORT*, April 1957, and is reprinted by permission of that magazine.

All these years I've wanted to get on the inside of a college recruiting case, one involving a big catch. In this case I did it, walked a gumshoe beat from the college (North Carolina State) to the farmhouse of Jimmy Moreland, daddy of the boy, Jackie Moreland.

I think I got as accurate a picture of how a major recruitment comes off as I can possibly get. I got, I think, as much gratification out of the actual leg work on the story as I did the writing. I talked to coaches, girl friend, store keepers around his town of Minden, Louisiana, and sat in the family living room watching the tears of his distraught parents.

You may note one thing: that I never actually talked to the boy. I was sure that was one thing I should not do. As partial as I am to fine, young athletes, and as much admiration as I have for them, I'd have been moved to such a point that the perspective I'd already gained might have been destroyed.

I enjoyed the working-out of the story, I think, because it became the one recruitment about which I could talk with positive conviction and without having to depend on second-hand knowledge. And, too, because it convinced me it

17

*was a rare case, that most of the recruiting that goes on in
college is on an honest-to-God level.*

FURMAN BISHER

This is a story of athletic recruiting in college. The central
figure is a very tall boy named Jackie Moreland who lives on
a farm midway between Minden and Homer, in the northwest corner of Louisiana, and who plays basketball.

Jackie high-jumped 6 feet and broad-jumped 21 feet, 6
inches for the track team at Minden High, to which he com-
muted ten miles each day. He hit .319 for the local semi-pro
baseball team and played first base so skillfully that the Baltimore Orioles were prepared to offer him a forty-five-thou-
sand-dollar bonus to sign a professional contract.

He was more than just an accomplished athlete at Minden High, though. He was also a student who showed every
prospect of becoming a worthwhile citizen. He was president of the senior class of 1955 and president of the student
council, staff member on the school paper, class favorite,
"Mr. School Spirit" and salutatorian. He missed being vale-
dictorian of his graduating class by less than one point.

Jackie didn't play football but the coach of the team at
Minden, George Doherty, a big, spirited fellow with a plump
face and a love for boys, said he was the best statistician
he'd ever had. "He fitted into everything that went on at the
school," Doherty said. "If Jackie Moreland had a fault, I
didn't know it."

But most of all, Jackie was a basketball player. He was
six feet, seven inches tall, going on eight. For three years
running he made the all-state class A team at Minden, a
never-never sort of thing in high school. College people who
watched them both through critical eyes said that Jackie
had class that Bob Pettit never had until he became an All-
America at Louisiana State. Jackie was more than just big.

He had finesse. He had a mind that functioned clearly, no matter how raging the heat of battle. He was completely ambidextrous and seemed to have a thousand different shots. In three seasons he scored 1,965 points. When a recruiting storm broke around his head and forced his name into the sports headlines prematurely, one famous college coach was asked why one boy should stir up such a furor.

"Simply," the coach said, "because he is the greatest basketball prospect in the country today."

Jackie Moreland's little world was about as orderly and as brilliantly promising as it could be. His family life was simple, for the Morelands are plain rural folk whose social life centers around the church and to whom everything outside the unbordered trade area called the Ark-La-Tex is foreign.

That was how it was before December 7, 1955, the date on which senior high school athletes became eligible to sign college scholarship grants. That was when the storm broke, when Jackie's world became muddled and confused, when his dreams were washed out and when the ideals he had lived by at Minden High tarnished like a forty-nine-cent bracelet.

Jackie eventually enrolled at North Carolina State College in Raleigh, about one thousand miles from home. Everett Case, a driving Indianian devout in his dedication to the favorite sport of his native state, has built a southern basketball empire at State. It takes a steady stream of incoming talent to keep the empire thriving and Case ranges from the Rocky Mountains to the sidewalks of New York on his hunt for the finest of the breed.

The Moreland kid was a natural for Case's empire, but Jackie will never play for N.C. State. Last November the policy council of the National Collegiate Athletic Association returned State to the probation list from which it had been paroled only the year before. This time the sentence was for four years, the harshest penalty of its kind ever in-

flicted by the NCAA. The reason: State's conduct in its recruitment of Moreland.

At the same time, the NCAA refused to grant Texas A&M
a shortened probation sentence it already was serving for a
football indiscretion until it had been dealt with on a
Moreland charge. The Aggies, the NCAA said, had violated
some rules and regulations of recruitment in their headlong
pursuit of the young man from Minden.

A few weeks later, Commissioner Jim Weaver of the At-
lantic Coast Conference, of which N.C. State is a member,
declared Moreland ineligible at the school which had fought
a determined recruitment fight for him and won. Another
storm blew up. N.C. State, with Chancellor Carey H. Bostian as spokesman, rose up in righteous indignation. "It is
our belief," said Chancellor Bostian, "based on the evidence
known to us at this time, that State College is not guilty of
the violations as charged."

There is a clause in the athletic code of the Greater University of North Carolina, of which N.C. State is a member,
that any member of an athletic staff found guilty of willfully
violating recruiting regulations as set forth by the ACC shall
be dismissed from his job. This projected two members of
the State staff, assistant athletic director Willis Casey and
assistant basketball coach Vic Bubas, squarely onto the seat
of jeopardy, for they had been assigned to the Moreland
recruitment campaign.

For that matter, the whole basketball program at State
seemed in danger. Ten years ago, this program was nothing. Case had only just arrived from Frankfurt (Ind.) High
School, where he had been the scourge of the Hoosiers, and
State played its games in an antiquated gymnasium that
could seat only 3000. Now State plays in Reynolds Coliseum,
a palace that accommodates 12,500 fans in comfortable the-
atre-style seats. In late December an invitational tournament called the Dixie Classic is played in the Coliseum and

draws close to 60,000 spectators. Because of State's initiative, basketball has taken a death grip on the Tobacco
Belt. And State has taken a death grip on ACC basketball
trophies. In seven of the last eight seasons, some covering
the old Southern Conference, Case's men have won conference championships.

Ditch all this for one tall farm boy from Minden, Louisiana? What kind of a set of values is this? Is this the kind of
judgment that goes into college recruiting? Who says N.C.
State and Texas A&M are guilty of indiscretions? What
kind of evidence does it take to get put on ice for four years?

"I'll put it this way," said Walter Byers, executive director
of the NCAA, one of collegiate America's most unwanted positions. "We must have enough concrete evidence to convince a board of eighteen men from all parts of the country.
In other words, our decisions aren't based on hearsay."

The NCAA detective on the case was A. J. (Dutch) Berg-
strom, former athletic director at Bradley University. A mystery gumshoe artist turned up in Shreveport, thirty miles
from Minden, one day last September and announced that
he had been assigned to the case. He was an elderly man
who identified himself as Billy Alston of Atlanta, Georgia,
but who refused to identify his client. It was later learned
that he was working for the University of Kentucky. At any
rate private eye Alston's report fell into the hands of the
NCAA and Commissioner Weaver of the ACC. It dealt both
N.C. State and Texas A&M a critical blow. It said that
State had offered Moreland an unrestricted (five-year) scholarship, a seven-year medical scholarship for a girl friend
from Minden, plus a one hundred-dollar clothing allowance
for the girl twice a year, and one thousand dollars a year for
Jackie.

The report said that Texas A&M representatives had offered Moreland a four-year scholarship, a scholarship to a
friend of his choosing, a scholarship for his girl friend to a

college in Denton, Texas, four hundred dollars per month while in school, and a new car on acceptance and another car on graduation.

The girl friend, a poised eighteen-year-old of statuesque build who is now a freshman at Centenary College in Shreveport, confirmed in an interview with this writer that a party representing N.C. State's interest had offered her a seven-year medical scholarship to a school of her choice, preferably Duke University in Durham, North Carolina. There she could be closer to Jackie.

"There was a lot of talk in my presence about money," said the girl, Betty Claire Rhea, a star witness for the NCAA. "I haven't told everything yet."

Why didn't she accept the scholarship, since Moreland did go to N.C. State? Why not choose Duke rather than Centenary, a little Methodist school of some one thousand enrollment?

"If we had been married, or even engaged," Betty Claire said, "it would have been different. But too much can happen in four years at our age. I didn't want to be under any obligation."

Texas A&M did accept a boy named Joel Smith on scholarship. Joel and Jackie were close friends, farm neighbors and once teammates at little Harris High School, where Jackie played before transferring to Minden's golden frontier. The Southwest Conference ruled Smith considerably below basketball standards for that level, and after this investigation Jackie's friend transferred to Louisiana Tech in Ruston.

Thus, there was more than circumstantial evidence on which the NCAA could build its case. Betty Claire was a focal point of the preliminary investigation. Later, after Jackie had enrolled at State, he was called before Byers and Weaver in a Raleigh hotel, confronted with the evidence, and was said to have signed a statement confirming all offers. Back on the campus later, he denied making a confession.

Fate allowed State just one good look at the vast potential of this Moreland boy. In a practice game against the varsity, he scored thirty points. The next week he was declared ineligible and to pour salt into the wounds, the ACC fined State five thousand dollars, remissible if Moreland stayed in school on his athletic scholarship terms and completed his non-athletic education.

The tall farm boy from Minden stood at the crossroads again. He could stay at State and be the greatest intramural basketball player in the country, or he could transfer to another school and play the kind of game he loves. Whatever he did, there was nothing in it for N.C. State.

How did this all come about? How did N.C. State, Texas A&M and Moreland get themselves hopelessly involved in this thicket of recruitment? What came over Jackie Moreland between December, 1955, and December, 1956? Where was the boy in whom George Doherty had been unable to discover a fault?

Jackie apparently had entered the danger zone of recruitment with clear-eyed resolution. It began on December 7 with a visit from Jack Heldman, an assistant coach from Vanderbilt. Next in line at the farmhouse on Highway 43, almost before Heldman was out of sight, was Harry Lancaster, assistant to Adolph Rupp at Kentucky.

Here, now, with Lancaster there, Jackie fulfilled a boyhood dream. He signed a standard Southeastern Conference grant-in-aid with Kentucky. "He's always wanted to go to Kentucky since he was so big," said his father, Jimmie Moreland, holding his hand about four feet above the floor. "That was his ambition."

But the recruiters kept coming. The family guessed that representatives of forty-three schools hovered around their Jackie. His Minden coach, Cleve Strong, a passive man with

grey-tinged hair and ulcers, said it was more. "It got so
bad," Strong said, "that Mr. Williams (the principal) quit
letting them see Jackie at school."

Little Centenary, where basketball is the major sport,
made a good pitch for Jackie. Jimmie Moreland liked the
Centenary coach, a well-scrubbed, down-to-earth young
man named Harold Mooty. They fished together. They
found companionship in each other. Soon Jackie was saying
he would go to Centenary.

Around the square in Minden, where Centenary is not a
big favorite, cynics charged that the Shreveport school offered Jackie more money than anybody. A Centenary official quite frankly said: "We offered Jackie a good job in the
summer, a very good job. We offered him the prospect of a
good future when he was graduated. Somebody said that
we offered him $36,000. I suspect that in the long run it
would have meant a lot more to Jackie than that, should his
future have panned out the way it could. But Walter Byers
knows all this."

Texas A&M made its sweetest overtures in the spring.
Jackie had assured Centenary he would be there when the
roll was called, but added, "I just want to look around a little more." A Texas A&M alumnus flew him to the College
Station campus for some of this "looking around." By this
time, it seems, Jackie had picked up some pretty worldly
advice on the matter of how to be recruited. "The first thing
he said when he got off the plane," said A&M coach Ken
Loeffler, once the builder of national champions (with the
assistance of Tom Gola) at LaSalle College in Philadelphia," was, 'What's the offer?'

" 'What do you mean, son?' I asked him." Loeffler reported.

" 'You know,' he said. 'An automobile, or something like
that.'

"I knew right then we had hold of a 'hot' one. He was too

big for A&M. He had indicated an interest in petroleum engineering, though, and we thought we might get him on that."

When Moreland actually did sign a Southwest Conference letter-of-intent with A&M, Loeffler was one thousand miles away at a boys' camp in Wyoming. The Moreland pursuit, however, was being carried on by some active alumni in Shreveport, with the surprising assistance of Paul (Bear) Bryant, A&M athletic director and head football coach. Bryant and four A&M alumni of influence showed up one day last summer at the Moreland farm.

"Mr. Bryant seemed awful nice," said Mrs. Moreland, a hardy woman of stout structure and the mother of six other children besides Jackie. "He did most of the talking. He offered Jackie a scholarship. He said, 'If you want a car, your daddy will have to buy it for you, or your granddaddy.' "

The NCAA investigators, however, charged that A&M alumni in Shreveport had pursued Moreland with more financial ardor. One, a mining and gas company official named Harmon Egger, became so incensed at whispered stories involving him that he submitted to a lie detector test in self-defense. He had been in Bryant's party the day of the visit to the Moreland farm.

The summer passed with still no final, conclusive decision by Jackie. Kentucky, Centenary, and Texas A&M all had his word that he was coming to their campus. N.C. State moved in at the climactic moment, setting up on Jackie's actual day of decision an almost fantastic series of concentrated uncertainty, promises, fast changes, bewilderment and, finally, the last emotional scene of an addled farm boy basketball player staggering barefooted the last few feet into the arms of N.C. State.

Jackie awoke that day, August 31, 1955, packed and prepared to make a departure for N.C. State, whose basketball administration had moved in an impressive task force to make the catch. The register at the Washington-Youree Hotel in Shreveport shows that Willis Casey, the athletic director's assistant, Vic Bubas, the basketball assistant, Harry Stewart, director of the Wolfpack Club, an alumni booster organization, and Ron Shavlik, All-America center at State the previous season, and his wife had set up camp there for three days. Together with a man named Dwight Laughlin, an ordnance plant employee who lives across the Red River in Bossier City, and who is a relative of Casey's wife, a State crew had visited the Moreland home the day before. Jackie had promised that he would be ready to leave at three P.M. on the 31st.

First, though, he had to tell Betty Claire good-bye. According to the Moreland family, "she pitched a fit" when Jackie arrived in Minden that morning to say good-bye. Somehow Betty Claire swung him back to Centenary, and they drove off to Shreveport to give athletic director Buzz Delaney and Mooty the good news.

Here a blackout develops, but it seems that Jackie and Betty Claire stopped at the Washington-Youree for one final word with the State task force. Here also, it seems, some of the last desperate counter-offers took place, because it is known that Jackie left the hotel with eighty dollars which had been handed him by Laughlin to pay for his plane fare to Raleigh. It was this eighty dollars that finally brought the ACC house down on State.

The trail continued to Centenary, where Jackie happily announced that he had made his decision. He would play for the Gentlemen of Centenary. His picture was taken with members of the athletic department and was splashed across the sports section of the Shreveport *Times* the next day, with an appropriately exuberant story of announcement. *Times* editions began rolling with a headline reading: "Moreland to Become Gent."

By the next morning the line had been changed to read:

"Moreland to Become Gent?" For by that time he was on his way to Raleigh.

Throwing the eighty dollars on Delaney's desk and asking him to get it back to the proper owners, Moreland and the girl friend set out for Minden. Before he got out of Betty Claire's sight, another change took place. "Mr. (Shorty) Long met him before he got around the corner," Betty Claire says. Long was Kentucky's agent, not an alumnus, but a self-appointed recruiter set on corralling Jackie for the Wildcats.

A hot reception was waiting for Jackie when he reached the farm. The State group had made their three o'clock appointment and left empty-handed. Jimmie Moreland, driven to his wit's end by the bewildering change of pace, charged his tall son with these words: "Damnit, make up your mind right now and let's get this mess settled once and for all. What do you want to do?"

Jackie pondered. What he wanted to do was to go to Kentucky. He said so. His father told him to call Shorty Long and tell him to come get the body. The Minden line was busy.

"That's how close Kentucky came to getting him," Jimmie Moreland said.

Before Jackie could call again, the State troops rode in again. In a few minutes Jackie said he was going to State again, and he stalked out of the house, toward the guests' station wagon, without his shoes. Someone reminded him of his oversight. His trunks were placed in the station wagon and he was rushed to the airport at Monroe, Louisiana, not to be heard from by his family or the press for the next four days.

"It's a wonder he didn't have a nervous breakdown," his father said. "You don't know what all of us have been through the last year. It's been somebody on our doorsteps or on our telephone all the time. We just took to lying. We'd tell them Jack wasn't here. I never did think I'd want him playing for that coach Rupp at Kentucky, but now I'm sorry he didn't go on there, where he wanted to as a boy. That Mr. Lancaster was a nice fellow, and Mr. Bubas was, too. But I never saw a bunch of people who seemed to hate each other so much."

The Morelands are unpretentious people of plain, humble, rural Claiborne Parish stock. Jimmie Moreland, in his middle fifties, works as a gauger in the oil fields near Homer. There is steel in his grip, honesty in his eyes and the undisguised trace of the out-of-doors life in his ruddy face. Two married daughters and a son no longer live at home. Another son is at Louisiana Tech. Two more, twins Joe and Ed, are juniors on the Minden High basketball team.

The Morelands are accustomed to a life without complexities. It is true that they had had a preview of this particular kind of turbulence. When Jackie was transferred from little Harris High School and its student body of some sixty students, to Minden, the Louisiana High School Association declared him ineligible until a thorough investigation could be made, causing him to miss a few games as a sophomore.

"We left the farm and moved into town to make it all right for him," Jimmie Moreland said. He and Mrs. Moreland and a visiting daughter sat in the dimly lighted parlor of their home. They had just finished decorating a little pine Christmas tree on a table in the corner. Jackie would be home in a few days.

"I drove twenty miles to work every day. We've made sacrifices for him to be able to play, then all this . . ."

Jimmie broke into tears and rubbed his calloused hands together in a gesture of helplessness. Mrs. Moreland, tearful herself, patted his knee sympathetically. This was a family emotionally uprooted by recruiting grief. In some manner, everybody concerned had contributed a fault to it. In the course of events, Jackie had become the prize beef at a cattle auction.

"We never gave him guidance," his father said. "We didn't know about things like this. But nobody ever talked to us about money. If he got any big offers, we don't know about it. But nobody believes us. All they ever talked to us about was education and how much Jack would like the school. We never knew it would be like this. Now Jack's ashamed to come home and face his friends."

Downtown in Minden, Jack Bridges' clothing store is the sounding board for local sports opinion. "Nobody blames the kid around here," Bridges said. "Everybody's for him. They know he made some mistakes. He shouldn't have told all those people he was going to their schools, but he did that to get them off his back. The kid's biggest mistake was that he didn't know how to say no. He would make up his mind he was going to one school, then somebody else would come by and he couldn't tell them he'd already made up his mind."

" 'But they've come from so far,' he would tell me," Mrs. Moreland said.

Somewhere, somebody in the background was giving the boy a good coaching job on how to be recruited. This is borne out in his shopping around after he had first signed with Kentucky, the pre-determined destiny of his ambition. There are plain, unvarnished facts, however, that would have eliminated this temptation to play the field, and they fall generally into the realm of the colleges' responsibility.

If no recruiter had offered more than the legal scholarship allows, the Moreland case would never have become an affair of notoriety.

If Kentucky's original grant-in-aid had been respected, the so-called cattle auction never would have come off. This is an argument for having the grant-in-aid, or letter-of-intent, be administered by the NCAA on a nationally recognized basis.

Club Fighter

by Jimmy Cannon

*Perhaps because he was raised in the slums of New York
City, Jimmy Cannon writes often of losers. He knows and
has compassion for the thousands of Lew Perezes in the
sports world. It comes as no surprise, therefore, that Cannon
selected "Club Fighter" to represent him in this book. It's a
vivid, poignant article—Cannon at his best.*

R. P. G.

I sat across from him at a table in the diner. He was a young
guy with a pudgy body and a rum-hurt face. It was a very
cold day, but he was moist with sweat. There was a wet rim
around the collar of his blue shirt. I asked him to hand me
the sugar bowl, and this started the conversation. He wanted
to know what I did.

"I work on a paper," I said.

"Printer?" he asked.

"No," I said. "The editorial department."

"You write up the editorials," he said.

I said, "I write sports."

"Sports?" he said, as though this were a word seldom used and he was uncertain of its meaning. "What kind of sports?"

"General sports," I said. "All kinds."

"Boxing?" he asked.

"I do a lot of boxing," I said.

"I used to box myself," he said.

"Where?" I asked.

"Around Jersey," he said.

"What name did you box under?" I asked.

"You wouldn't know me," this guy said, getting shifty when I tried to nail him down. "I was just a ham-and-egger."

"What did you weigh?" I asked.

"One hundred and thirty-five," he answered, and then I was reasonably certain he was a liar. Fighters usually say thirty-five or sixty and throw away the hundred.

"How many fights did you have?" I asked.

"Round thirty," the liar said. "I made a little money, and quit. I'm in the shirt business now."

The waiter brought my change, and I got away from him before he could give the lie any detail.

There are some men who believe that being a fighter makes you a special man. There are some fighters who believe that. One of them is Lew Perez. Once he was a semi-windup guy and he fought a few mains in his time. Now Perez boxes six-round preliminaries in neighborhood clubs in Brooklyn. He works in the daytime at odd jobs, but what he wants is to walk down the street in the slum where he lives and have the guys on the corner recognize him as a fighter. He walks by them, sharp in his zoot suit, the satchel in his hand, and if they say there goes the fighter, that is his reward.

Perez has been going eight years. There isn't anyone who will manage him. Matchmakers put him on a card because they like him. They know he doesn't quit or run and hide or stink out the other guy if he is hit on the chin. They give him fifty dollars for six rounds, and he cuts ten of it back to the second. He was born in the city of San Juan in Puerto Rico, and, after eight years of it, all he has is the right to say he's a prize fighter.

The club where he works most is the Ridgewood Grove. They have been fighting in this place for twenty-five years. Some of the young ones get good and leave it for the Garden and the other big arenas around the country. When they start going back, out of the Garden and the other important joints, they come back to the Ridgewood for a last shot. Perez has never fought in the Garden. The best he ever did was eight hundred fighting Wilfie Shanks in Albany, New York. By the time they cut him he didn't have much left, but it was one of the big nights of his life because it was a main event; he has had very few of those.

Guys like this live in a spectacular obscurity and enjoy a faceless celebrity. They are the guys who rebuke the sports pages and the fight racket of art and literature. They accept the poverty of their life, fascinated by the dubious ecstasy of hearing announcers shout their names in half empty arenas. They are always on the frontiers of starvation. They have no future in the cruelest of all sports. Winning doesn't help them. Losing doesn't tarnish their conception of themselves as anointed people.

They are the time-killers, the guys fighting as you come down the aisle to your seat. They are only half seen in their small moments of triumph, and their disgraces are vaguely remembered, like a joke told very late at night when everyone is drunk.

If they possess anything, it is the knowledge that a man once said there are no cowards in the ring. A fighter, said the unknown philosopher, must be game or he couldn't go through the ropes. Perez is typical of what he is. He is a pre-

liminary fighter who will never do any better. Change the
name, the birthplace, the weights, and each is alike, no
matter where they are fighting. It is not an extraordinary
story but a commonplace one.

At Ridgewood Grove, the fighters who work underneath
sat in a slope-ceilinged room on this night as they waited to
go into the ring.

If you go into rooms where athletes change their clothes
as much as I do, you would be disgusted by the way this
place smells. The customary odor of the locker room is a
healthy one and is dominated by liniments, sweat and soap
melting in the hot water of the showers. This room smelled
of poverty.

It is a peculiar smell because these half-naked bodies are
frequently cleansed by showers, and they are sound, young,
muscular. The flaws of these bodies are minor. The noses are
broken, and the breath creaks as it comes out of them. The
ears are swollen and, in many cases, shapeless. There are
usually clenched scars above the eyes, and the eyebrows are
made bald in places by the marks of old wounds—the way
a lawn might look if it were marred by a mower zigzagging
across it after it had been neatly cropped by a gardener.

The room is a sanitary place, policed by health officers
and sprayed frequently with disinfectant but the smell of
that gets out of your nose if you stay there for any length of
time. It is not a big smell, but you don't have to sniff to lo-
cate it. It is there, small and revolting, a mild smell of decay.
It is the smell of old men sleeping in lodging houses, but not
so strong. It confuses you because, in the lodging houses,
these bodies have surrendered to death and wait for it with
an eager hopelessness. But here in this fight club are young
men who use their bodies to survive.

It is the smell you get from unmade beds in furnished
rooms; from the impotent gas jets on the landings of tene-

ment stairways which now use electricity; from socks which
have been washed in the sink of a bus-station gents' room;
from sandwiches wrapped in newspapers and carried in
pockets; from clothes that dry on the body after being
soaked by the rain; from the benches in parks where no
flowers grow; from the overcoats panhandlers wear in the
summertime. It is the old smell of poverty that follows the
poor wherever they go. It is a smell you will recognize always if you were raised in the slums of a big city as I was.

Perez was sitting on a stool by himself, his street clothes
hung on the pegs up above him. He is a dark man, firm-
muscled, about twenty-four years old. His weight is 153
pounds, with the stomach wrinkled a little with furrows of
fat but still flat. He wears a mustache, and he snorts occasionally to clear his nose. There is a scar on his head and one
over his left eye.

"I was fighting with a guy," he said, pointing to the healed
wound in his head.

Johnny Schwartz, the second, a monstrous man with a
crushed face, who was dressed in a black sweater, black
pants and a dark sport shirt, interrupted the fighter by holding up his soft right hand.

"In the street," Schwartz said. "It was a street fight."

"In the street I was fighting with a guy," Perez said. "His
brother came and hit me on the head with a stick."

The second smiled contemptuously, pleased by his superior knowledge of the language.

"A bat he means," the second said.

"All right," Perez said. "A bat."

The second shook with laughter, as though humor were an
animal which frolicked inside his great body.

"A mustache he's got," the second said. "Lew Perez: next
stop, Hollywood."

Perez said Buddy Bailey put the gash above his eye.

"The first round," Perez said. "The referee wanted to stop

the fight. But I went the limit. I lost the decision. It never opened again. That is very good. It stays the way it is."

There is a theory that fighters with mustaches are the intellectuals of the ring. Hair on a man's lip is considered the mark of the scholar. The brown hand reached for the mustache as though it were an insect he was trying to brush off his face.

"I am a clown," he said proudly. "I am no cutie."

Perez, who came to New York when he was sixteen, first lived in the Spanish-speaking settlement in that part of Harlem which reaches to the northern end of Central Park.

"I have only one week in this country, and I not speak English so good," he explained. "One day I am fighting with a guy in the street. I am always fighting wtih a guy. Al King . . . a manager of fighters . . . is in an automobile and he sees this fight with a guy. He stopped the fight. He say to me: 'You want to make a couple of bucks?' I say: 'Sure. Why not?' He put me in the car, and he take me some place. I am fighting a guy in the street at five o'clock, and then in the ring that night. How do you like that?"

"Did you win it?" the second asked.

"I win it," Perez said. "The other guy quit."

"Why do you fight?" I asked him, because he knows as well as I do that this is as far as he will go and from now on it will get tougher.

"I like the sport of it," he said.

"You don't like being hit, do you?" I asked.

"No," the fighter said.

"Do you enjoy beating up the other guy?" I asked.

"No," he said. "I like the sport of it. I am working down the docks, on Pier 40. It's a good job. I make sixty-seven dollars a week. I get a fight. I quit. The sport appeals to me. I am a fighter. I work now in the daytime. I am a cashier in a carnival in the Bronx. My boss is good. He gives me a night to fight. I quit jobs all the time. In a laundry . . . dishwasher

. . . porter . . . stevedore . . . delivery boy . . . racking up balls in a poolroom . . . bartender. I do not like this. I just like to fight."

The second wheezed. "He likes to give people a laugh. But they stopped him. The commission suspended him for clowning. Is that a bad thing? Making people laugh? But what can you do? They took his license off him. He's got to be serious. A fine thing to do to a real clown!"

The fighter examined the knuckles of his hand while the second talked. The other fighters sat silently on their stools. They sat with the patience of men who turn up their suitcases and sit on them by the side of a highway, waiting for a hitch.

"It's rough," Perez said, talking about the fight racket as though it had just occurred to him that it was a dirty business. "It's rough, but I like it. I don't feel bad when I am losing. I like to be a good winner. A good loser. I like to have the people enjoy themselves when I fight. Some guy will say to me: 'Lew, you are a bum.' I find the guy in the crowd. I pick out the guy who says I am a bum. I bow to him. I tell him it is not an insult. This is to make him laugh. I am not a champion. I know that. But I fight my best all the time. That is being a fighter. Fighting your best all the time. I am going to fight all I can. When I think I got enough, I quit. I will never be punch-drunk. I take care of myself. If I have the money, I eat good food. I sleep. I hit the road. I run over the Williamsburg Bridge. I exercise on my roof. I do not like to pay money to train in the gym. But I will never be punch-drunk. I am too smart for that. The sport will not appeal to me when I am being hurt."

The first six was on, and the second came over to Perez and ran his fat hand over the muscles of the stooped shoulders.

"Lew Perez," the second said, "you're on your way to Hollywood."

The second held up a green-trimmed, red-satin bathrobe. It was faded from many washings, but clean.

"By this they know Perez," the fighter said and began to move his arms in the old motions. The other people in the room did not notice his departure. They did not speak to him as he left the dressing room and walked into the dusk of the arena.

There was a girl with high-arched eyebrows, raised in perpetual astonishment on her plump, powder-white face. She stood up when Perez passed her. She shouted to him, and he waved back to her. This was the fighter's wife. She is always there when he works.

There were not many people in the place at this time although they sold out that night. There were more people up against the bar and in the lunchroom in the foyer. They demand a lot for their money in this club, but the second six didn't interest them much. There was little excitement as Joe Bostic introduced the two fighters in the angular language used for preliminary guys. They save the descriptive adjectives for the main event. Comedy is not good when it is associated with a fighter. The people in the seats shouted bantering jokes to Perez; their crude humor did not displease him.

The guy he drew that night was Henry Robinson, who seemed embarrassed by appearing in public with only a pair of tights to cover him. He pulled them up as high as they would reach as he waited in his corner.

It was a bad fight. Robinson came cautiously from his corner, his right hand out in the pose of a left-hander. His advance turned into a sudden retreat when he discovered he was too close to Perez. Perez lunged at him, wildly, the offense without grace or pattern. Robinson cowered behind his raised arms, and a punch slipped through and grazed his chin. He fell down, writhing and moaning so loud you could hear him in the press row. The crowd laughed as he was

counted out. Perez bowed with a stately humor. Bostic
climbed into the ring and strolled over to the timekeeper.

"One oh six of the first round," the timekeeper yelled.

"Can you beat that," Bostic said. "Perez knocking someone out. Can you beat that?"

The people snickered as Perez came out of the ring. One
of them rasped: "Atta boy, Lew." The voice was very big
above the quiet savagery of the laughter. Perez searched
through the audience, located the man who had saluted him
and bowed again. He walked up the aisle to the dressing
room, alone. The guys in his corner were working the next
bout.

Perez went back to the dressing room, put his clothes on.
He met his wife, and they went to the box office and collected the fifty, less the ten the second took. They ate a big,
slow meal in a cafeteria near the club. They took the sub-
way home.

They live in a tenement on Rivington Street, near the
Bowery in a slum which is a disgrace to the city of New
York. Wash hangs on clotheslines in the small, three-room
apartment. The furniture is old but functional. There is a
bed to sleep on, a crib for the baby, a table to eat off, a stove
to cook on and enough chairs for them to sit in. The apartment is as bleak as despair, but there is steam in the pipes,
which is unusual, for this is a neighborhood of cold-water
flats. There was a pot of coffee on the stove, and it was good
coffee, strong without being thick and hot without scalding
your tongue. The baby was asleep in the bedroom, and they
sat in the kitchen.

"He is a crowd-pleaser," said Mrs. Perez, whose first name
is Phyllis. "He fought mains, too. But now he takes anything
they give him. Perez is a clown. I don't want anyone to take
advantage of him just because he's Puerto Rican. I don't
think that's fair. That's when I get mad. That's why I'm
there every time he fights. I know the business. Just because

he's only a preliminary boy I don't want him to come home with twenty dollars in his pocket. He can't express himself. He is good-natured. That's why I'm there."

The baby whimpered in his sleep.

"This apartment," Perez said, "I had two fights in one week so we could get this apartment."

The fighter's wife lit a cigarette. She inhaled deeply, gave it to the fighter. He took a drag.

"We do that all the time," he said.

The fighter's wife laughed.

"I used to go high after a fight," Perez said. "No more. I got the kid."

Memory caused her to frown, and her voice was thick with a remembered sorrow. "Many a time we don't have milk for the kid. He goes down to the trucking place in the store downstairs. He says to the guy: 'Put me on a truck so we can have what to eat.' He's good that way. He has a temper, but he is good to me. He knows I'm a friend, his mother as well as his wife. I leave it up to him the way he makes a dollar. If he wants to quit, let him quit. I'm not going to stand in his way. All I'm interested in is he knows he has a son and he has to support him."

Their son awakened and screamed. The mother went into the room and took him in her arms. He is a fat child with the features of his father. She came back to sit at the table, the child, wet-faced with tears, sleepy in her arms.

"Socks cost fifty-nine cents a pair," Mrs. Perez said. "The socks he wears in the ring, I mean. We had two pairs of them. But they were damp. We had to buy a pair for the fight last night. Fifty-nine cents a pair. It is a lot of money when you haven't got much. I could have married other fellows who would give me more. But Perez tries. He gives— he gives open. What he has. I knew him a month, and I married him. It's two years now. I met him at a dance, and he is the best rhumba dancer you ever saw. He is no fool.

He knows toilet water. He knows perfume. They call him
Killer Perez when he is dressed up."

The fighter's wife rose and handed the baby to the fighter,
and the child wept as the mother poured the coffee.

"What was the other name you had?" she asked.

"Buttons," the fighter said. "Buttons is a comedy book in
Puerto Rico."

The fighter said with a quiet bitterness, "I do a favor for
a Spanish guy. I give him the pair of trunks. I have no trunks
last night. They try to make me buy another pair of trunks.
I borrow the trunks from another guy. It is too much money
to spend. Five dollars. Too much."

The fighter's wife said spitefully, "They made him fight
hungry one time."

"I fight hungry a lot of times," the fighter said.

"I mean the time when he wouldn't trust you," the fighter's wife said.

"Not Johnny Schwartz," the fighter explained. "Another
one. I am hungry before the fight. I say to this guy: 'Give
me a dollar to eat.' This guy say to me: 'I don't lend money
to fighters.' I say: 'You are my second. You will make money
with me tonight when I fight.' He say: 'I wouldn't lend a
fighter a nickel if he dropped dead.' I fight that night
hungry."

The dignity of the State Athletic Commission baffles
them. They can't understand why the deputy commissioners
warn Perez not to attempt comedy while he is in the ring.

"They don't know what he is going to do next when he is
clowning," the wife said. "He comes out with a mouth full
of water and spits it right in the guy's face. He is the Al
Schacht of boxing. He is the Puerto Rican Max Baer."

"I do everything for a little laugh," the fighter said.

The fighter's wife is not troubled when he loses.

"I usually tell him his faults when he loses," she said. "I
always tell him: 'Lew, the next time you'll do better.' I tell

him: 'You shouldn't of done that.' I understand boxing. With him it is not a money proposition. He likes to do his best. He has no manager, so a lot of times they give the fight to the other guy. But he's never been hurt seriously. He is not afraid of anyone. He would get in there with Joe Louis to make a dollar."

"I will fight anyone to make a dollar," the fighter said.

The fighter's wife said, "It's been a real tough buck a lot of times. Like the time I was in the hospital. He's sick, too."

The fighter's wife nodded to him, and he started to tell the story.

"My hands hurt," the fighter said. "I had a high fever. I could hardly stand on my feet. But no money in the house."

The fighter's wife said, "I didn't want him to take that fight, but he said: 'It's a few dollars. We could use a few dollars. We got nothing.' He couldn't tell them how sick he was. The commission doctor wouldn't pass him."

The fighter winced with the ache of the past.

"Jimmy Mangia," the fighter said. "I lose the decision. I was in bed three days after the fight. I couldn't move."

"He's good," she said. "He's real good. Why don't someone bother with him? Why don't he get a manager? He never will be a champion. But he's Perez, the clown. He's a crowd-pleaser everywhere he goes. The people in the Garden would love him. Just a break is all he needs. Just one little break."

The baby fell asleep. She walked into the other room and laid the infant in the crib.

"I never had any affection," she said, embracing the fighter. "I wanted affection. I never had any friends or nothing like that. But I got everything I want right here."

The fighter said, "Maybe we get lucky."

Gene Tunney Today

This article first appeared in *LOOK*, July 10, 1956, and is reprinted by permission of that magazine.

On the Tunney piece: Tunney and I had been quite good friends for a number of years, and I also considered him an outstanding sports personality. People around LOOK *felt that this was one of the best pieces I had done.*

That's about the sum-up of the background of the story and why I submitted it.

TIM COHANE
Sports Editor
LOOK Magazine

Former heavyweight champion James Joseph (Gene) Tunney is the only man who ever mastered both Jack Dempsey and Will Shakespeare. For a long time, this earned Tunney only a pittance of esteem from most boxing followers, who idolized Dempsey and suspected Shakespeare. With the years, however, Tunney has grown both in stature as a champion and in personal popularity.

The high rank of Tunney as a ringman was underscored recently when Rocky Marciano retired as undefeated heavyweight champion of the world. Sportswriters seized on the fact that Rocky was following the wise example set by Gene twenty-eight years before. "Tunney had the good sense to stay retired," they added. "Will Marciano also make it stick?" (Gene, wiring Rocky congratulations, urged him to do just that.) The writers also pointed out that, of all earlier champions, Tunney was the one who had come closest to Marciano's perfect record: Gene lost only once. And they said that Tunney and Jack Johnson, of all past champs, were the ones with the best chances, on style, to have beaten "The Rock."

It was three decades ago that Tunney won and defended the championship in two ten-round decisions over Dempsey. The Manassa Mauler was the most popular fighter in history and the public could not be expected quickly to forgive the man who had toppled their idol. Then, there was the personality of Tunney himself. As a young man become champion, Gene threatened at times to fit the definition his friend George Bernard Shaw coined to describe himself in his twenties. "I was," said Shaw, "an arrant prig."

Today, Tunney is changed. The handsome, fifty-eight-year-old financier and gentleman farmer responds with courtly bow and smile when the hat-check girl greets him as "sweetie pie." Gene's tailor, Jim Greene, who has helped him select his single-breasted worsteds for more than twenty-five years, tells of a covey of Madison Avenue secretaries "oohing" and "aahing" at the former champ. Tunney gave his Homburg a cavalier tip. "Jim," he said, as they passed on, "I love people." And a lot of people get to see Tunney today. As a director of two banks and eight industries, he moves around the country almost as much as that restless restaurant keeper, Dempsey.

Dempsey and Tunney did not warm to each other, in or out of the ring, in their fighting days. But with the years, they have developed an authentic liking for each other and meet occasionally for dinner. Mrs. Tunney, who was Mary

Josephine (Polly) Lauder of the Carnegie Steel family, has a genuine fondness for Dempsey. Jack's older daughter, Joan, Mrs. Dennis O'Flaherty of Los Angeles, told her father after meeting Tunney: "Daddy, I like that man."

Tunney, like Dempsey, has kept his family away from his public life. Gene Lauder Tunney, 24, and J. (for John) Varick Tunney, 21, are Yale men. Jonathon Rowland Tunney, 19, who went to Lawrenceville Prep, is now in Okinawa as a marine, following the World War I example of his dad. Joan Lauder Tunney, 17, attends an exclusive school for girls near Baltimore. The boys all have a universal interest in sports and played tennis and football when they were at prep school. "They are too elongated physically," Tunney says, "to play football successfully at the college level."

Tunney's major athletic interest these days concerns the condition of America's youth. As director of the Navy's fitness program in World War II, he speaks with authority.

"We hold our own in athletic competition with other countries," he points out, "because we have more athletes to choose from. But statistics prove the average European youth tops ours convincingly in the various strength tests. Unless he takes up athletics seriously, an American boy tends to get little, if any, exercise. He becomes almost exclusively a spectator and a motorist. As a nation, we have lost the habit of walking.

"The answer lies in a good, compulsory physical-fitness program. In some of our larger states, we make our children go to school until they are 16. It is only another step to compulsory physical education. Why not give it a trial? It paid rich dividends with our military personnel."

And he has definite ideas as to how it could be done: "The Department of Health, Education and Welfare should create a Physical Fitness Division, headed by a qualified medical doctor, or a doctor of physiology or a doctor of physical education. States and municipalities should coordinate with the Federal Government in setting up a program and securing facilities."

In keeping himself fit today, Tunney carefully controls his weight. He weighs around two hundred and ten pounds, roughly twenty more than he carried against Dempsey for their second fight, in 1927. He retires at eleven P.M., sleeps eight hours, takes ten minutes of floor exercises every morning. His golf score has gone up ten strokes due to business pressures, but he still finds time to card a week-end low 90. For the brisk walk he used to take before dinner, he substitutes a sauna bath.

Except when a good boxing bout or a Wagnerian or Verdi opera keeps him in New York, Tunney leaves his office near the Yale Club on weekdays in time to catch the five-ten train to Stamford. He then drives to Long Ridge and his two-hundred-and-fifty-acre Star Meadow Farm. Gene has six-dozen white-faced Herefords and raises his own feed. The actual work is done by his farmer, Herman Zuern, and three hands. The help also includes a chauffeur, cook, upstairs and downstairs maids and a general handyman.

It is a very different story from the one you usually hear about boxing's former greats. Where did he get the money? Well, Tunney made one fortune in the ring; his two Dempsey fights netted him $976,534 and his final bout, an eleven-round technical knockout of Tom Heeney in 1928, $467,500 —this in the relatively taxless 1920's. He married into a second fortune. And he has acquired a third as a shrewd businessman.

Gene first demonstrated an aptitude for arithmetic in his late teens as a shipping clerk for a steamship line. He had learned early the value of money. He came up out of New York's Greenwich Village, and until he began to fight for fairly important purses, he had to husband his funds.

Today, he pays a staggering income tax and counts among

his friends financiers like Arthur Gray, retired banker, and Sidney Rheinstein, former governor of the New York Stock Exchange. Other intimates include Bernard Gimbel, the department-store owner; Stanton Griffis, former ambassador to Spain and Argentina; Dr. John Oliver La Gorce, president of the National Geographic Society and editor of the *National Geographic Magazine,* and F. M. Flynn, president of the New York *Daily News.*

An inquisitive mind, a universality of interests, a retentive memory and a set of positive viewpoints make Tunney a versatile and forceful conversationalist. He especially likes to discuss politics, finance, history, religion, music and art.

Although his formal schooling ended with the Christian Brothers' high school because he had to go to work, he determined to get more education on his own. By the time he retired from boxing, he had read H. G. Wells' *Outline of History* and all of Shakespeare several times. He continued to broaden himself by round-the-world travel with the La Gorces and by more reading. Today, only an occasional baseball game or Bishop Fulton J. Sheen lures him to the television set. He prefers to spend his evenings with biographies and modern fiction. His favorite authors are William Faulkner and Ernest Hemingway, another good friend.

Tunney's love of Shakespeare was rooted in his childhood. When he was a thirteen-year-old at St. Veronica's Parochial School, he played the Prince in the court scene in *Romeo and Juliet.* He rehearsed it so many times he knew everybody's lines. There is little Shakespeare he can't identify, and there is much he can quote. He was no *poseur* when he accepted the invitation of Prof. William Lyon Phelps to lecture on "The Bard" to his English class at Yale.

As a champion who discoursed on Shakespeare and who married a wealthy and comely heiress out of the social register, Tunney was something beyond the comprehension of the fight mob. He compounded his pariahhood by behaving at times as if he deemed himself the original discoverer of culture. His dialogues often advanced on stilts, as when he dismissed an objectionable fellow from his training camp with the castigation: "You are full of self-approbation and deceit."

Except for a few writers, notably W. O. McGeehan, who called him "The Golden Boy of the Golden Age," the sporting press did not take to Tunney. Some considered his erudition an act. His autonomy grated others. Besides, he had knocked over an idol, Dempsey. Even a ghost writer like Gene Fowler and a public-relations expert like Steve Hannagan couldn't sell Tunney. Gene aggravated his status when he hectored photographers and newsmen who tried to get near him and his bride on their European honeymoon.

"As I look back on it now," he says, "I was too hard on them. In fact, my attitude was juvenile. I did not take cognizance of the fact that they were only trying to do a job. I was irritated at them over the way they had received me. They had been my derogators. My reaction was expressed in a manner ascribable to my Irish temperament."

As a fighter, Tunney was unspectacular, but demoniacally efficient. He was a manufactured boxer—only his spiritual assets were natural. He had fragile hands. To strengthen them, he shoveled coal and hoisted five-gallon water jugs. "Even after he became champion," says Bernard Gimbel, "Gene used to squeeze small, hard rubber balls and exercise each finger five hundred times a day by using it as a lever to push his body away from a wall." Those hands forced on Tunney a style of hitting which was less likely to knock out a man than to cause ultimately a technical knockout from an accumulation of jolting, cutting blows.

From Benny Leonard, the lightweight maestro, Tunney borrowed the trick of shoving his left jab in a slightly upward plane, to sharpen its cutting edge. This method helped make a mess of Dempsey's eyes. The Tunney arsenal included also a fine right to the head, straight as a string, an enervating left hook to the liver and a hurtful right under the heart.

There never was a better conditioned fighter than Tunney, not even Marciano. Bearded, scowling Dempsey, with his fighter's beautifully proportioned physique, a heavyweight's torso on a middleweight's legs, looked stronger than Tunney, but it may be Tunney actually was the stronger. Where Dempsey, even in his prime, fought in spasmodic bursts out of a stalking weave and bob, Tunney was one of the few boxers who ever developed stamina enough to step around at top speed every second. But it was basically Tunney's iron will and frigid nerve that brought him to the title.

Few warriors would have stomached the full fifteen rounds of the only fight he ever lost out of sixty-eight as a professional. Tunney was defending the light-heavyweight title against Harry Greb. A cruel, ceaseless mixer, Greb went for Tunney with everything he had. He fractured Tunney's nose twice, opened cuts under his chin with head butts and practically punched him into a pulp. The blood Tunney swallowed, the adrenalin chloride which his seconds used to try to stanch his bleeding and the rum and orange juice with which they plied him . . . all combined to nauseate him, but he fought on. He collapsed only after he reached the steps of his dressing room.

The second day after the fight, with his face appearing as if he had slept in a busy cement mixer, Tunney visited the New York State Athletic Commission offices to post the challenger's bond of twenty-five hundred dollars for a return fight. "Son," Commissioner William Muldoon advised him, "forget about Greb. He is not a normal fighter. Fight somebody else." "Thank you," Tunney said, "but I still want Greb." He was to get Greb and to beat him, not once but four times.

After their fifth fight, Greb visited Tunney's dressing room. "Gene," he said, "I've had enough of you." "Come now, Harry," Tunney said, "Britton and Lewis fought any number of times." "Never mind that," Greb said. "I'll let somebody else fight you." Greb later won eight thousand dollars betting on Tunney against Dempsey.

Greb and all his other fights were to prepare Tunney for Dempsey. He had set his course for Dempsey as far back as 1919, when he was still in the Marines. His friend, Eddie Eagan, Rhodes scholar and Olympic boxing champion, who had seen Tunney win service championships, told him: "Gene, you'll never be any great shakes as a fighter. Why don't you come to Yale with me?"

"Eddie," Tunney replied, "I'm going to get an education, but it will have to be by reading. I won't have time to go to Yale. I'm going to be busy winning the heavyweight championship."

Tunney lived by the Platonic principle of knowing himself. He reasoned nobody could know him so well as himself. He arranged for his fights and decided how he'd train. Only Jimmy Bronson, a principled as well as shrewd fight man and Lou Fink (Dutch Louie), his trainer, had his confidence. Just before the first Dempsey fight, in Philadelphia, Tunney, the 3-1 underdog, fell asleep in a chair next to the shower. When it was time, Bronson roused him.

"Well, Jim," Tunney smiled, "what do you think?"

"You don't have to worry about the right," Bronson said, "but there's dynamite in the left. When he goes to throw the left, you'll get there first with your right."

Tunney nodded. After forty-five seconds of sparring, Tunney landed a smashing right to Dempsey's head that shook the champion and put Gene in charge. Back in his corner, he exulted: "Jim, I hit him hard enough to break my hand, but I didn't. I've won that title."

In twenty rounds—two fights—with Dempsey, Tunney

made only two mistakes. Each proved almost fatal. The first came at the beginning of the fourth round in the first fight. At the bell, Dempsey sprang tigerishly across the ring, readying the left hook. For three rounds, in planned pattern, Tunney had moved always to his left, away from the left hook. Now, for some inexplicable reason, he moved slightly to his right and angled into the ropes. The left hook came booming. If it had landed on his jaw, Tunney probably would have been counted out. It landed a little low, on his larynx. He experienced excruciating pain, but he was able to recoup automatically, move to his left and avoid further damage. Yet, the effects of the blow prevented him from speaking properly for a week.

The second mistake led up to the famous long count in the seventh round of the second fight in Chicago. Tunney was leading easily, when Dempsey feinted with a left and followed with a right to the head. Tunney stepped back from the left, but not far enough. The right thudded against his head. Then, Dempsey uncorked a thunderous left hook to the jaw that did the real damage, followed by a five-blow barrage to head and jaw.

Tunney sagged to his haunches. Both fighters had been warned that in the event of a knockdown, the man scoring it must go to the *farthest* neutral corner before the referee would begin the count. From force of habit, Dempsey delayed so long that Tunney was able to stay on the canvas with immunity for eighteen seconds. That's what the watch of the official timekeeper, Paul Beeler, showed, and Bronson, a strong Tunney supporter, so testifies. When Tunney got up, he was able to back-pedal for most of the round, and he went on to win the last three rounds and take a clear-cut decision.

"You simply could not make a single mistake with Dempsey and not pay for it," Tunney says. "Dempsey was always cerebrating. (Dempsey's comment: "Gene always did like them big words.") Greb was a clever fighter, but so was Dempsey, and he had the instinct to kill you. I do not subscribe to the theory, offered occasionally, that Greb would have outpointed Dempsey. Jack would have caught Harry eventually and knocked him out. Dempsey, to my mind, was the greatest fighter who ever lived."

As part of the build-up for a third Dempsey-Tunney fight, which he envisioned drawing $4,000,000, promoter Tex Rickard doctored the films of the Chicago battle so that postscript footage showed Tunney on the floor early in the long count, eyes glazed, while a training-camp shot presented Dempsey unmarked and smiling. Tunney, eager for a third fight, understood the build-up and said nothing. Dempsey did not want a third fight, for fear of incurring possibly permanent damage to his eyes. But the picture in the minds of most of the public added up to a conviction the Old Manassa Mauler had been rooked.

Today, the picture emerges in saner focus. Dempsey, who might well have beaten Tunney if they had fought when both were in their prime, was fairly defeated both times.

The years have enriched both in many ways. Dempsey is still "The Champion." As for Tunney, his revered Shakespeare sums him up well in the final scene of *Julius Caesar:*

> "..............................*the elements*
> *So mix'd in him that Nature might stand up*
> *And say to all the world, 'This was a man!'*"

The Greatest Matador
of All Time

Reprinted by permission of Barnaby Conrad. This article first appeared in *TRUE* magazine, February, 1956.

On the walls of my San Francisco bistro, "El Matador," there is a scrap of red silk encrusted with tarnished gold sequins framed against a small poster announcing: "Today! May 16, 1920, a grandiosa corrida in Talavera de la Reina featuring José Gómez!"

This valuable, bloody scrap of silk is a souvenir of the most terrible loss the bullfighting world ever suffered, for on that day José Gómez, called "Gallito" or "Joselito," was killed by the bull Bailador.

When I was a bull-mad young man of twenty-one in Sevilla I had the opportunity of knowing Joselito's family well and of learning the true story of the man who has now become a legend. I wrote this story and used it as the lead chapter in my book, "Gates of Fear" because to me Joselito seemed to embody all of la fiesta brava's *many elements: the passion, the technique, the dedication, the glory—and the horror.*

BARNABY CONRAD

It was May 15, 1920, the day before the man's last day on earth, and it was a bad day. The bull, the one that ran his total kills to 1566, swayed and crashed over dead, and the twenty-five-year-old matador down in the arena wiped his sweaty face, looked up at the Madrid crowd, and swore as they booed him.

This was José Miguel Isidro del Sagrado Corazón de Jesús Gómez y Ortega, known to Spain and the world as Joselito, or Joselito el Gallo, or Gallito, or simply—The Best. Although he was universally accepted by other bullfighters, experts, and historians as the most perfect bullfighter who ever lived, this afternoon the crowd was shouting insults and howling for his blood.

It's a recorded fact that as he walked away from the dead bull toward the fence, a woman stood up in the stands and screamed, "I hope a bull kills you tomorrow in Talavera!" A cushion struck Joselito on the arm, and as he looked up into the hate of the crowd, his melancholy eyes filled with tears. "This," he murmured to his sword boy, "this *must* end!"

The crowd had made the idol and, just as they were to do with Manolete twenty-seven years later, they were out to murder the idol they had created. The treacherous bull of the next afternoon, Bailador, wasn't really needed for the job. Joselito was already dead. He had been dead for some time.

He was an old-young man when he died. But he had always been old. Born near Sevilla on May 8, 1895, one of six children, little Joselito never seemed to be a child. Joselito was the son, nephew, and brother of gypsy bullfighters, and his kindergarten was in the unnatural shadow of the bullrings. His father, a good matador, died when Joselito was two.

"How—" he managed to rasp in his dying sentence, "how did Rafael fight today?"

Rafael "El Gallo," Joselito's brother, was a promising

young bullfighter then. Now seventy-three years old, colorful and revered, he told me most of this story of Joselito.

Another brother was also a novillero, and his three sisters
married toreros, so it was only natural that Joselito's first
photograph at the age of two shows him practicing an esto-
cada with a miniature sword. Joselito's mother, Gabriela,
was also from a bullfighting family, and she used to sigh and
say wearily, "The only ones who don't get gored by bulls are
the priests safe in the cathedral."

Gabriela fought to keep her youngest and favorite out
of the ring. "Let's save one," she pleaded. "Let's just save
one!" But she knew it was going to be a useless fight when
she saw "the child of her right eye" growing a pigtail at the
age of six.

Then at eight he began skipping school. Usually she found
him in the back yard of a painter named Cayetano who had
a spaniel trained to charge like a bull. The first time she
saw his already marvelously graceful body leaning into a
sweeping verónica, she knew she had a genius on her hands.

His first public success came when he was nine. It was
a festival at a little village called Coría del Río outside of
Sevilla. The arena was makeshift, formed by an enclosure
of heavy wagons, but the bullfighters—and the bulls—
were professionals. Joselito, wearing his first pair of long
pants and with a cap covering the pigtail pinned on top of
his head, perched up on top of one of the carts like the other
spectators, and his sad young eyes watched every move the
toreros made down in the arena. Inside his jacket he had
tucked a pair of cortas. These are banderillas that are cut
down to a third normal size; hence the person placing them
has to be that much closer to the bull, thus making the
maneuver much more dangerous.

It happened on the second bull. The veteran banderillero
was having trouble making the difficult animal charge the
way he wanted it so he could place the banderillas. Hold-

ing the barbed sticks ready over his head, he made false runs at the animal twice, challenging it gutterally with his voice and rapping the two long banderillas together to try to provoke a clean charge. The animal just shook his big horns and pawed the sand.

Suddenly a boy's voice was heard by the crowd.

"Where you're standing, man, it's never going to charge! Come, place yourself over there!"

The crowd laughed, and the banderillero looked up at the nine-year-old author of this statement and worked his mouth disdainfully.

Suddenly Joselito leapt down into the arena, and the crowd gasped. "Toro, hah-hah!" he called in as manly a tone as a treble can be, placing himself close to one of the wagons completely opposite to the direction the banderillero had been trying to force the bull's charge. He had the stubby banderillas in his hands, and he leapt up into the air once to attract the bull's attention.

The animal, twenty feet away, stared curiously at this new target in a different area of the ring, and then it charged hard. The boy stood there like a post, his feet flat on the sand, his back arched gracefully as the big animal bore down on him. The crowd screamed in crescendo, for it looked as though the horns couldn't miss. But when the sharp points were six feet from him, Joselito jumped his right leg out to the side, leaning his body with it, but without moving his left foot. The bull, thinking the target was escaping, veered off its course to intercept it. In that split second, Joselito sucked back his leg, leapt up over the lowered horns, and jabbed the darts into the animal's withers. Using the sticks themselves to push himself away and out of the bull's course, he pivoted and trotted calmly toward the barrier as the bull bucked and wheeled past him.

For a moment the crowd was too stunned to realize what they had witnessed. Then they set up a roar. But did you see it? A nine-year-old child. A pair of cortas al quiebro—and Espartero himself could have placed them no better!

Joselito held up his hand as he'd seen the professionals do and gravely acknowledged the applause as he climbed back to his seat. It was the first applause of his life. He liked it.

Word spread fast throughout Sevilla of the astonishing happening at Coría del Rio. "The youngest of the Gallos is a prodigy," was the verdict of the experts. How else could one explain that phenomenal pair of banderillas by a child who had never faced anything larger than a calf before?

That was a milestone for Joselito. The next came a year later at a tienta at the Miura ranch. Miura bulls are the most famous of all fighting bulls. A vicious, purebred strain raised exclusively for the ring for over a hundred years, they have killed more matadors than any other breed and have been labeled "the bulls of death." Tientas at the Miura ranch were highly exclusive, serious affairs, and Joselito pleaded with his brothers to be allowed to go. They kept him in the background during the testing of the calves, afraid of what old man Miura sitting up on the porch over the little arena would think about a child's being around and getting in the way. After the stubby-horned calves were caped by Joselito's brothers and the other aspirant toreros of fourteen and fifteen, a large five-year-old heifer with sharp horns was let into the ring. The toreritos, who a short time before were so eager, brave, and jealous with the two-year-olds, suddenly retreated behind the burladero shields and very generously began "you-firsting" each other.

And then they saw a figure flash by them with a magenta cape that was larger than he was. Joselito was out in the ring before his brothers could stop him, and he was holding the cape behind his body in the dangerous De Frente por Detras pass.

Old Miura, sitting up on the balcony, leaned forward,

tugged at his gray mustache, and watched incredulously as
he saw Joselito execute pass after pass with astonishing grace
and control. He sent for Joselito to come up to the big house
for tea. Before the afternoon was over he had given the boy
a horse and, most important, invited him out to practice
with the calves any time he wanted to. Joselito took the old
man up on his invitation, going out to "Don Eduardo's"
every chance he got. Miura became very attached to this
serious, honest boy who lived, breathed, and dreamt bullfighting and only bullfighting. He had never seen such dedication in anyone of any age, and he liked him for it. Once
Don Eduardo said affectionately, "It's as though another
son were born to me."

With every tienta, with every bullfight he witnessed, Joselito was learning and perfecting. When he was eleven he
said to his mother very solemnly, "Please let me become a
professional, since soon I will be too old."

His mother, horrified, managed to keep him at school one
more year. Then, when he was twelve, he fought in his first
organized fight, wearing his first "suit of lights" in his first
real plaza de toros. It was in Jerez, and he was to receive
ten whole reales (two dollars and a half) for fighting a pair
of small bulls along with two other young "fenómenos."
Joselito tasted triumph and tragedy that day. On his first
bull he was superb, graceful, and brave, and he had the
crowd that had merely come to watch a novelty act cheering as though they were watching a top "sword" in action.
He killed after two thrusts, and the crowd went wild, making him take several triumphant laps around the ring.

Then came his second animal. He couldn't kill it. "It's
made of concrete," he gasped to his brothers between trys.
Finally the warning trumpet blast sounded, and three minutes later the second, and then the last, and Joselito, with
tears of rage and frustration, watched the animal being led
out by the trained steers. Except for Bailador, it was the

only bull he ever took on that didn't meet death at his hands.

Joselito was miserable, but the critics overlooked the ending of the corrida because of the astonishing performance that preceded it. An impresario signed Joselito for sixteen fights in Portugal. He was on his way. He performed well in those becerradas—calf-fights—and turned the pittance he earned over to Gabriela with a manly flourish, saying as his father had said to her so many times, "Here you go, Mama—have a good time."

The next season he fought more, and by the following season he was being talked about all over Spain. But 1910 was his first really big year. Here's what the critics said of this fifteen-year-old-boy—and these reviews come verbatim from the newspaper files, not from the hazy memories of some old-timers bemoaning the passing of the "good old days when men were men and bulls were bulls."

Of his presentation in San Sebastián the critic Santo-Mano wrote in *Sol y Sombra*, the bullfighting bible of that era: "I never would have believed it possible! What this child did yesterday with a large and dangerous novillo!"

After his first fight in Valencia, the critic wrote: "Gallito III is nothing more nor less than a phenomenon. Why bother to detail the faenas he did yesterday? Let me just say that never in my life have I ever seen better fighting by anyone!"

The eminent don Ventura described Joselito's fight in Bilbao in a curiously anachronistic term "Positively atomístico [atomic]!"

The year 1911 was a repetition of success, with the addition of a feat unduplicated in the annals of tauromachy. On the fourteenth of May, just a week after his sixteenth birthday, this boy killed six novillos, instead of the usual two—all by himself! Before a crowd of ten thousand people he was awarded the ears off four of the animals; and this was back in the days when ears were very rarely awarded, no one yet having cut an ear in Madrid or Sevilla, for example.

The usually blasé *Sol y Sombra's* review of this fight of Joselito's in Cádiz starts out like something by a Hollywood press agent: "Un éxito inmenso, colosal, sublime . . ."

People in the rest of Spain were impressed by the fact, but they didn't quite believe it. "Cádiz is a small town after all," they said. "How would he do in a big city?"

The next year, Joselito's brother Rafael decided that the boy was ready to show them, and he arranged for a fight in Madrid. Appearing in Madrid for a torero is like making his debut in Madison Square Garden for a boxer, and the whole city was buzzing about the prodigy from Sevilla. "It's the result of paid newspaper propaganda," many scoffed. "He's just a calf-fighter. You'll see on Sunday what happens when he comes up against real novillos."

Joselito started the proceedings off in a highly unorthodox manner. The day before the fight he went to see the bulls in the corrals behind the arena. They were large three-and-a-half-year-old novillos, bigger than anything he'd ever fought. Joselito studied the animals snorting in the enclosure for a moment and then announced firmly, "I won't fight them."

"But why?" the impresario protested. "Certainly they're big, but I think you can handle them."

"They're too small," said Joselito. "I won't fight."

The impresario blanched. He had sold twenty thousand tickets for the next afternoon, and now his attraction was walking out on him. "But what am I going to do?"

Then Joselito looked over into an adjoining corral where there were half a dozen huge five-year-old bulls. "I'll fight those."

"But that's madness! Those are full-grown bulls—for full matadors next Sunday, not for a novillero who's never fought anything but calves!"

Joselito was adamant and got his way. His presentation in Madrid as a novillero was not with novillos, but with toros de verdad—true bulls. The first animal that blasted out into the sun to try to kill him was named Escopeta—Shotgun— and it weighed over fourteen hundred pounds! (Nine hundred is the official required weight these days.)

The first thing the monster saw was the slight figure of a boy kneeling alone in the center of the golden sand. Joselito's father had invented the dangerous larga cambiada, and Joselito was out to show Madrid whose son he was. He shouted at the bull as soon as it came through the toril gate, and it pounded toward the man, its head lowered to kill. Thirty feet, twenty feet, ten feet, and the boy stayed there unmoving on his knees, holding the cape spread out on the sand in front of him with his right hand.

When the bull was two yards from him he swung the cape over his head. The cloth leapt into life, blossoming out around his shoulders, and the bull veered off its course to slash at the cape. The bull's right horn passed just a few inches from Joselito's head as its momentum carried it a full fifteen feet beyond him.

After that Joselito did things that, according to his biographer Gustavo del Barco, "converted that august plaza de toros into a cage of howling maniacs."

He gave them everything. He placed banderillas three different ways, and people swore they'd never seen sticks placed like that, so elegantly, so surely, so dangerously. On the last pair he let the bull come into him so close that the horn split open his right eyebrow and he had to withdraw to the infirmary before continuing. For his opening muleta work he called for a chair, placed it in the middle of the arena, and, sitting in it, made the animal pass back and forth five times without standing up. Then he scratched an X on the sand with his sword, and, planting his feet on it, he did eight frightening natural passes without moving off. The tricks over, he settled down to the damnedest lesson in classic bullfighting ever seen in Madrid, ending up with a perfect sword thrust that dropped the bull instantly.

The next day one critic wrote halfway down his column: "I have run out of adjectives to describe the glory of this boy. For the rest of this review I will leave blank spaces and the reader can fill them in as he wishes."

Madrid had a new idol. For weeks afterward people discussed that incredible performance, jumping up in cafés to demonstrate how Joselito had placed the banderillas or to show how slowly and elegantly he manipulated the muleta. Three months later they went through the same thing again when Joselito took "the alternative." Usually calf-fighters graduate to the status of novillero and stay there for several seasons before becoming skilled enough to receive a doctorate of tauromachy and become a full matador. If they make the grade, it's usually when they're over twenty-one. Rafael el Gallo figured his brother had nothing more to learn about the science, so Joselito eliminated a long apprenticeship as a novillero and became a full matador de toros, the youngest ever to wear the title. This would be tantamount to a seventeen-year-old boxer's jumping from the Golden Gloves to top heavyweight contention overnight, without the educational fooling around in preliminaries and tank town main events.

The next season Joselito fought eighty corridas, and found himself the top sword in all the world. The only others who could be mentioned in the same breath with him were his unpredictable brother Rafael and Gaona, the Mexican.

What was this young man like, this eighteen-year-old who was well on his way to becoming a millionaire and who was already Spain's greatest hero? To most people he was an enigma. The most completely dedicated of men, he was dull, remote, and taciturn on any subject but his own. Nothing in the world interested him except bulls and the raising of them. Even in the years when he fought over one hundred corridas in a six-month season, if he found himself with a spare day when he wasn't either traveling to a fight or performing in one, his idea of a relaxing good time was to get out in the fields and cape heifers for a few hours.

He was superbly built, handsome with a thick-lipped brooding quality; women went mad for him. He had his women, plenty of them, and the best, but not for long. He liked to get away by himself out on the ranches, to ride on a fine horse through long fields of his beloved fighting bulls. He loved animals of all kinds, but especially the bulls. It's said that he inspired this dialogue in Hemingway's *The Sun Also Rises* between the matador and Lady Brett:

> "No. Don't do that. The bulls are my best friends."
> I translated to Brett.
> "You kill your friends?" she asked.
> "Always," he said in English, and laughed. "So they don't kill me."

Though he was often aloof and stern, men liked him. He was generous, fair, and "un gran compañero." "Here's a man!" wrote a member of his cuadrilla. "This is the essence of manliness we all hoped we'd grow to be when we were children."

He had thousands of admirers, but no one except his mother broke through that aura of greatness to be really close to him. He didn't ask for loves or intimate friendships from this life; he asked only to be The Best. And now he was, sooner than even he thought he could be, and life was good.

On July 3, 1914, Joselito reached the pinnacle. Alone, with no other matador, he killed six giant bulls in the Madrid arena (not young novillos as he'd done in Cádiz). As an added bonus he called for the substitute, killed that, and was carried out of the ring in wild triumph. He made 25 quités that afternoon, placed 18 banderillas, made 242 passes with cape and muleta, and never rumpled his hair.

A newspaper said the next day: "Nobody could applaud at the end because their hands were too sore, nobody could shout, only croak like delirious bullfrogs. The taurine Vatican has been opened and we have a new pope. If only Cervantes were here to describe it all accurately!"

Another one said: "Beethoven is music—Joselito is bullfighting. Genius like this comes along only once every three hundred years."

It looked as though Joselito would simply coast along, unchallenged like this, into immortality. But then something happened. Fate saw fit to produce a comparable genius, not only in the same century but in the very same period.

Juan Belmonte didn't look much like a genius. He was little and ugly and he stammered. Three years older than Joselito, he got a late start in la fiesta brava. There were no bullfighters in his family, but somehow he drifted into it, and at seventeen, an age when Joselito was already a seasoned matador, Belmonte fought his first corrida. He attracted attention immediately. With little science, he got contracts on guts alone for the first years.

"He's crazy," everyone said.

Literally, he was tossed every afternoon that he fought.

"This Belmonte spends more time in the air than on the ground," said one critic. "He's no matador, he's an aviator."

They called him "the torero of four oles and an *ay!*" because that's about how many passes he'd get away with before being tossed.

"If you haven't seen this madman Belmonte," they said significantly, "you'd better hurry!"

Some people realized from the first that Belmonte's style was revolutionary and that as it developed it was going to change all bullfighting. But most people wrote him off as *un suicida loco*—terribly exciting to watch, but not long for this mortal coil. How could anyone fight in "terrains" that no matador had ever thought of invading and expect to live? The old rule, first stated by the immortal Cúchares, had always been: "You place yourself *there*, and when the bull charges, you either move yourself in a hurry or it'll do the moving for you."

Joselito had modified that somewhat, but Belmonte, perhaps because of his deplorable physical equipment, didn't believe in dodging out of the way at all. He thought it made better sense to plant one's feet permanently and to move the bull out of the way with the cape rather than to move oneself. It didn't always come off, but when it did, and Belmonte wrapped the bull around his waist with no daylight between him and the animal, the crowds couldn't believe their eyes. But no one yet considered him any threat to the most technically perfect matador in the world, Joselito.

Then suddenly Belmonte arrived. On the sixteenth of October, 1913, he was given the alternative by the great Machaquito in Madrid. Whether or not it was because of the sensational performance Belmonte gave that day no one knows, but Machaquito returned to his hotel after the corrida and said, "I will never fight again in my life!" And he kept his word.

Overnight all Spain was arguing as to who was the better, Joselito or this new upstart. They fought together for the first time in March of 1914, in Barcelona. It was the most important fight held in decades, and special reporters were sent from all over Spain to cover the event.

When Belmonte had the crowd screaming on his first passes, Joselito's manager scoffed, "But just look at the bull the man's drawn."

Joselito whistled through his teeth admiringly, "Just look at the man that *bull's* drawn!"

As it turned out, they each cut ears, and were both carried

out of the plaza de toros on the shoulders of the crowd in complete triumph.

This was a historic happening, the beginning of what is always referred to as the Golden Age of Bullfighting, the greatest rivalry ever known in the bullring. Side by side they were to compete with each other for the next six years. Bitter rivals in the arena, they became best friends out of it. Never was there a better, more complementary pair. Belmonte, flamboyant, creative, frighteningly brave, gave the impression that he didn't know quite what hair-raising thing he was going to do next. One had the feeling that he was going to be tossed at any moment, and he usually was.

Recently I visited Belmonte in Sevilla, and as we sat on the porch overlooking his private bullring, I asked don Juan exactly how many times he had been wounded. He shrugged. "Twenty?" I suggested, but this just brought a smile to his lips. "Thirty?" He shook his head. "Forty? Fifty?" Then Belmonte's big jaw came out even farther as he said in his attractive, stammering way, "Fifty is a nice number. Yes, let's say fifty, because I like the number f-f-fifty." The only accurate way to find out would be to have a doctor count the white scars that form grim patterns over his entire body.

Competing against this daily attempt to commit suicide was the sure, unruffled calm of the master technician. Where Belmonte gave the impression that each pass might be his last, Joselito's every move, even when working a millimeter from the horns, seemed to assure the audience, "This is easy—anyone could do it."

Belmonte declared, "There is no cow alive who can drop the bull that could hurt Joselito."

And even Joselito's mother said, "Any bull that wants to hurt my José will have to catch him asleep in his hotel room."

This was not strictly true, since Joselito was gored five times during his career; but this was nothing when one considered the risks he took and the fact that once Belmonte received four almost fatal wounds in a four-month period!

And so these two completely opposite figures, the greatest pair in bullfighting's long history, fought on together almost every day during the season, and after each corrida the word would flash around Spain: "Juan gave Joselito the bath today in Valencia," or "José cut three ears to Juan's one in Bilbao," and the joselistas and the belmontistas would rejoice or lament according to the performance of their idol. More extreme than Dodger-Yankee partisans in this country, the aficionados went as far as wearing pins in their lapel proclaiming their loyalty, carving great profiles of their matadors in the cliffs outside Madrid, and sporting silver likenesses of them for radiator ornaments in their cars.

A famous story showing how vehemently everyone felt about the controversy tells how after putting up an extraordinary performance and cutting the first ear ever conceded in Sevilla, Joselito was carried on the shoulders of the crowd to the church of Santa Ana. There the mob tried to commandeer the platform base from under the Virgin in order to parade Joselito around town on it. The Guardia Civil prevented them from doing it, and the shocked priest berated the crowd, exclaiming, "What sacrilege! Imagine wanting to carry Joselito on the very platform of the Virgin!" He hesitated. "Now—if it were for Belmonte . . ."

Once a critic apologized as he was being introduced to Joselito, "I must warn you that I am a belmontista."

Joselito smiled warmly as he shook his hand. "That's all right, so am I."

Actually the most ardent belmontistas had to admit that Joselito was the more perfect and versatile torero, but they were overwhelmed by the fiery excitement that Belmonte generated and his startling disregard for the rules. Joselito studied Belmonte's revolutionary techniques, the lowered hands, the elbows close to the body, and the contempt for heretofore forbidden terrains of the bull in relationship to the man.

Belmonte was never strong, and he was limited by his physical shortcomings. ("My legs were in such a state," he once said, "that if one wanted to move it had to request permission from the other.") On the other hand Joselito was a superb athlete whose every movement in the arena was as smooth as an ocelot's. He quickly assimilated Belmonte's exciting new style and perfected it. And in a like manner Belmonte learned something from Joselito every afternoon that they performed together. He acquired more and more control; his faenas began to look more planned, rather than just a series of unrelated, foolhardy passes, and he began to be tossed less frequently. Belmonte even learned some of Joselito's seeming ability to read bulls' minds.

The stories of Joselito's extraordinary knowledge of the ways of a bull are infinite. A famous one is the episode of the white horse. He once drew a bull who refused to charge the picador. Nothing could induce it to attack. No matter how close the picador rode his nag up to the bull it refused to charge. Adjudged cowardly, the presidente ordered the animal withdrawn. Joselito requested a delay, had the picador's horse changed from white to black, and the bull charged the new mount immediately.

"I could tell the bull was not basically cowardly," said Joselito, so I guessed that the man who had tested it with a lance when it was a calf was riding a white horse. Bulls have excellent memories."

The test of a great matador is whether or not he can perform with a difficult bull. Too many matadors can shine only when they draw a pera en dulce—a "sweet pear" of a bull that charges unswervingly as though on rails. Joselito's greatest ability was in making nearly every bull that charged out of the Gate of Fear into a "sweet pear."

Sidney Franklin tells a good example of this in *Esquire:*

Once in Málaga Joselito found himself with a particularly cowardly bull. The animal kept hugging the barrier and refused to be attracted to the center of the ring. It looked like a poor fight. A lesser matador would have performed his capework around the perimeter of the ring, working between the animal and the center. Not Joselito. In this case he got between the bull and the fence, the most dangerous place in the ring, and jiggled the cape. The bull charged and smashed into the fence with a sickening crash, missing the matador by less than inches. Again Joselito called him. Another splintering collision of bull and wood. This required cool, pure daring, but it taught the bull a lesson: stay away from the fence. Thereafter the bull went to the middle of the ring of his own accord and Gallito was able to proceed with the fight in style.

The period leading up to Joselito's death is merely the telling of statistics and recounting of repetitions of triumphs: how he would tie his ankles together and give twelve passes of death in one spot; how he would fight entire faenas with his left hand, his right behind his back as though strapped there; how he fought 22 incredible corridas as the only performer (compared to Belmonte's one); how in 1916 he fought 105 corridas, killing 251 bulls in 210 days, more than anyone else had ever done in a single season. He seemed to get better and braver with each year, though everyone said it was impossible.

"You don't know the meaning of the word fear," a reporter once said in an interview.

Joselito smiled. "Nobody knows what I feel in my guts between the time the trumpet blows and the time that terrible gate opens for the bull to come in. Of course I know fear, but I hide it from the crowd—and the bull."

And Belmonte added. "If we matadors had to sign the

contracts one hour before the corrida was to start, there
would be no bullfights."

And so season after season the success continued. But, as
Fitzgerald says, nothing fails like success. In 1919, when
Fortune's Favorite Child was twenty-four and just attaining
the peak of his physical and mental prowess, everything
went wrong. First of all his mother died, and this was a
blow from which he never really recovered. "Without that
loving force," he said disconsolately, "I feel lost, untied,
purposeless, cast adrift."

Then in the same year, he fell in love, deeply and for the
first time. She was the pretty daughter of Andaluz nobility,
and although her father raised fighting bulls as a hobby, he
would hear none of her marrying a common bullfighter,
even if he was the best and richest torero in the world. This
was the first time in his life that Joselito realized the disturbing fact that there might be something else in the world
besides bullfighting.

He tried to forget her but couldn't. He grew moody and
restless. He went to Peru for a change and fought brilliantly
there. Then when he returned to Spain in 1920, he found
awaiting him a more fearsome adversary than any bull he'd
ever encountered: hostile crowds.

No one can say when and why the public turns against
an idol, but once it starts little can stop it. Joselito was fighting better than ever in his life; perhaps that was the very
trouble. One can forgive a man just about anything except
perfection. Gustavo del Barco says in his book on Joselito:
"In bullfighting, as in other arts, the sin of constant triumph
is unforgivable."

They were tired of applauding Joselito day after day, year
after year. It suddenly became more diverting, more chic,
more sophisticated to go to the plaza to boo him, just as it
was to happen in the last months of Manolete's life, twenty-
seven years later. Belmonte came in for some of the crowd's

hostility, but the attacks fell with the most savagery on the head of the one they had labeled The Invulnerable. Joselito was confused, hurt, uncomprehending, as any performer would be who daily tried to do his best for the people who paid to see him. Belmonte saw the reasons more clearly, and del Barco quotes him:

> The public began to tire of us, precisely because of the sensation of security and domination and the elimination of risk which we managed to give. This was worse for Joselito than for me since he gave the impression much more than I that he was completely invulnerable, that he never could be hurt. Seeing that time after time we filled the plazas and that neither of us managed to get ourselves killed, try as we might, the public felt defrauded.

At the start of their last fight together on May 15, 1920, the Madrid crowds began to boo them before they'd even started the parade into the ring, and Joselito was unnerved. A group of threatening spectators advanced on the toreros. "Gyppers! Thieves!" they kept yelling.

"But what have we done?" Joselito exclaimed to Belmonte.

Later in the fight, after the cushions rained down and a woman had yelled that she hoped a bull would kill him the next day in Talavera, Joselito talked to Belmonte. "I'm going to get out of all this," he said bitterly. "It's time for me to retire. I don't know how to fight this."

The next day, eight days after Joselito's twenty-fifth birthday, was the corrida in Talavera de la Reina. Originally, Joselito had no intention of performing in this second-rate arena, but he accepted the fight at the last minute to help out a friend. He took the train there, booked a room in the hotel, and napped until three when his sword boy, Paco Botas, and his brother Fernando woke him up. They remembered later that, though he had been terribly depressed by

the crowd's attitude the day before, now as he dressed in
the gold and scarlet "suit of lights" he seemed almost gay.
He joked with them about several things and kept singing
a bit of cante jondo from the "Coplas del Espartero."

> Little Miura bulls fear nothing now,
> For El Espartero, who used to kill them so well,
> Is dead, olé, olé, olé!

When his superstitious brother chided him for singing
such depressing songs Joselito laughed and pointed to his
pigtail saying, "Why worry? This is coming off very soon."
(A matador ended his career when he cut off his pigtail.)

When he kept singing Fernando said, "The truth is I don't
like that song."

"Well, Fatty," Joselito said good-naturedly, "I like it," and
he continued to sing.

"What goes for you goes for us," said Fernando.

The fight started much like any other corrida in the prov-
inces. They left the hotel at quarter past four and drove
through the gaily decorated town. "There he is, there he is!"
the crowds who lined the streets shouted. Joselito was the
most exciting thing ever to happen to Talavera.

It had been cloudy, but the sun came out as the toreros
paraded into the arena, and the band blared and the five
thousand people cheered. They seemed so much less hostile
than the Madrid audience that Joselito said to the other
matador, his brother-in-law, Sánchez Mejías, "Let's really
give them something today."

But Joselito's first bull from the Viuda de Ortega ranch
was impossible to work with, and even he could do little
with it. The second bull was a little better, and Joselito let
his brother Fernando make some passes with it. Fernando
was a wastrel, fat and completely inept, but Joselito felt
sorry for him and took him around as part of his cuadrilla.
(The famous pasodable "Gallito" was actually written about

Fernando, when he gave promise as a novillero, and not about Joselito, as is generally believed.)

Sánchez Mejías' second bull was the best and bravest of all, and he invited Joselito to put in a pair of banderillas. This Joselito did while standing on the stirrup board, his back up against the fence, and the crowd wildly cheered the magnificence of the maneuver. This was the last sweet ovation the man was to hear.

The fifth bull was named Bailador-Dancer. It came into the ring fast and low, corral dust blowing off its black hide, a big O branded on its flank and the number 7 on its side. The moment Joselito saw it he sucked air in through his teeth, and his green gypsy eyes never left the animal for a second.

"Get behind the fence and don't come out," he ordered his brother. "Everyone look out with this animal. Get on those horns and you won't get off."

Bailador was comparatively small, 259 kilos dressed, which was about half the size of the bull of Joselito's presentation in Madrid. But Bailador had a killer's horns and a treacherous killer's charge, which Joselito spotted immediately. He also discerned that the animal didn't see well close up, but at a distance its vision was good; "burriciego," the toreros call it, and it's a dread thing since bullfighters depend upon the bull's seeing well, so that they can control it and make it choose to charge the cape instead of the man.

In the act of the picadors, Bailador, small as he was, killed five horses in six vicious charges. After the banderillas, which were placed with great difficulty since the bull was completely unpredictable in its charge, the animal took a stand in its querencia. A bull's querencia is an arbitrarily chosen spot in the ring where the animal feels secure for some reason of its own, perhaps where it killed a horse or tossed a man. In its querencia it will fight a defensive, impossible, come-in-after-me type of fight instead of the long, hard charges that both the crowd and the matador want.

When Joselito was handed his sword and muleta by his sword boy, he dedicated the bull. "It goes for the memory of my father who fought the inaugral corrida in this plaza so many years ago," he said as he doffed his montera and tossed it elegantly onto the sand.

The banderillero had managed to lure Bailador out of its querencia by repeatedly trailing capes in front of it, and Joselito pointed with the sword to where he wanted the bull placed. Then he ordered the banderilleros to leave him completely alone with the dangerous animal. He draped the muleta over the sword in his right hand and advanced on the animal. "Toro, ah-hah," Joselito chanted as he walked. "We'll teach you how to charge, little bull."

Fifteen feet from the animal he stopped and shook the muleta. The bull, seeing well at this distance, lowered its head, attacked hard, and Joselito gave it a beautiful trincherazo pass. Three more passes, and the animal was charging straighter and easier on each one, being controlled and learning how to charge from the master teacher. But on the fifth charge it suddenly broke away from the man and trotted back along the boards toward its querencia. It had been attracted by one of the banderilleros who had disobeyed his master and hadn't left the ring.

"Hide yourself, Enrique," Joselito called exasperatedly, "he's with you and won't take the muleta!"

Joselito went after the bull, headed it off, and gave it two more passes, but the capricious animal had lost interest in the muleta now and was looking around distractedly for the banderillero. Joselito blew out a weary sigh and retreated fifteen feet from the animal and wiped the sweat from his forehead. He took the muleta in his left hand, and, looking down at the cloth he shook out the folds and started to redrape it over the sword in his right hand.

Then it happened. Joselito, by withdrawing those five yards from the animal, had stepped into the area where the bull could see well. Suddenly and without warning, it lunged forward, heading straight for the man's body. A banderillero cried out, and Joselito looked up. At that long range it would have been no trick for him, the greatest athlete the ring has known, to have dodged out of the path of this animal. But he left his feet planted on the sand as though they were nailed there, and standing straight and gracefully, he flared out the muleta to distract it off its course as he had done with so many hundreds of other bulls.

But with the surprise of the attack he had forgotten for a fatal moment that this animal had a visual defect. Though the bull had seen the man clearly at a distance, as it came closer the target became more and more blurred until it saw neither the man nor the flared-out muleta designed to make it swerve. Without even seeing its victim, the bull crashed into Joselito. Its left horn hooked into the man's right thigh, and he was slammed up into the air.

As Joselito spun on the horn, the bull chopped its head from side to side viciously, and the right horn ripped open the man's lower stomach. He hung doubled up on the bull's head for a second, managed to push himself off the horn, and then fell to the ground.

The other toreros lured the bull away and ran to Joselito's aid. He struggled to sit up on the sand and was clutching his stomach when the sword boy reached him. There was terror and disbelief in the matador's eyes.

"Ay, madre mia," he moaned, "my guts are coming out!"

"Don't talk like that, Matador!" said the sword boy as he started to pick him up. "It's not true!"

But as he said later, "The truth is, I could see in the mouth of the wound a green ball . . . ."

As he was being carried, Joselito tried to hold his viscera in with his fingers. "Mascarell, Mascarell!" he cried as they rushed him out of the arena toward the infirmary. This was the name of the great horn wound specialist in Madrid.

Once in the infirmary, the two regular doctors and two Madrid surgeons who happened to be in the audience slashed off the matador's "suit of lights." He was breathing feebly, his eyes closed.

"Leave the wound alone," ordered Dr. Pastor. "Take care of him first!"

They injected blood serum, caffeine, and camphor oil into his arms and sides. But the man was slipping away. His cuadrilla was allowed into the operating room, and they wept when they saw the look of death coming on the man. At eight minutes past seven Joselito opened his eyes.

"Madre, me ahogo!" he said. "Mother, I'm smothering, I'm smothering!"

Then he died. The doctor explained later that the wound, in spite of its horrible aspect, wasn't necessarily fatal, but that Joselito had probably died of shock, that his heart had given out upon seeing himself so badly wounded. "He had begun to believe, as we all did, that he was invulnerable."

The sword handler, sobbing like a baby, ceremoniously cut off his dead master's pigtail. All night a steady stream of weeping people from all walks of life filed past the dead man to pay their respects. His brother Rafael arrived from Madrid, but, though he tried three times, he was too shaken to enter the room.

Joselito was taken through Spain to Sevilla with the largest funeral cortege the country could remember, and there he is buried in a tomb topped by a magnificent monument by Benlliure. It depicts nineteen life-sized figures in bronze, weeping gypsies, bull breeders, and toreros carrying the marble, godlike form of the dead matador.

Today, all these years after his death, Joselito el Gallo is far from forgotten. Every May 16 the newspapers in Spain devote pages to his memory, featuring odes by famous poets,

paintings, photos, and editorials. And every May 16 you will
see the toreros wearing black arm ribbons in the big annual
fight in Talavera. It's impossible to pick up a bullfighting
magazine in Spain or Mexico without finding new Joselito
anecdotes or comparisons between him and the current crop
of toreros. There have been hundreds of songs and volumes
written on his life and art. To show what a truly living hero
Joselito is after all these years, the top popular song in Spain
two seasons ago was not about him, but about his mother!
Called "La Gabriela," the verse starts out: "Fernando is
fighting in Puerto, brother Rafael is fighting in Jerez, but
what really chills poor Gabriela's heart is that little Joselito,
all by himself, in Cádiz, is facing six Miuras."

Nearly every young boy in Spain dreams of being as great
a torero as Joselito. And there are many Gabrielas today and
there will be more tomorrow whose hearts will be chilled as
they watch the "child of their right eye" swirling a cape in
front of a trained dog and hear him sing "Coplas del Espartero," but changing the words to:

> Little Miura bulls fear nothing now,
> For Joselito, who used to kill them so well,
> Is dead, olé, olé, olé!

The Louis-Schmeling Fight

Reprinted by permission of International News Service. Written exclusively for INS, June 22, 1938.

The second Louis-Schmeling fight built itself toward its eventual climax in a way no other fight of our time ever did. This was no "war hero vs. slacker" fight, as the Carpentier-Dempsey match was preposterously billed in advance (thereby helping to create the first million dollar gate). Louis-Schmeling had the impact of a great crisis in history. Max, after his surprise upset of Joe in their first meeting, had returned home to find himself a Nazi hero. In time he himself believed in the Super Race and the Thousand Year Rule. The night he entered the ring against a representative of a race a successful Hitler would have enslaved or liquidated, Max was a symbol of the hob-nailed arrogance of his Leader. Joe took on the robes of Right.

Against that background, the blazing, sometimes almost terrifying fight started. For the next two minutes and four seconds, I think Louis could have beaten any heavyweight who ever lived.

BOB CONSIDINE

Listen to this, buddy, for it comes from a guy whose palms are still wet, whose throat is still dry, and whose jaw is still agape from the utter shock of watching Joe Louis knock out Max Schmeling.

It was a shocking thing, that knockout—short, sharp, merciless, complete. Louis was like this:

He was a big lean copper spring, tightened and retightened through weeks of training until he was one pregnant package of coiled venom.

Schmeling hit that spring. He hit it with a whistling right-hand punch in the first minute of the fight—and the spring, tormented with tension, suddenly burst with one brazen spang of activity. Hard brown arms, propelling two unerring fists, blurred beneath the hot white candelabra of the ring lights. And Schmeling was in the path of them, a man caught and mangled in the whirring claws of a mad and feverish machine.

The mob, biggest and most prosperous ever to see a fight in a ball yard, knew that here was the end before the thing had really started. It knew, so it stood up and howled one long shriek. People who had paid as much as one hundred dollars for their chairs didn't use them—except perhaps to stand on, the better to let the sight burn forever in their memories.

There were four steps to Schmeling's knockout. A few seconds after he landed his only punch of the fight, Louis caught him with a lethal little left hook that drove him into the ropes so that his right arm was hooked over the top strand, like a drunk hanging to a fence. Louis swarmed over him and hit him with everything he had—until Referee Donovan pushed him away and counted one.

Schmeling staggered away from the ropes, dazed and sick. He looked drunkenly toward his corner, and before he had turned his head back Louis was on him again, first with a left and then that awe-provoking right that made a crunching sound when it hit the German's jaw. Max fell down, hurt and giddy, for a count of three.

He clawed his way up as if the night air were as thick as black water, and Louis—his nostrils like the mouth of a double-barreled shotgun—took a quiet lead and let him have both barrels.

Max fell almost lightly, bereft of his senses, his fingers touching the canvas like a comical stew-bum doing his morning exercises, knees bent and the tongue lolling in his head.

He got up long enough to be knocked down again, this time with his dark unshaven face pushed in the sharp gravel of the resin.

Louis jumped away lightly, a bright and pleased look in his eyes, and as he did the white towel of surrender which Louis' handlers had refused to use two years ago tonight came sailing into the ring in a soggy mess. It was thrown by Max Machon, oblivious to the fact that fights cannot end this way in New York.

The referee snatched it off the floor and flung it backwards. It hit the ropes and hung there, limp as Schmeling. Donovan counted up to five over Max, sensed the futility of it all, and stopped the fight.

The big crowd began to rustle restlessly toward the exits, many only now accepting Louis as champion of the world. There were no eyes for Schmeling, sprawled on his stool in his corner.

He got up eventually, his dirty-gray-and-black robe over his shoulders, and wormed through the happy little crowd that hovered around Louis. And he put his arm around the Negro and smiled. They both smiled and could afford to— for Louis had made around $200,000 a minute and Schmeling $100,000 a minute.

But once he crawled down in the belly of the big stadium, Schmeling realized the implications of his defeat. He, who won the title on a partly phony foul, and beat Louis two years ago with the aid of a crushing punch after the bell had sounded, now said Louis had fouled him. That would read better in Germany, whence earlier in the day had come a cable from Hitler, calling on him to win.

It was a low sneaking trick, but a rather typical last word from Schmeling.

Football's Greatest Loss

This column first appeared in the New York *Herald Tribune,* August 28, 1955. Copyright 1955, New York Herald Tribune Inc.

The reason I selected Plainfield State Teachers as my favorite story is because of the delightful fantasy involved. Nowhere in sports has there ever been a football team to compare with Plainfield, nowhere will they ever find a back as great as the fabulous John Chung.

Though the actual Plainfield story broke in the newspapers in 1941, I didn't treat it as column material until some fifteen years later. By that time, almost everyone had forgotten the tale and it amounted to making another so-called "news" story out of a theme that had been in the paper fifteen years before.

BOB COOKE

The entire football world was saddened the other day when Morris Newburger announced his retirement from football. Oh, you've heard of Knute Rockne, Walter Camp, Alonzo Stagg, and the like, but I'll make a bet you never thought of putting Newburger up there on the list. Fact is, I'll wager you never heard of Newburger.

81

Football was blessed with Newburger many years after Rockne, Stagg, Camp, and their kind had become famous in song and story. It remained for Newburger, a citizen of quiet renown, to provide an everlasting memorial to the game as we know it today.

Newburger was always a fellow who shied away from praise. He never played football. He is not a spotlight seeker. Yet, the advent of a football season, with no mention of Newburger, is more than a fan can stand.

Newburger once coached a team that was never beaten, never tied. He needed no assistant coaches, no stadium, no customers, and no players.

It was in the fall of 1941 when Newburger was seized by an uncontrollable desire to build an undefeated eleven.

So he created one which he called Plainfield State Teachers. Sounds like a college, doesn't it? Newburger thought so, and so did a number of metropolitan sports writers.

Having founded Plainfield State, Newburger needed only a schedule to get his season started. Swiftly he improvised some "tough opposition," not to mention, "traditional rivals." When he had completed his work, Plainfield State had an eight-game itinerary against such teams as Scott, Chesterton, Fox, Randolph Tech, Ingersoll, Benson, Appalachian, and Harmony U (home-coming).

The above institutions were as mythical as Plainfield State, but they appeared to be football teams. Newburger, working fiendishly, had given them names which carried a trace of the familiar thus leading to the illusion of the authentic.

In the opener against Scott, Plainfield State got off to a "terrific" start by whipping its "bigger opponents," 20-0. At this stage of the game, Newburger displayed a talent amounting to genius.

After he'd phoned the result of the Plainfield State-Scott

game to the New York *Herald Tribune,* the New York *Times,* the Associated Press, and other news media, he created the celebrated fullback, John Chung.

"Can't have a miracle team without a miracle player," Newburger whispered to himself as he began to make an accounting of Chung's assets.

Chung was a 205-pound, full-blooded Chinese fullback. He was the star of the Plainfield State team, the crowbar which pried victory from defeat, the shining white horse on which the team rode forth to battle. According to Plainfield State's statistics, Chung gained an average of nine and three-tenths yards every time he carried the ball, due largely, so Newburger said, to Chung's habit of eating rice between the halves.

Herb Allan, former sports writer on the New York *Post,* received a publicity release on Chung and wrote a glowing feature about the star of the Orient. This was one week prior to the revelation that neither Chung nor Plainfield State existed.

Six victories had been recorded before Caswell Adams, then of the *Herald Tribune,* scooped the town with his story of the Plainfield State hoax.

Plainfield had trampled on Scott, Chesterton, Fox, Randolph Tech, Ingersoll, and Benson. Appalachian was to have been beaten, 20-2. Then, in the final, Harmony was to put up a great game but was to succumb to Chung's wizardry, 40-27, before an enthusiastic home-coming crowd.

The cancellation of the games against Appalachian and Harmony saddened Mr. Newburger. He was also downhearted over the sudden end to the career of John Chung, the indestructible Chinese. So retirement has claimed Mr. Newburger.

Always and forever, Newburger will recall the time he telephoned a local paper with the score of the Plainfield

State-Randolph Tech game. The score was Plainfield State Teachers 35, Tech 0.

"Where's Plainfield State?" asked the rewrite man. "In Plainfield, New Jersey?"

"No, just outside," said Newburger and hung up.

Archie, You Were Magnificent!

by Bill Corum

This column first appeared in the New York *Journal-American*, September 22, 1955, and is reprinted by permission of that newspaper.

Bill Corum, like most sportswriters, rarely saves or even looks at a column once it has appeared in the newspaper. This makes selecting a favorite piece difficult. "Fortunately," writes Corum, "to refresh myself on fights, I do sometimes keep fight stories of my own and others, and I think the attached is a first-rate piece and not out of date."

R. P. G.

I speak now of big prize fighters as I have seen them since Dempsey fought the Orchid Man of France—Carpentier—back of the billboards in New Jersey.

I speak of them only as fighters, all of them, through these many years and in the light of last night's memorable encounter for the "Big One" in Yankee Stadium.

And I speak to two all-the-way game men directly, and in this fashion:

Champion Marciano, you were invincible as always.

Archie Moore, you were magnificent!

As your conqueror said of you in the ring and into the microphone when it was over: "He wasn't just talking up there in North Adams."

And you, in your turn, Archie, said: "It was a pleasure to have fought him."

Just one night, to paraphrase slightly what you said about the postponement, "is a little time in twenty years."

But time enough for you, Archie, an often lonesome traveler of the vagabond trail of boxing, to thrill a nation.

It just couldn't have been, Archie, that you didn't thrill the oldsters—such as I—since you proved, for sure, that it isn't always the hot-blood of youth that can walk into the guns with a steady tread.

Oh, yes, I know what you said to Doc Nardiello, when he came into your corner at the end of the eighth round, when your legs were gone, and hope of victory was gone, and even the glaring white light over the ring must have seemed dim to the one eye that you still had entirely open.

You said, and I quote:

"Please, Doctor, don't stop it. Let me try once more with a desperado."

And Doctor N., who, too, has been a long time around these things, which are just boxing bouts, of course, even though there must always be in them some sort of measure of a man, replied:

"Okay, Archie, if that's the way you want it."

And that was the way you wanted it.

You knew full well by then, Archie, what was going to happen. You had learned, as had others before you, that the sweet science of boxing, at its sweetest, can befuddle and confound at times the great champion of the world who is Rocky Marciano, of Brockton, Mass.—the ugly duckling, fighting-wise, who never turned pretty, but who always winds up the boss of where he stands.

Still, as I say, you knew full well by then that the feints, the moves, the almost artistic slipping of punches, which you had given the folks a look at for more than half a minute once in the fight, when Rocky had you against the ropes and swung, and swung, and swung, hitting nothing, were of no avail.

He'd swung until his arms were plainly weary and heavy. But, unhappily for you, Archie, his heart still was light. He comes on that way, The Rock. Missing often, floundering often, no Pavlova he. But he is so strong, and he is such a man in his remarkable body and in his concentrated and never-questioning mind.

Rocky's is the simple philosophy of a guy who brought a pretty girl to the dance. He has a lovely wife and nice youngster. I'm sure that his lady will understand that what I'm saying is figurative and far from personal.

But his attitude toward the world's heavyweight championship when he takes it into the ring is: "I brought the girl and I'm going to take her home."

Nor ever for a fleeting second in any kind of trouble— and last night he had some trouble, make no mistake—does he doubt that he is "going to take her home."

Moore rode with punches, slipped 'em, tried to fend Rocky off with the jab—a good jab but not strong enough— "suckered" him, too, quite often in the right moves, as they were known to the Marquis of Queensberry.

The trouble was that Rocky didn't know it, and never doubted or waivered, or even remotely feared for a moment. A fighter who can do that comes to be a real tough man to beat. And Rocky Marciano does it.

Up to now, he just "ain't heard about losing." So, up to now, he's never lost.

There was some small talk in the champion's dressing

room to the effect that he might "hang 'em up." Skip it. As of now, at any rate, he won't. The world's greatest financial matchmaker, a man named Sam, will bring him back again.

There was no reporter named Napoleon at ringside last night. But a man named Napoleon wrote the story of the fight long ago, when he said: "God is on the side of the heaviest artillery."

That was it. Switch the power in their punches, if it could be done, then give me Moore and all that sweet 4-1 that I could take.

After last evening, I'd concede the years and even Archie's plainly tired and rebellious legs. But, if Archie's legs often sagged and buckled, as they did, his heart marched to the cadence.

The never-beaten champion won. In common sense, barring a star-bright break in luck, who else?

But the "Old One" came to meet him and fought him, and punched with him, and tried him for all he had learned over so many long, lean years.

And when all was said and done, and he had crumpled in a small heap for such a big man on the last knockdown—and the kayo—he, ol' Arch, still was asking his legs to give him one more chance.

Then it was over. And the actor, and wandering minstrel of the boxing glove still, Archie ran his comb through his henna-touched and marcelled hair, and came out to say: "It was a pleasure to fight him."

What do you want, Sir Beerbohm Tree?

You got frapped, Arch, but, for very sure, you didn't freeze.

They tell me the fight drew 61,574 paid, with a gross of $948,117, and a net of $820,935. Add Theatre TV, the radio, and what should be a highly-successful picture, and, Promotor Norris, you had a great fight. But, sir, you deserved it.

I never saw a better promoted fight, a cleaner one, a better regulated and controlled crowd. Or more thrilled people than I saw leaving the Stadium.

It was something of which to be proud, all around.

International Crisis

by Arthur Daley

This article first appeared in The New York *Times*, November 2, 1947, and is reprinted by permission of Arthur Daley.

A sports columnist sometimes finds his material in strange places—in this case, the United Nations. Arthur Daley writes that he was introduced to this story by a Times *U.N. correspondent, who suggested he would find Australia's Colonel Hodgson an engaging subject. "Hodgson talked, I listened," writes Daley. "International Crisis" was the result.*

R. P. G.

A ringing challenge to America was delivered yesterday by a delegate to the United Nations. For a change, though, it wasn't a Russian who was doing the delivering. Nor did the challenge bristle with indignation, vituperation and scathing invective. It came from a merry-eyed son of the British Empire, Col. William R. Hodgson of Australia. If the truth must be told, he undoubtedly was engaging in what an Englishman might describe as "pulling your leg a bit, old chap." That's what it seemed to add up to, anyway.

"Where do you fellows get off calling your world series for the championship of the world?" asked the colonel. "We have some baseball back home, you know. It's pretty good baseball, I might add." The colonel set his jaw firmly and his visitor, still uncertain of his ground, had to proceed cautiously.

"The way you chaps do things," continued the colonel with an airy wave of his hand. "You play bridge and the winners are world masters. Everything is at least for the championship of the world. You can't truly have one in baseball, you know, until you play Australia." He gave that last word the fascinating pronunciation which strikes the American ear as sounding suspiciously like "Austrilya."

Since the visitor was fully aware of the fact that Colonel Hodgson was a rabid baseball fan who never missed an opportunity to see a major league game, his opinions merited attention. "If the teams from Down Under are that good," he was told, "arrangements could undoubtedly be made to have games here as soon as the world series is over."

"Play here?" exploded the colonel in astonishment. "Why should we come here? Why not Australia? The Sydney Cricket Grounds, you know, will accommodate 100,000 spectators. After all, the Yankee Stadium holds only 70,000." He smiled in superior fashion. His visitor rolled slightly to absorb that unexpected verbal punch.

"Don't forget," continued the colonel, pressing to the attack in true army style, "that our chaps more than held their own with the Giants when they toured Australia." Ahem. That took place only some thirty-odd years ago when John McGraw's Giants and Charley Comiskey's White Sox made a round-the-world tour. And no big leaguers have been there since.

"It would be tremendously stimulating to the sport back home," resumed the Australian delegate, his simulated pugnaciousness giving way to a natural wistfulness, "if we could have your chaps on tour again. It would lead to great public interest. That's the sort of stuff we need."

The colonel's bold front was starting to show signs of cracking at the seams. He'd become, for the moment, merely an ardent sports fan, the representative of a section of the world that probably has more athletic addicts to the square inch than any other part of the globe. Vishinsky never would have made so damaging an admission. In all probability it demonstrates how decadent capitalism really is.

"To tell you the truth," said Colonel Hodgson, sadly, "there's just no comparison between our brand of baseball and yours. Your teamwork and precision is a revelation and the way your lads handle the double play is unbelievable. After all, our ball players are mostly cricketeers who have a go at baseball during the off-season in order to keep in shape."

Cricketeers playing baseball? The provincial Americans always had held to the theory that any major league team could go anywhere in the British Empire and beat a top-flight cricket team. After all, Pop Anson took a group of ball players to England before the turn of the century and supposedly beat the famous Marylebone team at cricket, 107 to 105. Sharper and better fielding did it—or so the rumor ran.

Colonel Hodgson blinked incredulously. "Our cricketeers are top-flight fielders," he protested, "and good fielding plays a large part in the game. You chaps talk about the Williams shift and the Dimaggio shift as though you invented massed defenses. We've been doing that for more years than I care to remember. We've always filled the gaps to counteract rival strength."

The Australian leaped to his feet and began to swing an imaginary cricket bat, carefully protecting an imaginary wicket. "If a man is strong on the 'off' or on the 'leg' or on the 'drive'," he explained, "we set our fielders out to protect the spots where he's most likely to hit. Not only can they catch a ball but they throw with a typical baseball motion —all but the bowler, of course."

It wasn't pertinent to the discussion, of course, but the Danes once had an event on their track and field program called "throwing the cricket ball for distance," the record being held by some Englishman. A touring American track team visited Copenhagen many years ago and two of our heroes mischievously entered the event.

A flag near the far wall at one end of the stadium marked the record heave. Pete Bowen, a quarter-miler from Pitt, promptly threw the cricket ball over the wall, to the vast astonishment of the local populace. But Leo Sexton, the Olympic shot-put champion from Georgetown and the New York A.C., arched the cricket ball clean out of the stadium, clearing the ramparts by so much that his new record never could be measured.

Colonel Hodgson seemed unimpressed. "We have a lot of professional running back home, you know, and we've always been very keen on horse racing. Wrestling is very popular and we get all your leading wrestlers. But the sport has to be dinkum or we won't go for it." Wrestling that's dinkum or correct in a genuine sort of way hasn't been seen in these parts for at least a generation. However, there can be no doubt about the fact that it thrives Down Under.

The colonel looked at his watch and began to peel off his coat. "I have to go now," he said, presumably on affairs of state. Since he was in his hotel suite and since he seemed to be staying rather than going, his visitor took the hint and headed for the nearest exit, the international crisis settled. It seemed the dinkum thing to do.

Home on the Football Range

This article first appeared in The New York *Times*, December 10, 1935, and is reprinted by permission of Allison Danzig.

If anything I have put on copy paper in the course of a wayward career as a sports scribbler has any literary merit, this is it. In writing straight news reports under the gun of a deadline there is little opportunity for getting fanciful or delving into antiquity. There was such an opportunity here and also the challenge of doing one of my first pieces in trying to fill the space belonging to the peerless John Kieran. It is the one time, I like to think, that I ever remotely approached the master.

ALLISON DANZIG

Not so long after the turn of the century, about the time the Cotton Palace came to Waco and the Great Emancipator was established first in the thoughts of the nation's tender youth as the figurehead on the copper coin of the realm, a barefoot boy found himself on the gridiron of Baylor University and came down with a hopeless case of kick-and-buck fever.

After that, the standing order with the family doctor to stop by on Sundays to remove a fish hook from the toe of the said barefoot boy was rescinded. Along with the tackle that he had dropped every weekend into the Brazos for catfish and perch, his shotgun was put away, to gather rust in the garret.

From that day on there was never any question of where to find the urchin of a Saturday afternoon or any other afternoon from September to December. The bacillus Pedinan (pigskin Latin) had entered his bloodstream and football now became his chile con carne and drink.

The family doctor dropped around from force of habit. He had studied medicine in the North and he had wondrous tales to tell of the mighty football teams of Yale, Harvard, Princeton, Cornell, Penn and Syracuse. The barefoot no longer boy, who now insisted on sleeping with his cleats on, listened entranced. It was more thrilling than anything in Grimm or Bullfinch. Yale, in particular, became the object of his new-found apotheosis.

More wonderful than knights in shining armor riding a Bucephalus or slaying a Medusa were Frank Hinkey, Pudge Heffelfinger, Tad Jones, Tom Shevlin, Gordon Brown, Brinck Thorne, Jim Hogan and the new sensation of the day, Ted Coy. They were all so many heroes of mythology to him, so supernatural seemed their deeds and so far, far removed were they from the narrow orbit of his existence.

And then, out of a clear sky, the barefoot boy learned that it was Eastward, ho! for the family lares and penates. Grabbing the household cat by the tail, as per instructions of a knowing pickaninny, he sought, for good luck, to heave the clawing pet over the homestead roof—a forward pass that failed dismally—and said good-bye to Waco.

The barefoot boy grew up and forgot all about Texas, except when he saw Benny Boynton of Williams, Eddie Kaw of Cornell, Bill Cunningham of Dartmouth and, later, Waco Jack Buckler of Army in action. It made him proud to think that all-America material could come out of his homeland, but, shucks, they had to come East to become real heroes. Who ever heard of an All-America player on a team in the Lone Star State?

Gus Dittmar, center on Texas from 1913 to 1916, was the only one he could recall that had got the slightest tumble from Walter Camp. Yes, sir, it was get along East, young man, if you wanted to make your way in the football world.

A week ago Saturday Southern Methodist and Texas Christian played a game of football at Fort Worth. The barefoot boy who set out from Waco to see some real football in the East sat high up in Franklin Field, with the greatest sports spectacle of the season, the Army-Navy game, before him, and mourned his luck. His thoughts were with the game far off in the Southwest, where two of the greatest teams of the year were meeting in what amounted to civil warfare, with a Rose Bowl invitation as the prize.

From all parts of the country fans poured into Fort Worth on a hegira to a new Mecca of football. Verily, the mountain had come to Mohammed. Texas had come into its own, its stature on the national gridiron horizon established second to none and its Bobby Wilsons, Darrell Lesters, Sammy Baughs, Truman Spains, John McCauleys, Bill Wallaces, Iron Man Wetsels and Harry Shufords marching down the same corridors once sacred to the immortal cleats of the Hinkeys of Yale, the Mahans of Harvard and the Poes of Princeton.

S.M.U., Princeton and Minnesota are the only three unbeaten and untied major teams in all the land, the Mustangs remaining in this august company by virtue of their triumph over Texas A&M last Saturday. On New Year's Day, when Southern Methodist enters the Rose Bowl stadium at Pasadena to engage Stanford, the day of the new deal will have dawned for Texas football. A battle second only to that of the Alamo will have been won.

That battle for national recognition has been going on for

years. Football has been played in the Lone Star State for nearly half a century. Some of the most illustrious coaches have taught the game there. They include Ray Morrison, at S.M.U. in 1915, 1916 and from 1922 until he left for Vanderbilt this year; Francis Schmidt, who went from Arkansas to T.C.U. in 1929 and remained there until called to Ohio State in 1934; and Dana X. Bible, at Texas A&M in 1917 and from 1919 until he went to Nebraska in 1929.

Others have been Sol Metzger, at Baylor in 1904; Charley Moran, at Texas A&M from 1909 to 1914; John Heisman, at Rice from 1925 to 1927, and Clyde Littlefield, at Texas from 1927 to 1933. Hugo Bezdek coached at Arkansas, now a member of the Southwest Conference, from 1908 to 1912.

Most of the coaches now holding forth have been on the job for two seasons at the most. Matty Bell stepped up from the job of assistant to Morrison at S.M.U. Leo (Dutch) Meyer came up from freshman coach to replace Schmidt at T.C.U. Jack Chevigny left St. Edward to succeed Littlefield at Texas last year. Jimmy Kitts got the job at Rice in 1934, when Jack Meagher went to Auburn, and Homer Norton came from Centenary at the same time to Texas A&M, where Bell had followed Bible. Morley Jennings has been at Baylor since 1926.

No team has ever won the conference title two years in a row. The Aggies, Texas, Baylor and S.M.U. dominated the group in the 1920's until T.C.U. broke through in Schmidt's first year, 1929. Schmidt produced another champion team in 1932, and in 1931 his eleven ruined the Rose Bowl hopes of S.M.U. by holding the Mustangs to a 0-0 tie. Rice won the title for the first time in 1934, Kitts' first year, and now Bell has produced a champion in his first season.

The biggest day in Texas football, until S.M.U. and T.C.U. met on November 30, was October 6, 1934. On that date Texas defeated Notre Dame, Rice conquered Purdue and S.M.U. tied Louisiana State.

Next year Texas will celebrate its centennial with the biggest sports festival in its history. The barefoot boy is getting a bad case of nostalgia . . . and say, wouldn't a bowl of real chili taste good, with a side helping of hot tamales? Jeeves! my chaps and sombrero and saddle up Pinto.

Requiem to Rickard

The Rickard poem was written in haste, as are most newspaper pieces. Pegler and I had gone across the street from the MORNING TELEGRAPH *(of which I was then the editor) to the Garden, where Rickard's body lay in state. Neither of us liked to look at dead friends; so we sat in the gallery as the people moved below us. I was for a short time in 1928 the publicity chief for the Garden (having succeeded Ike Dorgan), and my regard for Tex, always high, was increased. The poem was an impromptu memorial, nothing more.*

GENE FOWLER

Not before the altar and the choir of the Cathedral,
With surpliced boys intoning,
And dirges of holy bells beating down on the con-
gregation;
Nor with cross bearers and robed clergymen
marching;
Candles burning and sunlight groping feebly
through stained glass while swaying censers
are uplifted—

99

But beneath the high and bare girders of the hip-
    podrome hall—
With twice ten thousand seats strangely empty,
And the chill of a January day stalking through the
    bleak corridors—
There, in a bronze coffin, lies the tall and silent
    Texan.

In the high hall he built, he lies in state.
Along the torn-up avenue, the laborers peer at the
    silk-hatted men leaving their motor cars and
    at the throngs passing into the black-draped
    foyer—
And near the ring-space is a floral platform and a
    bronze box.
And here is his Peace, where only yesterday—and
    again tomorrow—the bodies of boxers were wet
    with straining and their flanks were cramped
    and tired from the blows,
While gutturals of the gallery men, sadistic, growled
    like the surf of the Rockaways.

Not the Gothic sanctity of the Cathedral with its
    somber ecclesiastics and the rituals—
But the stolid policemen in the hippodrome hall
The crepe-festooned lobby, where the mourners pass
    the picture gallery of the champions—
Portraits of muscular celebrities: Muldoon, his
    arms folded and his loins draped bravely in a
    lion's hide and posing in a studio setting simu-
    lating the arena of the Caesars;

Hairy-chested Jeffries in his ponderous crouch,
    poised for a left-hand rip to the liver.
Huge, phlegmatic Willard, his unwieldy biceps
    flexed and his steam-shovel fists framing a va-
    cant face;

Dempsey, when his tapering legs were yet alert
    with youth and when his body was a symbol
    of power;
Jack Johnson, the incorrigible black genius of de-
    fense;
Corbett in white tights, his pompadour suggesting
    a cockatoo's crest and his darting left extended.
Skinny-legged Bob Fitzsimmons with his grotesque
    bald pate and his abnormal shoulders—
The Maulers' Hall of Fame—and beyond it, in the
    high hall, the sleeping Texan.

Upstairs, in the locked drawer of the bronze desk,
    are the dry and shriveled gloves Battling Nel-
    son wore when bludgeoning the consumptive
    Gans;
And a trophy head of an African buck given by the
    younger Roosevelt, and a rhinocerous hide
    cane presented by T.R.
And an empty chair made from the horns of steers;
And a brass cuspidor the Texan seldom hit with his
    tobacco thrusts.
And drawn blinds on the wide windows fronting
    Forty-ninth street, where he often listened to
    the voices of playing children.

His friends—the millionaire and the beggar, too,
    come in to see the Texan.
The gate is shut forever between him and them
    and there is only Memory.
Lament and January Day—tomorrow the Spring,
    and flowers newly-blooming on a grave.
Not beneath the vaulted roof of the Cathedral,
But under the high and bare girders of the hippo-
    drome hall,
There, in a bronze coffin, lies the tall and silent
    Texan.

Inside the Inside

by Paul Gallico

Paul Gallico was in Europe while this book was compiled and requested that a piece be selected for him. After going over a good number of Gallico's magazine stories and newspaper columns, I came back to my original choice—"Inside the Inside"—the finest, most penetrating analysis of a sport and its appeal that I have ever read.

R. P. G.

Baseball can be the most fascinating game in the world to watch and also the dullest, depending very often upon circumstances—that is to say, the quality of the play, the caliber and situation of the competing teams, and also what you yourself bring into the park. All games are alike in form and intent. One man tries to beat another man, or one group of men try to worst another group through skill, courage, and physical condition. It is merely the materials with which they are provided for this purpose, the rules, and the playing grounds that differ. The more intricate the game

102

and tangled the rules and complicated the materials, the more difficult it is to understand, but the more fascinating it becomes when you do understand it.

When two men face each other in a boxing ring with gloves on their hands and begin to fight when the bell rings, and stop fighting when it rings again after three minutes, it is reasonably obvious to anyone what is going on and what they are trying to do to each other and the means they are employing. The struggle is a simple hand-to-hand trial for complete mastery within certain time limits, and because the struggle sometimes gets atavistic, abysmal, and terrifying, with show of blood, it is arresting and arousing. The novice spectator becomes an expert after witnessing his first prizefight or boxing match because everything is plain and simple and easy to see. It takes rather longer to know what is going on on a baseball field, what the trials and the problems of the various players are, what can be done and what cannot be done; and even so, many people who have been going to games for years do not know exactly what it is all about because they have never taken the trouble to find out. They love it, though, because they do realize that there is a fine balance struck between offense and defense and that, by a lucky accident in the laying out of the playing field and the development of the game, you may sit by and witness the development of real drama and the working of keen wits in fast bodies.

Baseball talk is a great bore, baseball-players are not exactly intellectual giants, and baseball figures, box scores and averages even duller. But the things that take place on the field in a tight game played to the hilt by a couple of major-league clubs can be completely captivating.

If games as a whole bore you, you will never like baseball. But if you can take pleasure in the story of conflict unfolded before your eyes, it is only necessary to become a little more familiar with the materials used by baseball-players and the rules under which they operate to find something that can be quite as fascinating, for instance, as the theater. In one afternoon at the ball yard you may, if you know where and how to look for it, come upon half a dozen split-second races between a running man and a thrown ball, in which the hundredth part of a second is all the difference between success and failure, dozens of examples of skill triumphant, skill defeated, traps baited and snapped shut upon victims, human courage, human folly, and human cowardice, narrow escapes, heroes, villains, individual deeds that verge upon the miraculous, bits of co-operation between two men or among three or four that are really beautiful to see in their rhythm and perfection, heroes turned suddenly into clowns and goats, clowns becoming heroes, speed, grace, and sometimes even a curious beauty, the beauty of the perfection of a well-pitched, well-defended game.

The patterns of the game are of themselves interesting and pleasing to the eye. The rich chocolate-brown or pale tan of the infield is contrasted with the fine soothing green of the outfield. The base paths are neatly geometrical, and the white foul lines on either side of the home plate start their diverging roads towards infinity. There is a place for everyone and every place is neatly marked off with white lime. There is a base at each corner of the square, and a player stationed at, or close to, each base. The outfield is divided into three sections, right, center, and left field, and each field has a patrolman stationed in his appointed place. Pitcher and catcher stand on a line that is the hypotenuse of the right-angle triangle made by the three bases, home, first, and second. And pleasingly anti-geometrical is the shortstop, who is placed with no heed to design at all, midway between second and third base, upsetting the whole scheme of regularity like a tiny beauty mark on the cheek of a pretty girl.

One team dresses in white, the other in gray. And the

action is static rather than fluid, with sharp, refreshing changes from tension and immobility to quick, brilliant bursts of motion. You may see this curiously exaggerated in newsreel photographs of ball games, because the camera cuts in usually just a second before the flashes of action on the diamond. You catch a glimpse of them stock still first, and then suddenly men are streaking around the bases, heads down, legs twinkling, while fielders glide in to make their quick, graceful defensive moves.

But the plot behind the patterns is even more exciting. Let us take a simple example; the score is tied, there is one out, a runner is on first base, and a heavy hitter is at bat, crouched a little over the plate, waving his mace back and forth gently but menacingly. And, incidentally, he doesn't do this in hopes of frightening the pitcher. He is merely keeping his bat moving because the action he is to be called upon to meet is so fast that he will be hopelessly beaten if he hasn't begun to move a little in advance of it.

There they are, then, the eleven men involved at the moment in what from the point of view of the eventual outcome of the game may be definitely the crisis. The first baseman is dividing his attention between keeping the runner at his base from gaining too much of a lead, and still covering his territory defensively. If the ball is hit, the runner on first will come charging at full clip into second base. Depending upon where the ball is hit to, either the second baseman or the shortstop will have to get there to take the throw and the shock. Or he may not even wait for a hit, but try to steal in the little bit of time between the start of the pitcher's delivery and the passage of the ball to catcher and thence to second baseman. The shortstop is intent upon the delicate problem of starting a successful double play and retiring the side. The third baseman has moved in a little to speed up the fielding of a possible bunt or roller in the infield, and yet he must not leave the space around his base unprotected through which a sharply driven ball may scoot for two or three bases and disaster.

The outfielders have shifted their positions to suit the known batting habits of the hitter. The burly, powerful figure squatting behind the bat, the catcher, is the man in control of the entire situation, and the pitcher is his tool, obeying his brain and his strategy, telegraphed to him by means of finger signals. Or perhaps the catcher is merely an intermediary who transmits the signals and will of an even better strategic mind in the person of the manager sitting on the bench. And the batter is one lone man playing the other nine men, their speed and skill, the intelligence of the catcher in playing his weaknesses, and the control of the pitcher and his ability to obey the orders of the catcher, combined against him. Every move that follows will have a direct bearing upon the outcome of the game. Nothing is unimportant. A double play will badly hurt the morale of the side thus retired with victory in its grasp. A hit or an error or a stolen base may equally upset the equilibrium of the defending team. But still more fascinating and exciting is the fact that all of the men involved are playing a match against time and distance and dealing with the smallest fragments of seconds that can be split on the dial of a delicate stop watch.

The baseball diamond is no diamond at all, but actually a square set up on one of its points, and the bases, home to first, first to second, second to third, and third to home, are each exactly 90 feet apart. The pitcher's box is 60½ feet from home plate. The distance from home plate to second base, which is the line on which the catcher throws in the attempt to catch a man out who is stealing, is a fraction over 127 feet. And the entire science and thrill of the American game of baseball, developed from an old English game called rounders, lie tucked away in those measurements. They are very rarely examined, and still more rarely thought of, even by the players. Most of the men who play the game haven't the vaguest notion of the miracles of timing and precision that they perform.

The infielders, for instance, have a fraction under three seconds in which to field a batted ball and get it over to first base ahead of the runner, because the batter only has to run a distance of thirty yards to reach first. From a standing start a fast man can do it in three and two tenths seconds, and a left-handed batter perhaps one or two tenths of a second faster, because he is on the right-hand side of the plate and a yard closer to his goal. If the fielder can get that ball to first base in just under three seconds, the runner is out. A few tenths of a second over the three seconds and he is safe and a potential run is menacing the defense.

Now, look at the second hand of your watch and note the time it takes for three seconds to tick off—one . . . two . . . three and gone. In this time, the infielder judges the speed and direction of a ball hit with all the weight and force behind the body of a man, moves in to meet it, figuring the hop as he does so, and the number of steps he must take to reach it, catches it and throws it again all in one motion while still moving forward. There is nothing prettier for timing and rhythm in any sport than to watch a shortstop or third baseman (whose problems are greater because, of the infielders, they are farthest removed from first base and have a greater distance to throw) come in fast for a slow roller, and as he is moving, swoop on the ball like a gull dropping for a fish, and with a continuation of the same movement with which he picked it up, get it away on a line for first base with an underhand throw across his forward-bending body. So precious and vital are those tenths of seconds that if he tries to straighten up, or draw his arm back to gain more speed and accuracy, the play is over. The runner has crossed first base.

How much faster, then, and more beautiful in speed and

execution is the double play when three men handle the ball in the same length of time and retire two runners on the one play, the man speeding to second (and he has a good head start) and the batter heading for first. Three seconds flat or better, and yet the shortstop fields the batted ball, or rather scoops it over to the second baseman, who sends it on to first. It would take a delicate timing instrument to measure the fraction of a second that the shortstop actually has possession of the ball. Crack! goes the bat. Step, and flip, goes the shortstop! The second baseman in that time has run from his position perhaps five or six yards from the bag as the ball is started towards him by the shortstop. Ball and man meet on the base, and likewise with the same motion, in which there is no check or hesitation, the second baseman whirls and lines the ball down to first. He can whip that ball the ninety feet from second to first in three fifths of a second. And he is lucky to have that much time left.

The catcher has a pretty problem to throw out a man who is trying to steal. A good base-runner will take a lead of from two to three or four yards from first base before he suddenly ducks his head and breaks for second with every ounce of speed he can muster. He can make it in something around three seconds flat, or even a tenth or two under. Unlike a force-out, where it is merely necessary to touch the bag once the ball is in the fielder's possession, the second baseman or shortstop, who receives the throw at second, must touch the runner with the ball before his spikes cut into the bag or he hooks it with his leg. Here is a fine, brisk bit of juggling with time. The runner starts his dash with the wind-up of the pitcher or, as he rarely winds up with a man on base, with his first move to pitch the ball to the batter, usually the first tension or drawing back of the arm. From that time on, the hurler is committed and must go through with the pitch.

The ball travels the sixty feet to the plate, and, just to be mother's little helping hand, the batter takes a cut at it to make it more difficult for the catcher and throw him off if he can. The catcher must receive the ball perfectly, straighten up, whip off his heavy mask, draw back his arm, and fire the ball on a line, not in the general direction of second base, but to the foot of the bag, about ankle-high, so that the receiver is spared that precious tenth of a second or more in getting it onto the sliding runner. If the maneuver is completed inside of three seconds and the throw is accurate, the runner is out. Anything over that and he is safe. It takes a ten-second man to steal a base successfully these days—that is, a man who can run a hundred yards in ten seconds. And every inch of ground that he can chisel by increasing his lead off first without getting caught at it and thrown out at first, is important and vital to the success of his maneuver and has a direct bearing upon the eventual outcome of the game. Those seemingly endless throws that the pitcher makes over to first base to hold the runner close to the bag are not made for exercise or to annoy the customers. The purpose is to reduce those inches. The inches otherwise will be translated into hundredths of a second around second base and spell the difference between safe and out. A man can score from second on a single. Runs depend upon those tiny measurements.

As a matter of fact, no game in the world is as tidy and dramatically neat as baseball, with cause and effect, crime and punishment, motive and result, so cleanly defined. The consequences of a single error or failure pyramid inexorably as the game goes on and finally prove to be the events that have won or lost the day, exactly as the minor unnoticed incidents unfolded at the beginning of a well-constructed play suddenly loom up as prime and all-important to the climax.

Pretty, too, is the personal duel between pitcher and batter, or rather between the pitcher and his alter or commanding ego, the catcher, and the man who is trying to hit. The problem of the batter seems tremendously magnified when one considers what might be termed the ballistics and forces under which he operates.

The distance between the pitcher's box and home plate, as has been noted, is 60½ feet. And a fast ball will make the trip from the hand of the thrower to the mitt of the catcher somewhere between three and four tenths of a second. That doesn't exactly give a batter much time to turn the matter over in his head and make up his mind whether he will take a cut at it or let it pass for a ball, though it is true the average pitch is somewhat slower and the ball takes four to five tenths of a second for its flight. The average baseball bat is only about three feet long, and the batter's arm permits it to extend for another foot or so. Actually, out of that entire distance of 60½ feet that is traversed by the ball in less than half a second, it is in position to be hit safely by the batter for only three feet of the journey. That brings the time element in which a ball remains in a position where it may be met with the bat close to an absurdity, an impossibility; something around two one-hundredths of a second, which is cutting it rather fine. And still the batsmen manage, on an average, to hit safely one third of the baseballs thrown at them.

To assist the batter and to strike a better balance between him and the pitcher, the latter is forced, if he wishes to register a called strike, to throw the ball to the hitter down a groove a little more than a foot wide, the width of the home plate. And if the pitcher throws more than four of them outside this groove, the batter, as everyone knows, is entitled to the equivalent of a hit, a free passage to first base. The batter is further permitted two misses without penalty. If he misses the third time he is out.

Thus, the activity centered on home plate is really very simple to understand; three strikes out, four balls a walk.

But the drama that is packed into that simple arrangement of figures, the swift changes of fortune and situation whereby first one and then the other finds himself in difficulties which with stunning suddenness are liable to mushroom into the loss of the game, explain a good deal of the fascination of the sport.

For instance, the so-called three strikes allotted the batter are a great snare and delusion. In point of fact it is only two strikes, for he is allowed to miss the ball only twice, but nobody but the batter ever thinks of that. The third time he misses it he is out. And yet there is magic in that number "three" and he strides to the plate with great confidence in his allotment of three strikes, a confidence that is only slightly dented upon the calling or taking of the first one, because, after all, there are still two more chances left. Two strikes and he is in for it. Now he *must* hit. The margin of possible failure has been wiped out. The pressure has suddenly become almost unbearable. And three chances had seemed such a safe margin when he first stepped up to the plate!

But note how the balance of power seesaws between pitcher and hitter. Batter up! The first one comes over—a ball. The batter smirks and pounds the plate with satisfaction. The advantage lies with him now. If the pitcher throws another wide one it means that three out of his next four pitches must be in that groove or the batter walks. Very nice. And so the next throw will bear looking at very closely, because the chances are it will be a strike. There is a little pressure on the pitcher and none whatsoever on the batter. He can afford to relax a little and let the pitcher commit himself on the next ball. He does. Ball two! Ha! Two balls and no strikes. Lovely. The batsman begins to preen himself a little and the pitcher to perspire. That man serving 'em up from the little mound is in for it now. Strike one! Oh, oh! Now the batter is doing a little more thinking. The next

one will be more of a problem. Shall he let it pass and hope
it will be a third ball, putting the pitcher definitely on the
spot, or should he reason that the latter will try to burn it
over and get *him* in the hole? Ugh! Strike two! Swung at it
and missed by a foot. Guessed wrong. The pitcher fooled
him (or rather the catcher). He should have let it go. Out-
guessed. Now the batter begins to sweat. The advantage
lies with the enemy now. Two balls and two strikes and the
pitcher has another ball to waste and can tease him with a
bad one, or take a chance of breaking a fast one over the
corner of the plate and getting him out. Hardly a moment
ago the batter had the situation well in hand. Now he is in
a mess. That confounded pitcher is just playing with him.
Look at him grinning up there on the mound. All the confidence has oozed out of the hitter and into the hurler. Here
it comes—zip! Has the umpire's right arm flashed up? No!
A ball! Three and two! Switch again. Now the pitcher is
in deep trouble, although the batter is not feeling any too
good about the situation. But the odds have passed to the
batter because the pitcher must commit himself first. Once
that ball leaves his fingers it is irrevocable. There is no calling it back or changing his mind. True, the hitter has only
that tenth of a second in which to make his decision as to
what he will do with the next pitch, but in a game of such
delicate fractions of time it is a decided advantage. He
knows that the pitcher cannot afford to walk him, especially
if there is only one out, or none, or another man on base
already. And if the bases are full the corresponding pressure
upon the pitcher is all the greater. No, he must throw the
ball down that nice, one-foot groove in which the bat may
work to deadliest advantage. His only chance is to put so
much spin, or "stuff," on the ball that when it meets the
bat instead of rifling off onto the outfield for a clean hit,
it will deflect to the ground and give the fielders a chance to
scoop it up, or glance off high into the air to be caught on

the fly. But he might decide to risk it and make the eager hitter bite at one and strike out.

This goes on every minute of the game, and never seems to be twice the same, as the individual duels go on, inning after inning, changing in their nature and intensity according to the situation of the game. Pitching to batters with runners on base increases the pitcher's worries and problems a hundredfold. Batting in pinches piles pressure upon the batsmen. The situation is always different, and they drive on relentlessly, piling up and piling up to a certain climax as the final innings of the game are reached, increasing in intensity as the pitcher begins to tire and it is a question how long he can respond with accuracy and control to the dictates of the brain behind the bat.

The game is as full of surprises as a mystery play. The plot and its ending may be perfectly apparent up to the ninth inning and the last man at bat, and then with stunning suddenness change entirely and go on to a new ending. A pitcher will often be the hero of a closely fought battle in which his side leads 1-0 for eight innings and the rival batsmen have been looking sillier and sillier as they fanned the air, clawing at curves and drops, or standing with their bats on their shoulders while the ball broke across the plate for perfect called strikes. A batter in the hands of a masterful pitcher is a pitiful sight, anyway. He releases enough energy with each swing to cave in the side of a building and it does nothing but create a mild breeze as bat fails to meet ball. He swings himself clear off his feet and sits awkwardly in the dust from the force of his useless blow. Or he stands looking like a big zany, with his ears turning a beautiful shade of cerise, while a perfect third strike burns past his bosom and the umpire calls him out and the catcher laughs sardonically and makes unpleasant remarks out of the side of his mouth.

These are moments of pure glory and unadulterated satis-

faction for the pitcher and his battery mate and their ad-
herents in the grandstands. Or the batter actually connects
with the ball with a mighty swipe destined to rip the hide
from it, but all that happens is that the ball takes one hop
into the hands of the second baseman, who, to show his
contempt for the puny effort, tosses the ball underhand to
the first baseman.

Even in the ninth inning when an obviously astigmatic
umpire, with two out and none on base, calls what was obviously a third strike a fourth ball, and a man reaches first
base, there is no cause for alarm. The batters that day are
lugging useless timber to the plate and have had no more
than three safe hits the entire game. They might just as
well have match-sticks in their fingers. And the next man
up, the final hitter, is a weak sister, relegated to the lower
half of the batting order because he has no reputation or
record as a dangerous slugger. The crowd is already beginning to head for the exits, chuckling to themselves at
the helplessness of the batters, admiring the skill and control of the pitcher. The catcher calls for a sizzler over the
plate, loaded with spin. The weak hitter will ground it to a
fielder and the game will be over. In anticipation the pitcher
is already standing beneath a cooling shower, listening to
the laudatory words of his comrades, and reading the
"SHUTOUT" headlines in the morning papers. Next year
he must ask for a raise. He winds up—let the man on base
go down to second if he wants to. Now he is in a knot. Now
he unwinds. Now he pitches. And now, too, it happens. For,
working silently and without warning, the poisons of fatigue
in that arm that seemed to be made of steel and whipcord
have worked their changes. The pitcher has given the same
twist, the same flip of his wrist, the same leverage and fol-
low-through with his body, only instead of slanting towards
the batter with blinding speed, the ball comes floating down
the groove, all stitches showing, and looking just a shade

smaller than a full moon. The batter doesn't have to be a Babe Ruth to nudge that one. He says: "Oh, baby, come to Papa!" laces it into the grandstand for a home run, and that is that.

The game is over. The pitcher has lost 2-1. All he could do was stand there with his hands on his hips, feeling his ears growing long and furry, watching the ball sail over the whiskey advertisement affixed to the top balcony. The fielders cannot even make a play for it. The right fielder dutifully has his rump pressed up against the right-field wall, but he would have to be a hundred feet tall to get his hands on that ball and he can do little more than wave it a regretful farewell as it disappears into the crowd.

There you have it. One, tiny, uncontrollable slip and the hero has become the dunce, the goat, and the villain. All the failures of the batters that day are forgotten and forgiven, wiped out by that one blow. The sportswriters, some of them, angrily tear sheets of paper from their typewriters, on which they have already begun to write: "In one of the most masterful exhibitions of plain and fancy hurling ever seen at the Polo Grounds, Joie Dokes, diminutive southpaw of the New York Giants, shut out the St. Louis Cardinals 1-0 here yesterday afternoon, letting them down with three hits," etc., etc., insert a fresh piece of paper, and start all over again: "Elmer Crabtree, veteran shortstop of the Cards, hasn't been hitting the length of his cap all year, but yesterday afternoon in the ninth inning of a brilliant pitchers' duel, he stepped to the plate with two out, the score 1-0 against him, and a comrade on base due to walk, and with the count two and two on him," etc., etc., etc.

There are hundreds of these situations brought on during the course of the game, and one could write endlessly of them. I don't mean to do so. But that is why I have liked baseball and always will. It is endlessly intriguing, and when the human element is added to the wierd mechanics of the sport, the wise, foxy veterans, the brash, cocky young kids, the eccentric and screwy characters who play the game, it becomes truly a part of the national scene.

But I like, too, the freedom of baseball and the physical and emotional simplicity of the relationship between player and spectator. It is the only game in the world where the onlooker is permitted to heckle, hoot, cheer, and advise the player to his heart's content. I am not particularly concerned whether it is sportsmanlike for an individual concealed beyond hope of detection in some section of the crowd, to howl, purple-faced, as a batter retires from the plate with his tail between his legs after having fanned in a clutch: "Oh, you bum! Go lay down, you bum, yah yeller. Oh, you bum!" but I know that it makes the abusive individual feel wonderful, because I have sat next to him and watched him wipe the sweat off his brow with a damp handkerchief after his tirade, tilt a bottle of pop to his lips, and then look around him to take in the admiring glances of some of the less daring and articulate fans. He has established himself as an expert and a critic. He has hoisted something off his chest. I know him, the poor little man; not man, but mouse. In the office he sits under the thumb of his niggling superior and at home under both thumbs of his wife. Taxi-drivers curse him as he scuttles out from beneath their wheels, waiters ignore him, policemen bawl him out, nobody loves him, nobody pays any attention to him. But in the ball park he can rise up on his hind legs and abuse a player. It's good for him, and it doesn't hurt the player any.

So, too, the crowd as a whole plays the role of Greek chorus to the actors on the field below. It reflects every action, every movement, every changing phase of the game. It keens. It rejoices. It moans. It jeers. It applauds and gives great swelling murmurs of surprise and appreciation, or finds relief in huge, Gargantuan laughs. I can stand outside of a ball park and listen to the crowd and come close to telling exactly what is happening on the diamond inside. That quick, sharp explosive roar that rises in crescendo and is suddenly shut off sharply as though someone had laid a collective thumb on the windpipe of the crowd, followed by a gentle pattering of applause, tells its own story, of a briskly hit ball, a fielder racing for it, a runner dashing for the base. The throw nips the runner and the noise too. That steady "Clap-clap-clap-clap-clap . . ." Tight spot. Men on base, crowd trying to rattle the pitcher. A great roar turning into a groan that dies away to nothing—a potential home run, with too much slice on it, that just went foul. The crowd lives the actions of the players more than in any other game. It is a release and something of a purge. It is the next best thing to participation.

The Great Emancipator

This article is reprinted from *ESQUIRE*, September 1934. Copyright by Esquire, Inc., 1934.

I am, frankly, pleasantly surprised at the way this piece stands up. It marks an occurrence of historic significance in sports and I think that the Hagen contribution pretty generally has been forgotten.

I think, of course, the admission of pro athletes into the higher stratas of society was inevitable but nobody else could have done the job for the pros as smoothly as Walter did it.

HERB GRAFFIS

In the very old days professional athletes were slaves.

Then the best break a pro got was to be permitted by holders of Roman arena ringside seats to nominate the lion to gnaw on his meat and framework.

Things softened up a bit for pros when practices of slugging each other with lead-ballasted cesti or plunging runt swords into gladiatorial vitals were introduced. The softening consisted of slightly delaying the inevitable finish of the athletes which were by sack to the glue works.

It took almost ten centuries before professional athletes advanced in status enough to separate the names of the vanquished in any athletic contest from obituary notices; defeat and death were one and the same in the simple times prior to that flowering of civilization represented now by such developments as boxing and wrestling commissions.

Then it required almost another ten centuries before professional athletes were allowed to prowl on the loose, subject only to the commands of the sporting nobility that willed them to perform in contests of more brutality than skill.

It was not until the sparkling nineties that the professional athlete achieved some social standing and then merely as a museum piece for men only. Basket-busted, pumpkin-fannied chorus girls beat pro athletes into society and happily blended a restorative element of virility into the get of many a prominent family. Unfortunately the robust coryphees did not feel it incumbent upon them to bring into the upper social strata those brawny pugilists, handsome young men on the flying trapezia, or shifty, speedy professional foot racers with whom the choristers had whiled away tinseled hours of maidenhood.

So the pros again were left out in the murky, hoppy limbo of transfer corner saloons, which were not much of an improvement over the bloody arenas of the Roman days.

Here we have, roughly, about two thousand years in professional athletics with the pros having gained for themselves during all this time only the right to keep living among the lower species.

Then Mr. Hagen arrived. In ten years after the time Hagen won his first national golf championship, at Midlothian Country Club, in the southern fauborgs of Chicago, in 1914 the condition of professional athletes improved more than during the two thousand years prior to the Hagen début as an athletic notable. True, there were professional baseball players, for instance, who were accepted socially before Hagen registered in, but their social conquests were limited to acceptance by persons in trade. Polite society had not been polite to workingmen athletes.

Hagen changed all that. Well, maybe Hagen and conditions, but you can't blame a fellow for having been born at the right time and taking advantage of it.

Walter's playmate, the sage Tommy Armour, jests with Hagen by calling Walter "The Great Emancipator," but in a serious vein Armour stands solid on this verdict. Had it not been for the effrontery of Hagen in proclaiming by word and deed the doctrine of equal rights for the man who makes his living by athletics, all pros might still be competing with bus-boys for a rung near sea-level on the social ladder.

Hagen was Mister Hagen by his own introduction to his public long before he was Walter. He did not allow undue familiarity on the part of either peasantry or plutocracy while he was in his early twenties. Recall, that this was back in the days when American newspapers and magazines referred to professionals in golf stories by the raw address, Bill Mugg or Jock McGoof, and to the amateurs always with the respectful title of "Mister," a practice that now has vanished even in England and which disappeared mainly because of the Hagen influence.

It was at Midlothian, when Hagen came to win his first championship, that the old caste system classifying professionals as untouchables was first swept aside by the self-sufficient Dutch-Irish boy. The golf professionals had nails in the clubhouse basement on which to hang their coats. They could change to golf shoes either outside the clubhouse or in the basement. The golf officials and club members didn't care which, and the pros thought nothing of being neglected or scorned. Hagen had been a full-fledged professional golfer only three years but the Rochester ex-caddie paraded blithely into the Midlothian locker-room selected a vacant locker in a conspicuous and convenient spot and made himself at home with the members and amateur contestants. Then he went on the golf course, gave the Liberty Bell lusty yanks, the golf ball deft smacks and won the championship. From that time on, in golf, the professionals have sat down at the first table with the white folks.

Golf as the favored sport of the wealthy and influential gradually let down the barriers of twenty centuries that had prevented professionals from mingling with the select populace. After golf had succumbed because of the Hagen action, the sports of lesser social standing promptly approved the credentials of their professionals.

Pugilists married into society and cow-punchers became polo players; society and polo getting the long end of what pugilists and cow-punchers had been perfectly willing to have go as a draw decision. Tennis amateurs formally turned professional, college football players graduated into professional football instead of becoming cappers for "security" houses, sweet girl swimmers brought to the movies some genuine grade A curves of the human form divine instead of unprofitably slapping at the water for expense money and the dear old A. A. U. Slavery days for the professional athletes were over. Hagen had fought the civil war for the pros single-handed. He cocktailed his way to victory at Shiloh, danced triumphant engagements at Lookout Mountain and Gettysburg, and played well-bred bridge hands marching through Georgia. Time after time he outsnooted the shock-troops of society snobs until they signed papers of unconditional surrender.

In the diplomatic phases of the war for pro freedom he never lost a skirmish. Even the Prince of Wales played along with Hagen and it helped the Prince socially, commercially and athletically. When Walter shot his first game with the Prince each shot taken on the course was a shot heard 'round the world. Now the American golf professional who has visited England and hasn't played with the genial Edward P. is considered a distinguished character; Walter having done that well for his comrades in the cause. Edward's grand-pappy, King Edward, was a very democratic guy, especially with the dolls, but had he so far violated social regulations to be publicly the playmate of professional athletes it is doubtful that he would have perpetuated the divine right of kings in Albion.

The subtle and subconscious campaign Hagen conducted for professionals' release from bondage was unquestionably one of the most unusual in military history for it was conducted on a financial basis that at times showed more red than all the blood that ever drained into the Marne. Hagen has made well over a million dollars with his golf clubs alone. The testimonial silver that rained on Hagen when the advertisers were going strong in this department of copy, amounted to a soaking shower for two years but with Walter's facility for putting legal tender into circulation he stood in this downpour and dried out almost instantly. Hagen's amazing contempt for money has one lovely aspect: when he is flush he pays off with great joy that people should be so delighted to put their hands on something that is merely an item for poor people to worry about; that's Walter's idea of money.

When he sailed for England in 1928 to win the third of his four British Open titles Walter could have floated his entire cash assets out to sea on a cigarette paper, but he traveled in style. At the dock as he sailed were so many evil-looking men with writs for Hagen in their mitts that it appeared as though the troops were sailing.

Engineering the departure was the companion and business manager of Hagen's golfing activities for many years, Robert Harlow. Hagen played the Grand Duke role for the team and Harlow was simply Comrade Harlow, a stalwart,

epicurean ex-newspaperman who disclaims having been
Hagen's "manager" because, he makes clear, no one could
manage Hagen.

The Hagen-Harlow combination had put its hands on approximately $6,000 for the English trip, including $1,500
which was to be wagered in a 72-hole match with Archie
Compston. Harlow bought the transportation and pushed
the $1,500 wager ahead to England. The Grand Duke and
Comrade Harlow reasoned that the $1,500 would become
$3,000 immediately after the match with Compston was
played. Therefore there would be no need of funds other
than for tips en route. Having arrived at this logical con-
clusion, the patriots decided to spend American money with
Americans and personally conduct their own farewells, each
according to his manner. The Grand Duke held open house
for three days, working twenty-hour shifts each of the days.
Comrade Harlow, gypsy evangelist of the Great God Gut,
spent his percentage of the commune's funds at excellent
eating places.

Harlow parked early in his cell on the boat, cramming his
quarters with medicinal waters, indigestion tablets and philo-
sophical volumes in which authors go to great lengths to
prove that man is not born to waste in toil.

Leisurely concluding his packing for the journey, Hagen
left his hotel suite with an allowance of less time for making the boat than the New York fire department would set
for the run to the pier. With the Grand Duke was a Hagen
associate in the golf club and ball business named Walter
Ring. Ring's build is about that of Hagen and he rather re-
sembles the Grand Duke in contented and well-fed features.
While Hagen had been packing Ring selected a gaudy suit
of Hagen's, which had been given the Great Man by an en-
terprising tailor who recognized Hagen's standing as the ace
male mannequin of the age. Hagen not only would give a
fellow the shirt off his back, but coat, vest, trousers, shoes,

hosiery and tie to complete the sartorial scheme. Thus it happened that Ring was to outward appearances another Hagen as the taxi jerked to a screaming stop at the wharf. Ring recognized the enemy at the docks. He stepped out of the cab, hailed porters who grunted the Hagen luggage aboard and serenely accepted the papers shoved at him by the process-servers as Hagen followed out of the cab after an interval and modestly edged aboard. As the boat swung out into the channel with Hagen safely aboard, Ring turned to the group of men who had presented him with papers.

"Now, gents, what can I do for you?" he asked.

"Stick around and kick in, I guess, Mr. Hagen," volunteered one of the serving men.

"But I'm not Hagen," explained Ring.

Whereupon Mr. Ring and the process-servers adjourned to a tavern and from a comfortable distance from Mr. Hagen wished Mr. Hagen bon voyage.

That journey did not work out as planned. Compston dusted off Hagen, 18 and 17—the worst defeat Hagen ever suffered. The $1,500 blew then and the team was playing strictly from scratch. But Hagen, who had trained on champagne, scotch and seltzer and sharpened his vision by staying up to see the English sunrises, hired a bodyguard to shanghai him into sleep at reasonable hours. Shortly after the defeat by Compston Hagen won the British Open with 292. His compatriot, Sarazen, was 294 and Compston was in third place with 295.

In exhibition matches played during a few weeks after his British Open title Hagen earned about five thousand dollars but when he and Harlow steamed into New York harbor, home-coming, Harlow craned his neck over the steamer-rail looking for a welcoming pal who would get the champion out of hock. Fortunately, Eddie Conlin, a famous tennis official turned golf-ball sales manager, was on hand to see the circus come to town.

Harlow energetically beckoned Conlin aboard. Conlin dug down for bail; Hagen lavishly tipped the boat staff and the conquering hero landed. In a bit more than a month Hagen had played in eleven thousand dollars with his golf clubs and played it away, but not with his golf clubs. He was perfectly happy and tranquil. Hagen likes to live.

When Hagen is opulent—and those periods are becoming more frequent again as the depression drags to the rear—he is perhaps the softest of all targets for touches. When he spent part of his winters in Hollywood he ran a relief station for impecunious actors and actresses, conducting the operation in a manner that aided without embarrassment. The mob scene would be put on in Hagen's suite, around dinner time, with Hagen signing tabs the size of the national debt. Then there would be some social bridge. When the Thespians won Hagen paid off in cash. When Hagen won the score was written on Hagen's cuff and vanished the next day when the hotel laundresses busted the suds with the Hagen shirts.

During those times when the Grand Duke's funds can not be seen with the naked eye he considers the situation in a very logical manner—a manner worthy of wider adoption. He reasons: "My only troubles are money. I have no money. Therefore, I have no troubles. Q.E.D." Comrade Harlow would differ slightly with Hagen concerning that decision about no money—no worry, and arrange exhibition tours among the nobility and the mujiks. The rubles would roll in again and all would be at peace.

Hagen and Harlow joined forces in 1922 at Pinehurst. Hagen then had won the United States Open championships of 1914 and 1919. His first start in the British Open— that of 1920—had resulted disastrously; he didn't finish among the first 50. His second attempt, in 1921, brought him in a seven-cornered tie for sixth place. In 1922 after he and Harlow had agreed to investigate the commercial possibilities of exhibition golf Hagen won the British Open. He was the first American-born professional to win that title.

With Hagen, the lion-tamer, as the big attraction to ballyhoo, Harlow quit his job under Sheriff Bill McGeehan on the New York *Herald* sports staff, and the two set out on what was supposed to be a business but actually was the greatest money-making ten-year holiday any two fellows ever enjoyed. It is true that when they slipped the knot of their business tie in 1932 both of them were behind the eight ball, financially, but in view of what had happened in American finance, they called themselves lucky for not having wasted time saving.

There have been two reunions of the conquistadors; one when Harlow managed the Hagen-José Jurado exhibition tour and one in the Florida 1932–1933 season when L. A. Young, Hagen's angel in the golf club and ball business, put up fifteen hundred dollars in prize money for an open golf tournament Harlow promoted in Jacksonville. Both of these foregatherings made sport page copy. Hagen turned in a blazing 33 for the last nine holes of the tournament Young and Harlow had christened for him, and won his own event. First prize money was three hundred dollars which the Grand Duke airily waved aside for the man who finished in second place to collect. Hagen then gave his last five dollars in cash to his caddie; laughed, talked and drank with the locker-room crowd and then drove off into the golden Florida night. What difference? Money is only money. There had been a time when Hagen had given a fifty-dollar bill—a crap game trophy—to a filling station attendant and received change for five dollars. Ten miles away, at a roadhouse, Hagen discovered the mistake but was having too much fun to think about sending back for a pittance like forty-five dollars.

Harlow handled Jurado's publicity campaign so the

Hagen-Jurado combination drew customers at a rate reminiscent of the rich old days in exhibition golf but the serious, wiry Jurado couldn't stand the grind of trouping with the Grand Duke. Night after night Hagen and Jurado would be entertained by the élite and go back to their hotel quarters to find late revelers in waiting. Jurado kept up for a time because he thought it was the custom of the country. It was the custom of the country with Hagen, who flourished and scored well on this routine. After two weeks, Jurado, normally one of the world's best golfers, was ready to be shipped back to the Argentine on a stretcher.

Olin Dutra, the present National Open champion, a sturdy young man, also has found that Hagen is a person of most amazing endurance. Dutra and Hagen started out on their tour and in a week after the tour's start Dutra was in bed in Chicago under doctor's orders. Part of his illness was a backfire from the amoebic dysentery but probably he would have recovered in stride had it not been for his endeavor to keep pace with Hagen in showing contempt for the clock. Let Dutra tell about it.

"Walter asked me to go out with him one evening to visit at the home of some of his friends on Chicago's gold coast. He told about what charming people they were and I went along, although I knew we might stay a little later than I wanted to.

"After we'd visited with the host and his wife and their other guests until the wee hours, I was dead and suggested going home.

"Walter eventually got started and as we were driving back to our hotel I thought a sandwich and a glass of milk would go good, so I said to Walter, 'Let's eat.'

"'A swell idea,' he agreed, but instead of going to some lunch counter and grabbing a hamburger and some milk quick as I wanted to do, we went to a night club at Hagen's

insistence and got back to the hotel around six A.M. I am a
working man and husky, but that Hagen would kill me in a
week if I tried to run along with him."

The Grand Duke is not much of a drinker, contrary to the
popular belief. He will play with one drink for an hour or
more in the same deliberate manner he does everything
else, but he will do his share right along with relays of the
merrymakers and go for weeks without looking at a time-
piece. That disregard for sleep is something that only one of
his playing companions on exhibition tours ever was able to
match. Hagen and Tommy Armour brightened the land one
year with a tour that is still discussed where fellows get the
good song ringing clear. They played astonishingly good
golf, shattering course records at most of the places they
played. After the afternoon pastiming for which they were
paid, the real business began. Their suite always looked
like night sessions of conventions were being held. Most of
their sleeping they did in automobiles between country
clubs.

At one city along the line of march a wealthy golf enthu-
siast put up $1,500 in prize money in addition to the guar-
antee the club made for the exhibition. The $1,500 was to
be paid out as follows: $500 if either player broke the course
record of 70; $500 if either player scored 70, and $500 if
either player equalled the course's par of 72.

Playing in a near-by city the day prior to this fifteen-
hundred-dollar added money performance Hagen and Armour were given the eye by two striking young women. Be
it said for the Grand Duke when in his prime and for Armour, when likewise, that no striking young women ever
gave them the eye without being given an eye for an eye.

Whilst striding between shots the Grand Duke talked
over conditions with one of the dazzlers.

"You boys must get very lonely and homesick in the evenings," she remarked.

Hagen thought that it was a perfect opening but as a discreet stranger, let it go with a nod of agreement.

"Possibly some young women whose social standing is not very high importune you," the lovely young thing added.

Hagen guessed he knew what importune meant so what could he do but say "yes"?

"Tonight is going to be different. My friend and I are going to call at the hotel for you and Mr. Armour and I am sure that we will pleasantly entertain you." When the Grand Duke heard that from the obviously high-class female native, he made haste to acquaint Armour with the happy tidings. Instead of lingering after the exhibition Hagen diligently passed around word that he and Armour were leaving town immediately and it was no use to expect them to be central figures in the usual evening frolic.

Promptly at eight that evening the telephone rang in the Hagen-Armour quarters. In patrician tones and accent one of the two lovelies announced they were waiting with a car by the hotel entrance. Walter and Tommy couldn't have made the lobby quicker if they had slid down a brass pole in a fire station.

Through the midsummer evening the quartette drove for a half hour while spots of interest in the city were pointed out and polite persiflage exchanged. Night fell.

"Well, where are we going now?" asked Hagen of the charmer who was driving.

"Oh, we're going to take you boys where you'll really enjoy yourselves. We're going to the Wednesday evening lecture of the Exegesis Culture society in the parsonage of the First M.E. church."

"Oh no. We have to go back to the hotel," protested dazed Mr. Hagen.

"Yes. I don't feel well," said Armour weakly.

"Well, then we'll be late for the meeting," pouted one of the girls.

"No you won't," Hagen assured them. "We're getting out and walking. It will do Armour good to walk back himself."

So Walter and Tommy walked back to the hotel and were sound asleep by nine o'clock. After this indulgence in sane slumber they went out the next day after the fifteen hundred dollars. Armour shot 77 and Hagen a 78; absolutely the worst golf either of them had shot in two years.

This was one of the very few times when the Grand Duke went wrong seriously. He is far smarter than his casual manner indicates. Walter began changing his swing years ago when he realized that time was going to make his muscles stiffer and his bones more brittle so he would be unable to take the sweeping slash that distinguished the playing style of the younger Hagen. He is still good—very good, despite his unhappy performance in the 1934 National Open at Merion Cricket club.

But whether he wins any more major titles or not, he will be the shining star of the golf galleries for years to come, partially because of his personality, partially because of his performances, but mostly because he is today's one professional athlete of stellar social significance. He is the one who showed all other professional athletes it was possible to eat their pie up in the sky, instead of being unjustly compelled to retain their traditional status as muscular menials.

Fellow Named Archie Moore

This column first appeared in the New York *Journal-American*, December 27, 1955, and is reprinted by permission of that newspaper.

The Archie Moore piece represents, really, not much more than a vagrant thought at a year's end; a memory of a man, for whom I have a great personal liking and a vast respect as a professional, reaching his peak after years of striving and, although defeated, emerging no less the gladiator he was when he entered the ring. Basically, I wrote it because I had to have something in the paper on December 27, 1955. If I hadn't, it might never have been done.

FRANK GRAHAM

Looking back on the sports year now rapidly dwindling to a close, it stands here that the most beguiling figure to walk through it was Archie Moore. Not, of course, that Archie was a newcomer on the scene. He'd been around for a longer time than he cares to admit, so long, indeed that he'd become the old man of the ring, an almost legendary figure who had fought and beaten men whose names remain in the book but whose achievements have been blurred by time. But this was Archie's finest year. He made it so—and, in or out of the ring, he made the most of it.

He made it by his constant challenging of Rocky Marciano and his forcing of the match with no help whatever from his manager, financing his campaign with money borrowed from his friends, and clinching it with his stunning knockout of Bobo Olson in June. The Olson fight was a daring gamble on his part. His light heavyweight title was at stake and, more than that. How could he be accepted as a contender for the heavyweight championship if he lost to an overstuffed middleweight? He couldn't, of course, but he was of no mind to let anything like that happen, and knocked Olson out in the third round.

Al Weill, who hadn't believed a fight between Moore and Marciano would draw the kind of money to which, as manager of the heavyweight champion, he had become accustomed, now was convinced that it would, and so the match was sealed for the Yankee Stadium in September and Moore went to North Adams, Mass., to train. It was there that Archie played to the hilt his role as the contender.

"With his tufted chin," Red Smith said, "he looks like a road company Othello."

"He is," Harry Mendell, the camp publicist said, "the greatest con man I've ever known. I am certain that before we leave here, he'll sell the Mohawk Trail to a stranger."

And a couple of weeks later, when someone asked Harry if Archie had unloaded the Trail, he said:

"No. But I hear the Taconic is gone."

One of Archie's early stories of his reason for choosing North Adams as his training site was wound 'round the Mohawk Trail.

"I came here in 1949 to box Esco Greenwood," he said. "I arrived the day before the fight and drove up on the Trail and sat there looking down on the town and this beautiful countryside. I said to myself that if I ever could get a big fight in Boston, I would come here to train. I didn't have much money then and I knew I would have to pay about eight dollars for a room at the hotel, so I pulled my car off the road up there on the mountain and slept in it."

It made a delightful picture, the vagabond fighter who was destined to meet Marciano for the championship six years later sleeping in his car on a mountain top because he couldn't afford a hotel room, but Tom McShane, sports editor of the local newspaper, innocently blasted a gaping hole through it. When someone asked him if he remembered Archie coming to town to box Esco Greenwood, he said:

"Oh sure. Very well. He stayed in a little hotel just down the street from here."

Still, as someone else said at the time, Archie had planted the seed of a story that never will die. Forever it will be told that the night before he flattened Esco, he slept on the mountain top.

There was, too, the morning that, on a weedy tennis court at his camp, he enacted the first Marciano-Walcott fight, playing the parts of both Rocky and Old Joe with the greatest of ease.

As he talked, and gestured, you could see the great Municipal Stadium in Philadelphia, and hear again the rumbling and the roar of the crowd. You could see the knockdown in the first round as Walcott came out of his crabwise shuffle and hit Rocky on the chin. You could see Walcott turning his back on the fallen contender and strutting to his corner and, at the end of the round, Marciano slumping on his stool, a kitchen chair having been placed on the court long beforehand as a prop for the drama that Archie had devised.

This was one of Archie's "messages." Telling of his fight with Olson he had said:

"I hit him with a right hand in the first round. It was high. But Bobo got the message."

This time the message he conveyed to his spellbound audience of eight reporters, a chauffeur, the driver of a baker's delivery wagon and a small boy, was that if he knocked Marciano down he would not lose him, as Walcott did. He also dropped at various times, messages about the science of boxing and the science of living, impelling one of his fascinated listeners to say one day:

"The guy leaves more messages than a kid from the Western Union."

But the night of the fight, the mountebank, the con man and the teller of tall tales had been left behind. That was a fighter who came out of his corner to meet Marciano when the bell rang.

Archie couldn't win because he didn't have the equipment for it. He knocked Marciano down and stunned him and hurt him, but lost him even as Walcott had lost him. But, battered as he was, he gave furious resistance through round after round until he could fight no more, and it was a just and honest compliment Rocky paid to him when he said:

"You're a great fighter, Archie."

And so, that night, he was. Brave, resourceful, skillful and dead game.

Death of a Race Horse

This article first appeared in the New York *Sun,* July 28, 1949, and is reprinted by permission of W. C. Heinz.

I suppose I shall always have a fondness for this piece because it had its origins in a time when I was a sports fan who wanted to be a sportswriter. In those days of poring over the sports pages I repeatedly came across stories of the race track recounting how, in the course of a race, a thoroughbred had suffered a broken leg. Somewhere, in all of those stories, there was always one line or one sentence that reported that the animal had been—to use their word—destroyed.

In time I came to resent this. I don't believe I was ever so naïve as to think that horses ran around ovals for their own sport or even to confuse the reasons why men make them run. It did seem to me, however, that there were these times when the price a horse paid did not show on the tote board, because the price was his life, and that some day someone should define that overworked word of dismissal—destroyed.

It was not important to me who wrote the story, just so that it be written for the record. Eventually I did become a sportswriter and I was at Jamaica on a hot and humid afternoon in July of 1949 and the accident described in this piece did occur.

"What's the quickest way for me to get to the stable area?" I asked one of the track's representatives.

"What do you want to go there for?" he answered.

"Because they're going to destroy that horse," I said.

"My God!" he said. "You're not going to write about that?"

Well, I did write about it, and there it is. Some months later a national magazine asked me to submit what I believed to be my best column. I was pleased to submit this, because it would give this record wider circulation and, to be honest about it, because they were going to pay me, just to reprint a piece, what my pecunious employers were paying me for a month's work. Some weeks after the submission, however, the column came back with the explanation that the editor felt that women would fail to understand it. This I submit . . .

W. C. HEINZ

They were going to the post for the sixth race at Jamaica, 2-year-olds, some making their first starts, to go five-and-a-half furlongs for a purse of $4,000. They were moving slowly down the backstretch toward the gate, some of them cantering, others walking, and in the press box they had stopped their working or their kidding to watch, most of them interested in one horse.

"Air Lift," Jim Roach said. "Full brother of Assault."

Assault, who won the triple crown . . . making this one, too, by Bold Venture, himself a Derby winner, out of Igual, herself by the great Equipoise. . . . Great names in the breeding line . . . and now the little guy making his first start, perhaps the start of another great career.

They were off well, although Air Lift was fifth. They were moving toward the first turn, and now Air Lift was fourth. They were going into the turn, and now Air Lift was starting to go, third perhaps, when suddenly he slowed, a horse stopping, and below in the stands you could hear a sudden cry, as the rest left him, still trying to run but limping, his jockey—Dave Gorman—half falling, half sliding off.

"He broke a leg!" somebody, holding binoculars to his eyes, shouted in the press box. "He broke a leg!"

Down below they were roaring for the rest, coming down the stretch now, but in the infield men were running toward the turn, running toward the colt and the boy standing beside him, alone. There was a station wagon moving around the track toward them, and then, in a moment, the big green van that they call the horse ambulance.

"Gorman was crying like a baby," one of them, coming out of the jockey room said. "He said he must have stepped in a hole, but you should have seen him crying."

"It's his left front ankle," Dr. J. G. Catlett, the veterinarian, was saying. "It's a compound fracture, and I'm waiting for confirmation from Mr. Hirsch to destroy him."

He was standing outside one of the stables beyond the backstretch, and he had just put in a call to Kentucky where Max Hirsch, the trainer, and Robert Kleberg, the owner, are attending the yearling sales.

"When will you do it?" one of them said.

"Right as soon as I can," the doctor said. "As soon as I get confirmation. If it was an ordinary horse I'd done it right there."

He walked across the road and around another barn to where they had the horse. The horse was still in the van, about twenty stable hands in dungarees and sweat-stained shirts, bare-headed or wearing old caps, standing around quietly and watching with Dr. M. A. Gilman, the assistant veterinarian.

"We might as well get him out of the van," Catlett said, "before we give him the novocaine. It'll be a little better out in the air."

The boy in the van with the colt led him out then, the colt

limping, tossing his head a little, the blood running down and covering his left foreleg. When they saw him, standing there outside the van now, the boy holding him, they started talking softly.

"Full brother of Assault." . . . "It don't make no difference now. "He's done." . . . "but damn, what a grand little horse." . . . "Ain't he a horse?"

"It's a funny thing," Catlett said. "All the cripples that go out, they never break a leg. It always happens to a good-legged horse."

A man, gray-haired and rather stout, wearing slacks and a blue shirt walked up. "Then I better not send for the wagon yet?" the man said.

"No," Catlett said, "Of course, you might just as well. Max Hirsch may say no, but I doubt it."

"I don't know," the man said.

"There'd be time in the morning," Catlett said.

"But in this hot weather—" the man said.

They had sponged off the colt, after they had given him the shot to deaden the pain, and now he stood, feeding quietly from some hay they had placed at his feet. In the distance you could hear the roar of the crowd in the grand-stand, but beyond it and above it you could hear thunder and see the occasional flash of lightning.

When Catlett came back the next time he was hurrying, nodding his head and waving his hands. Now the thunder was louder, the flashes of lightning brighter, and now rain was starting to fall.

"All right," he said, shouting to Gilman. "Max Hirsch talked to Mr. Kleberg. We've got the confirmation."

They moved the curious back, the rain falling faster now, and they moved the colt over close to a pile of loose bricks. Gilman had the halter and Catlett had the gun—shaped like a bell with the handle at the top. This bell he placed, the crowd silent, on the colt's forehead, just between the eyes.

The colt stood still and then Catlett, with the hammer in his other hand, struck the handle of the bell. There was a short, sharp sound and the colt toppled onto his left side, his eyes staring, his legs straight out, the free legs quivering.

"Aw—" someone said.

That was all they said. They worked quickly, the two vets removing the broken bones as evidence for the insurance company, the crowd silently watching. Then the heavens opened, the rain pouring down, the lightning flashing, and they rushed for the cover of the stables, leaving alone on his side near the pile of bricks, the rain running off his hide, dead an hour and a quarter after his first start, Air Lift, son of Bold Venture, full brother of Assault.

I Play Baseball
for Money—Not Fun

In collaborating, a sportswriter must accept a fact he might reject at any other time. The collaborator's own opinions are valueless. His job is simply to phrase and to organize the thoughts of someone else.

Duke Snider and I talked about baseball as he saw it for many days and many nights. Then, when I thought I understood his outlook, I whipped out a thirty-five-pound tape recorder I just happened to have handy and we went to work. Three tape spools later, we had enough.

This article, which provoked some little controversy, is an edited version of Snider's conversation for the record. I don't think it's the smoothest article I've done and it's certainly not the most complex, but it is a favorite because it represents a difficult assignment in a unique medium, which seemed to work out well.

ROGER KAHN

My wife and I began to hear the question right after our first baseball season together. We'd just gotten back home to California in the fall of 1948 when Beverly's high-school friends started asking what baseball life was *really* like. For a while, Bev made an honest mistake and tried to tell the unglamorized truth.

"It was a kind of rugged summer," she would say. "You see, Duke started with Brooklyn but he got sent out to Montreal and then called back by Brooklyn again. That meant we had to move three times. Once it was in a rush and Duke flew so I had to pack and load the car by myself and . . ."

Usually, the friends would interrupt at about this time and make some smart remark about complainers. It wasn't long before Beverly caught on. Nowadays when anyone asks about baseball life, she just smiles, says it's fine, thanks, and how are the kids? That changes the topic before someone has a chance to tell us what a picnic we've got, and before I have a chance to get steamed.

The truth is that life in the major leagues is far from a picnic. I'm explaining, not complaining, but believe me, even though deep down I know it isn't true, I feel that I'd be just as happy if I never played another baseball game again. I have my reasons. I can tell you a couple pretty quick:

There are youngsters who throw skate keys and marbles at my head when I'm backed up close to the stands at some ball parks.

There are the older fans at other parks who bounce beer cans off my legs during dull moments in the games.

There are the sportswriters who know just as much baseball as my four-year-old daughter, but who write expert articles about what's wrong with me every time I go a few games without a hit.

There is the travel that makes me spend half my life in

strange towns, a thousand miles away from Beverly and the kids.

You know, it isn't just these things or any of my other reasons by themselves, but when they all come at you at about the same time, when you get off a train after a couple of hours' sleep, and a manager snipes at you before the game, and the fans during the game and the writers after it, you begin to wonder about baseball as a trade.

It's like anything else. From the outside it looks great, and when you're a kid dreaming, it looks like a helluva dream. Then you grow up, you're in the major leagues and all of a sudden baseball isn't so great—and sometimes it can be a nightmare.

I remember when I was a boy around Los Angeles I used to dream about playing in a World Series. It was my biggest and most important dream. Last autumn when I played in my fourth World Series, I was still dreaming. Only the dream had changed. While we were beating the Yankees, I was dreaming about being a farmer. I'm looking forward to the day when baseball will allow me to settle down to raising avocados in the California sunshine.

Often I try to put my finger on the one thing that turned my boyhood dream around, or the one time when it happened. But I can't. There are a lot of things, a lot of times. I can't even be sure which is most important. Different ones seem "most important" different days. Maybe travel is the biggest problem. I know it's the one that's steadiest.

The first time I traveled across the country on a train, I was so excited I could hardly sleep. That was in 1944. Now I've come across the country twenty-five times and moved around the National League circuit about thirty, and I'm not excited about train rides any more. But I still have a terrible time falling asleep. Even sleeping pills don't help much. Pee Wee Reese has the same kind of difficulty.

With the Dodgers, I have to spend as many as twenty-five nights a year on trains, sometimes six or seven in a row. Sleeping gets to be a real serious thing if an afternoon game follows an overnight train ride. I get about four and a half hours' sleep on those rides, and you'd be amazed how fast big-league pitching is, even for a well-rested batter. When you're short of sleep, you better bunt and hope.

The eating is as mixed up as the sleeping. When you play a day game, you eat a big breakfast, a light snack in the clubhouse around noon and the big meal at six-thirty. When there's a night game, it's brunch, a light snack around four and that big meal at midnight. Luckily I have a rugged stomach. With baseball schedules the way they are, a ball-player needs a good stomach as much as a good throwing arm.

But right here I want to set down the other side of the record. I've mentioned the bad parts of baseball. Just the same I don't want anybody to think I'm running down the game or trying to say it hasn't helped me.

I've made great friends, fellows like Pee Wee Reese and Carl Erskine. I've made great contacts with businessmen, nicer types of fans, even with some sportswriters. And I've made an awful lot of money.

With endorsement fees, my salary and my winning World Series share, I earned about fifty thousand dollars last season. You can put up with a lot for that kind of money. I did. I mean the pay is good, but they take it out of you in sweat and worry. Baseball in the big leagues isn't like the baseball you play when you're a kid. I mean it wasn't like I stole that fifty thousand dollars.

Sometimes you hear talk about "the good old days when there were fellows like Ruth and Cobb who really loved baseball." Maybe they did, but they didn't exactly go broke playing it. Besides, neither one of them ever had to play a night game. Now, I *like* baseball. It's a good clean living, and it's been good to me even though it's rough on my family. Living out of a suitcase, fighting for sleep, making peace with your stomach and all the while staying in shape to play is a part of the job ballplayers should force themselves to accept. What hurts me most is something else. It's being away from Beverly and the kids.

This year Bev stayed in California with the children when I went to spring training in Florida. Kevin, my oldest boy, is in school now, and he's had to switch from California to Brooklyn schools in the middle of the spring term. We thought that switching from California to Florida to Brooklyn would be too much and might hurt his marks.

In all, we have three children, and spring training kept me away from them for six weeks. Now that the season's under way, it's going to be two weeks with them, in the place we rent in Bay Ridge, then two weeks on the road, and it'll be on and off like that pretty much until October. To put away as much money as I want, I know I'll have to have five more good seasons. I'll miss the chance of watching even Kurt, my youngest child, as he grows a little day by day.

Ballplayers are not the only people who have to travel, any more than they are the only people who work for managers. But there are times when the combination of a suitcase life and managers can get rough. If a manager gets on you, he ran really make you squirm, and on the road you can't play with your kids to forget your troubles.

A couple of years ago in Philadelphia, a bunch of us went to see *The Caine Mutiny* one afternoon. The movie started pretty well, but it was when Captain Queeg came in that it got great. We watched the way Queeg ran his ship and we all had the same thought: Charley Dressen.

Dressen had managed the Dodgers the year before, and the movie made us all remember an incident on the team like the scene where Captain Queeg blows his top over one quart of strawberries. Charley blew his over one order of creamed cauliflower.

At the hotel in Philly you can hit double figures at dinner if you order an extra pat of butter for your bread. It's a good thing the ball club lets us sign our checks there, instead of trying to make us get by on a meal allowance. Anyway, this one time somebody had ordered cauliflower à la carte. We had a night game, but around six o'clock it started sprinkling a little. That was all Charley needed to keep us in the clubhouse. It was a cinch he was going to make a speech.

"Creamed cauliflower," he opened up. "You blank wise guys got nothing better to do than order creamed cauliflower at seventy-five cents extra. You eat that way at home?"

It wasn't far from game time, and the rain really wasn't hard enough to hold up play. But when Charley started one of his speeches, you could never tell whether or not they'd have to move up game time so's he could finish. Not that Charley said much. He just said the same thing six or seven times.

About the fifth time around, I began thinking we were going to have to play without a warmup. "Say, Charley," I said. "What say we get out on the field?"

We were all sitting around, but Charley was standing. He made a kind of run toward me and stuck his face near mine. "What you trying to do," he hollered, "run this ball club?"

"Heck, no. I just wanted to get out on the field and loosen up."

"You'll loosen up when I tell you," Charley shouted. "Now about this here creamed cauliflower . . . you listening, Snider?"

"Look," I yelled. "I didn't even eat at the hotel last night. I ate in a restaurant on my own money. Why don't you deduct the seventy-five cents that blank cauliflower cost from the six bucks I didn't use?"

"Listen, you wise guy . . ." Charley began. My ear still bleeds when I think about what followed.

I laugh about the cauliflower now, but when I think of the run-in I had with Charley on my birthday in 1951, that seems pretty serious. Probably you remember that in '51 we were thirteen and one-half games ahead of the Giants, we started to slip and ended up blowing the pennant in the play-offs. We were slipping pretty fast that September. My birthday is September 19th.

Don't ask me why, but I always hit well on my birthday: a homer, a lot of runs batted in, or some such. In 1951, I spent my birthday in St. Louis. I was fighting a slump and the team was going sour and I figured this was going to be my day. I was wrong.

When I came out on the field to loosen up, I passed close to Stan Musial, a fine guy. "Hey, Duke," Stan said. "You ought to be about ready to break that slump today."

"Not today I won't," I told him. "I'm not playing."

"You hurt?" Stan asked.

"Nope. Just benched."

"Why?"

"Ask Dressen."

After warmup I stuck my glove in my hip pocket, loosened my pants around the knees and sat down in a corner of the dugout. The Cardinals went ahead, and in the eighth inning a situation came up when I knew we were going to use a left-handed pinch hitter. Dressen walked toward the dugout. I took the glove out of my pocket and began hitching my pants. Then I heard Charley.

"Russell," he shouted to Jimmy Russell, a utility outfielder just recalled from Montreal. "Get in there and hit."

He turned to me. "Snider," he said. "Go down to the bull pen and warm up. You're playing center field next inning."

I wanted to hit. I felt I could hit better than Russell. "You want to lose the game?" I said under my breath.

"Get down to that bull pen!" Dressen yelled. He hadn't heard me.

"I ain't going," I said. "I don't need a blank warmup to play the blank outfield." Then I put the glove back in my pocket.

Actually, even though Russell struck out, we won. Besides, Charley was calling the turns and I was wrong, but in a pennant race with thousands of dollars at stake, when you think your manager won't let you help the club, you can lose your head.

I don't blame Charley, and I don't think Charley blames me for sassing back at him when he stuck a needle into me. It was a terrible situation because he always seemed to needle me just when a pat on the back was what I needed most.

But before Charley left Brooklyn, my batting average had improved, and we were getting along so well we even went to a show together. I mean he wasn't really as bad as Queeg. I guess he meant well. At least I hope he did.

Even with a rough, loud guy like Charley, a ballplayer can hold his own if he's got backbone. The situation with sportswriters is different. Like Charley, most sportswriters mean well. The big problem I've found with writers is their habit of stretching the truth to back up what they call "an angle." Nearly all the writers I've met stretch facts a little. All right. But a few stretch them till they bend.

A couple of years ago, a big national magazine wanted an article about me. Their angle was that I was baseball's problem child. Well, I've had my fights with managers and I've been wrong a lot, but not often enough to support a lame-brained angle like that.

Naturally, I tried not to give any quotes that would make me look silly. But do you know what happened? I was quoted as blaming some of my baseball problems on my father and mother because they spoiled me when I was a

child. Now, I never would say this about my folks; it con-
demned them as parents in the eyes of millions of Americans. It didn't make me look like much of a son, either.

Then there's that silly business with Willie Mays. Newspapermen keep comparing us and trying to trap me into
knocking Willie, and they probably bothered the life out of
him, too. Look, he's had some good years and I've had some
too. Why can't credit be given where it's due, without comparison all the time?

There are a few writers around the league who like nee-
dling and second-guessing and experting just as much as
they like reporting. I remember a fellow writing, when
Dressen benched me one day four years ago, that the
Dodgers were certain to cut my salary and were probably
going to trade me. The team was in Cincinnati when the
story came out in a New York paper, so Beverly, who was
back in Brooklyn, saw the thing before I did. As soon as she
read it, she picked up a telephone and called me long-
distance. I knew the story was out of line and I told her so.
Still, I've seldom heard Beverly more upset.

After I'd calmed her down I knew only one thing. I
wanted to get my hands on the writer. I guess he knew it,
too. He stayed out of my way for a long time.

Of course, it's not right to blame one writer or one manager for the problems a player like myself faces in baseball.
It isn't a matter of individuals. It's the pressure the whole
system builds up.

There's as much pressure to produce in baseball as there
is in anything else in the world. If you make a mistake in
your office, maybe your boss calls you down. If I make one
on the field, there are a couple of million people waiting to
call me a bum. A lot of them think of baseball pressure in
terms of choking up—getting so scared you can't swallow.

I choked up in the 1951 All-Star game when Ted Williams
hit a long fly to center, but no one in the stands could tell I

was choking. I went back full speed and got to where I could reach the ball with a good leap. Then I thought that this was the All-Star game and Williams had hit the ball and I froze. The ball went just above my glove. Everybody thought I'd made a great try. Only I knew I'd choked. I don't believe I've choked since. Choking isn't what I really mean by pressure.

I found out about pressure and realized baseball was a business in 1947 when I was twenty years old. I'd played one year of low minor-league ball, served a hitch in the Navy and played less than half a season in the Texas League, but in 1947 I went to spring training with the Dodgers. The first time you go to training camp with a major-league team is the first time you learn that baseball isn't fun. I got sandwiched in pretty tightly.

The Dodgers were building their postwar club and they wanted every star they could get. They tried to make me fill a role. Branch Rickey told the sportswriters that I had a perfect swing; not just good, but perfect. I didn't have ordinary legs, either, he explained. My legs were "steel springs." Naturally, the sportswriters ate this stuff up. They need any angle they can find to fill space during spring training, and I filled a lot of space that spring.

Stan Musial had hit .365 the year before, but by opening day Rickey was still talking, the writers were still writing, and I was being billed as another Musial. It was a real situation. The club wanted to sell tickets and the writers wanted to sell papers. Another Musial would help them both and there I was, squeezed from the outside and pressing on the inside. The first time I ever saw Ebbets Field, I was playing in it. I started badly. The fans only know what they read, and when I struck out a lot, they got on me.

I want to make it clear that I don't blame anyone for this. I was simply a victim of baseball circumstances. My "perfect swing" was imperfect against curve balls. My "steel

springs" didn't help my batting average. The fans booed because I wasn't another Musial, and I brooded because they
booed. I stopped sleeping well. I didn't lose any full night's
sleep but dozing off became a problem. I was restless, nervous, everything.

I hadn't learned then to pop off so I just kept to myself
and sulked. The more I sulked the worse I got, and the
worse I got the more I sulked.

The manager? Well, Leo Durocher had just been suspended from baseball for a year and his replacement, Burt
Shotten, was doing all he could to hold the team together.
Rickey? Jackie Robinson was breaking in and Rickey had
his hands full with that. You know, everyone has problems
of his own, even in baseball. When I was hitting .241, they
farmed me out to St. Paul.

The pressure was different, but no less tight, the following
spring. Rickey had decided that I couldn't tell a strike from
a ball, and he sent me from the regular training camp in the
Dominican Republic to the little Florida town of Vero Beach
for a special course.

In Vero I saw Pete Reiser taking a course, too. Pete, an
outfielder, was trying to learn how to play first base. He had
run into a lot of fences trying to catch home runs and the
battering had about caught up with him. I suppose there
were a lot of things we might have talked about, but Pete
was quiet and worried. He was in pretty bad shape, besides.

In one exhibition game at Vero Beach, Pete hit a triple, or
what should have been a triple. Halfway between second
base and third, he fell down. His legs gave out on him.
As I say, he was in pretty bad shape. When I looked at
Reiser, it seemed to me I was seeing a guy who was washed
up at twenty-eight. I said to myself that in the outfield I
could never let myself make a mistake. I had to be thinking
whenever I went for a fly ball; thinking where the wall is.
Otherwise, I knew, I might end up like Pete.

I stuck with the Dodgers at last in 1949, and it was that year that I learned how to withstand the pressure to succeed. In the '49 World Series, which lasted only five games, I struck out eight times. That tied an all-time record, and we lost to the Yankees, of course. Back home a few weeks later, I thought things through. It went something like this:

"Well, here I am right now after the biggest disappointment of my life. I always wanted to play in a World Series. It's always been my biggest and most important dream and now it's my biggest disappointment. I can't do any worse than I've done and I'm still alive, still got friends, and the finance company hasn't taken away the car. This is the bottom, but it's not as bad as I was afraid it would be. So either I stay here, which isn't bad, or I move up, which is better."

I went into the next season wth all the confidence in the world. Although my confidence has been shaken any number of times since then, I don't think I've ever lost it.

I don't brood any more and I don't sulk. Last year when the Brooklyn fans weren't supporting the club, I popped off. I hope I never have to pop off to the public again, and I certainly don't want to.

With writers, I plan to handle it this way. If a writer says something bad about me and I don't think it's justified, I'll tell him so, like I did last year. I wouldn't pick a fight or tell him how to write, just give him my side of the story.

Handling these headaches is no fun, but it's better than suffering the heartaches of a sour press and hooting fans. In the majors, headaches, like hitting and fielding, are all part of the job. You can be happy in baseball, when you learn to live with them. But the learning is rugged.

As I've said, I hope to play for five seasons after this, which ought to leave me pretty well fixed. Then Bev and the kids and I are going to live on the farm I've bought way south of Los Angeles. We've got a house on a hilltop and almost any day you can see the ocean a long way off.

When I'm watching the Pacific ten years from now, I know I'll miss my baseball friends. Maybe I'll even get a twinge when I hear about some other Dodger center fielder helping some later Dodger club to a pennant. But the first time one of my neighbors drops around to tell me how soft I used to have things, I'm going to get that neighbor into a chair. Then we can have a little talk.

Baseball Memories

This article first appeared in The New York *Times*, July 19, 1927, and is reprinted by permission of John Kieran.

Extract from a letter to the Editor from John Kieran, printed with his permission.

I'm glad you liked the column about John McGraw. How it came to be written is disclosed in the text. It was McGraw's twenty-fifth anniversary with the Giants and they were making an afternoon of it. I waive the fee for reprint rights and I must ask you to waive any introductory remarks by me. I would be embarrassed to choose any piece I wrote and explain why I thought it was good. I never wrote a piece that I didn't think should have been much better.

JOHN KIERAN

BALLAD OF BASEBALL

Give me a ballad of sport's romance,
Pipe me a tune that is blithe and gay,
Never mind Pennock or Dazzy Vance,
Sing me a ditty of yesterday;
Carol a lyric, historical lay,
Tell me of Bowerman and McGann,
Back through the seasons lead the way;
Those were the days for the baseball fan!

153

Tell me of Tinker, Evers and Chance,
Kling and his wealth of tricky play,
Steinfeldt and Sheckard led the dance,
Schulte and Evers led the fray.
Three-fingered Brown was good, I'll say.
Overall, Ruelbach—man, oh man!
Fierce were the Cubs of an early day;
Those were the days for the baseball fan!

Who was it fought them, sword and lance?
John J. McGraw, ere his hair was gray,
Shouting his war-cry: "Go to—France!"
Ready to cut and thrust and slay;
Ready to fight, and no delay,
Dahlen and Gilbert, Bresnahan,
Matty, McGinnity—come what may,
Those were the days for the baseball fan!

L'ENVOI

Lads, though my rhymes be far astray,
Feeble my verses, poor of plan,
This is the slogan I display:
Those were the days for the baseball fan!

Unpublished Memoirs

Extracts from a speech which will not be delivered at the
McGraw Silver Jubilee Celebration at the Polo Grounds this
afternoon:

"So they're giving you flowers, are they, Mac? And a big
silver cup, no less. And best wishes, and maybe love and
kisses. Think of that after the stormy battles of younger
days. The umpires shook your hand today and wished you
well. I saw it with my own incredulous eyes. I remember
when no umpire would come within a stone's throw of you
except under injunction. They doted on your very absence.
They loved the sight of your back. And Barney Dreyfuss
sends congratulations on your jubilee, the same man you

called 'Hey, Barney!' years ago and who was going to send you greetings from the Sheriff for disturbing his dignity.

"Everybody is polite these days, but there was politeness in the old days, too. Remember the Cincinnati fan who reached in the carriage and was thoughtful enough to lift Bowerman's cap off before swiping him over the head with the pop-bottle?

"The boys were so accustomed to fighting in those days that they used to fight each other when nothing better offered. Didn't Bresnahan once say to Devlin, 'You ain't stopped a thing in a week!' And didn't Devlin reply, 'You're so good at stopping, stop this one?' Which Bresnahan did, the same being a punch on the chin.

"But the fight you enjoyed was the fight you didn't see, wasn't it, Mac? The big battle among your ancient enemies, the old-time Cubs. Zimmerman was giving Chance 'what for' when the other boys piled on to help their leader. It came to a halt when Zimmie cracked Sheckard over the crown with a bottle of rub-down, and Sheckard was carted to the hospital. You sent flowers, didn't you? To Zimmerman, I mean.

"The great Cub battle was a close secret until Bresnahan kicked at a called ball with Chance at bat at the Polo Grounds. 'You kick too hard,' said Chance. 'I don't kick as hard as Zimmerman, do I?' said Roger. And then the story went around the whole circuit.

"You had some queer lads in your day, Mac. You had Bugs Raymond and you hired a keeper for him by the name of Dick Fuller. It was only a week ago that Sergeant Smith of the Regular Army reminded me of what Bugs used to say to his keeper: 'No matter how full I get you will always be Fuller.' Remember the time you gave Bugs the new ball to warm up with and he sneaked out of the grounds and sold it to buy himself a half dozen scoops of beer?

"There was poor Phil Douglas, too, who wrote that fool-

ish note to Les Mann about going fishing. And Big Fred
Toney, who collapsed in the third inning in St. Louis one
day, and when you checked back you found he had eaten
two steaks, an order of liver and bacon, a side dish of cab-
bage and four pieces of pie for lunch.

"And you had Ferdie Schupp, who relieved Rube Schauer
so often that Heywood Broun said: 'It never Schauers but it
Schupps.' Queer lads they were, and that's the truth.

"Well, it was grand fun. You had your battles with the old
Cubs, and maybe they got a bit the better of it. But you
won plenty of pennants all the way down the line. You had
some great infields. You won with Devlin, Dahlen, Gilbert
and McGann. You won with Herzog, Fletcher, Doyle and
Merkle. You won with Groh, Bancroft, Frisch and Kelly.

"You fought the Pirates year after year, and you say
that Honus Wagner, the man with the hands like hams and
the feet like crates, was the greatest player of all. And you
should know. You fought Connie Mack time and again, and
Connie says you are the greatest figure in the whole game
of baseball. And Connie should know.

"You had Matty, Wiltse and McGinnity. You had Marquard. You have no pitchers like them these days, John,
more's the pity. When they were talking of what to give you
at this jubilee party, Willie Collier said: 'Give him two
pitchers who can go nine innings.' Well, you can't have
everything, and you can't win every year. Some of the boys
in the bleachers forget that.

"I don't know what's up ahead for you, John, but you've
earned this party, and more besides. You were a great
player and you've been a great manager. You never forgot
a friend, and it's no wonder they're remembering you this
afternoon.

"You fought for what you got, but you always fought in
the open. You've a fight on your hands this minute, and you

haven't got Matty, Devlin, Dahlen, Wiltse, Burns, Young, Marquard and others like that to help you. But you'll keep on fighting as you have for twenty-five years and more. And, John, here's happy days!"

Babe Ruth Has a Birthday

by Al Laney

This article first appeared in the New York *Herald Tribune*, February 8, 1942. Copyright 1942, New York Herald Tribune Inc.

Al Laney is recognized as one of the best feature writers in the business. This human, touching piece on Babe Ruth's forty-seventh birthday should give an idea why that reputation is deserved. With sensitive writing Laney has made a basically routine story memorable.

R. P. G.

It was Babe Ruth's birthday yesterday, and the great man got out of bed to receive his guests and submit to the photographs they still want to take of him. He has been ill with grippe for nearly three weeks and he was not really up to the usual birthday interviews, but he went through it in the same old way.

There were not so many reporters and photographers present in the rather luxurious apartment on Riverside Drive as there were a year ago. Every year there are fewer and no doubt one day the great man will sit alone in his splendor on February 7 and wait in vain for them to come. That day,

however, has not come yet. There was quite a respectable
turnout and they put the ailing Babe through a long workout.

He came into the tastefully furnished living room along
the Drive in red silk lounging pajamas and minced along in
that same ridiculous little walk of his that used to carry
him up to the plate. He stopped in the middle of the room
and rattled the windows with a Gargantuan cough that
racked the barrel chest and caused him to collapse in an
armchair. He took out the handkerchief that had been carefully folded into his jacket pocket and blew a blast through
his broad blob of a nose. His eyes were glassy and feverish
and anyone could see he felt terrible.

"I got the damnedest cold," he said in a squeaky voice.
"Any you fellows want a drink or something? Nora! Bring
me some orange juice. Big one. Can't shake it off. Usually
takes me only a few days. It sure gets you, don't it? Well, I
suppose I got to think up ideas for you guys as usual."

The Babe took a long swig of orange juice and began to
brighten up a bit. Before long his voice came back to him
and he talked in the same boyish direct way he has always
talked. He told the photographers to go on in the bar and
see if they could think up something new for a change.
Then he just talked along.

He didn't say anything much. The Babe no longer gives
out statements about re-entering baseball. He said he hadn't
any plans. He was leaving last night with Mrs. Ruth for
North Conway, New Hampshire, where their daughter and
her husband run an inn for skiers, and then in a couple of
weeks he would go to Florida to bake out in the sun and
play a little golf. He would get back to New York about the
time the golf courses open up.

The Babe gave the impression that he has no great enthusiasm for this round of things that fill his life. He is really
a simple man and it does not occur to him to try to con-

ceal what he is thinking or feeling. He is a man of substance. His future is secure. But it appears that he is not a happy man. It appears that he thinks quite a lot about not having a job of work to do and worries some too, although he does not speak of these things any more.

"Both girls are married now," he said. "Sure miss those kids round here. We got fourteen rooms. It's too big."

The Babe got up and said to come on in the bar and see what those picture guys were up to. He was a little shaky on his legs and his face was flushed, but he posed for nearly an hour while they shot him from every conceivable angle. He had the maid bring in a huge birthday cake someone had sent him and fifty times without complaining he went through the act of cutting it.

The bar is a little room filled with the Babe's trophies and pictures and you could see that he loves it in there. It reminds him of the great days and he lives a lot in the past now. Pointing to a big frame on the wall inclosing sixty baseballs with a name and date on each one and a picture of the Babe in the middle, he said:

"I want to introduce you to some of my relatives. All cousins of mine."

The names on the baseballs were those of the pitchers off whom the Babe hit the sixty home runs in 1927.

The Babe is forty-seven years old and out of the limelight a long time as such things go. But he is still an altogether engaging fellow and a good deal of the old magic still clings to him. He has not changed much. His moon of a face is still ugly and maybe a little coarse, and when he grins he still seems like an impish but lovable child.

If he were still out there where they could see him the millions would still adore him. It is sad to think they are forgetting the Babe. He is still a great man. He came to the door and stood there in his red pajamas while the elevator was coming up to the fifteenth floor. Just before the door closed he said:

"See you fellows next year." And, after a pause, "I hope so."

The Sack of Shelby

Reprinted from WHITE HOPES AND OTHER TIGERS by John Lardner and used with his permission. This article first appeared in *The New Yorker*, June 19, 1948. Copyright 1948 The New Yorker Magazine, Inc.

Soon after the second World War ended, under the winy influence of peace, I wrote for THE NEW YORKER *some chapters of a history of the aspect of boxing that had always interested me most: the non-athletic side of it, the part that is played in this spectacularly human and corrupt game by rascals, politicians, reformers, parasites, sutlers, wits, and adventurers. My special hero was that great complement of the great bruiser, the fight manager. My truest pleasure as a sportswriter had come, as it still does, from watching the work and drinking in the reminiscences of men like Jimmy Johnston, Dan Morgan, Joe Gould, Dan McKetrick, Joe Jacobs, Jimmy Bronson, Billy McCarney, and Jack Kearns. I think that the art of the fight manager reached its zenith in Kearn's adventure with Dempsey in Shelby, Montana, in 1923.*

The story, which I merely pulled together, is an epic of the picaresque; it describes what may have been one of the last stands of the independent, romantic hustler against the "state." Kearns looted the state of Montana, to the best of his ability. In doing so, he also acted out a conscious bur-

lesque of the Lewis & Clarke tradition, of the winning of
the west. He produced a hell of a story, and I've never had
more fun in sports writing than in writing this one.

JOHN LARDNER

Jack Kearns became almost legendary in the prize fight business between the two world wars because of his ability to
make money in large, bold scoops without recourse to day
labor. After the second war, to show that his hand—green
thumb, prehensile fingers, and all—was still in, he repeated an old trick by steering still another fighter to a
championship. The fighter, Joey Maxim, who became
world's light-heavyweight champion under Kearns, will
not shine brightly in history books. He is just a footnote sort
of fighter—cute but pedestrian, the critics agree, and
practically punchless. I remember that there was something
like boredom in Kearns's voice, one day in the late nine-
teen-forties, as he sat on a desk in Madison Square Garden,
shortly before Maxim's bout with the Swedish heavyweight
champion, Olle Tandberg, and delivered a routine hallelujah
to his latest means of support.

"This kid is better than Dempsey," said Kearns. His soft
blue eyes stared vacantly at the floor. "He don't hit quite
as hard as Dempsey, but otherwise he's better."

Since Kearns managed Jack Dempsey when the latter was
heavyweight champion, it may be that he thought he held a
lifetime dispensation from some celestial chamber of commerce to misuse Dempsey's name for advertising purposes.
It may be that he was right; at any rate, no thunderbolt
split the ceiling to strike him down for his blasphemous
words. His audience, composed of managers, trainers, reporters, and press agents, shifted its feet and withheld comment. There was nothing to be said—nothing polite. Then

one of the managers, an old-time boxing man, began to warm to the recollection of the team of Dempsey and Kearns. He turned the talk to happier times.

"Remember Shelby, Doc?" he asked. "You and Dempsey broke three banks in Montana."

Kearns's eyes came to life.

"We broke four banks," he said. With rising enthusiasm, he went on to describe his withdrawal after the sack of Shelby, Montana, in 1923, with two bags of silver in a railroad caboose. His listeners drew closer. The career and prospects of Joey Maxim were, for the time being and without regrets, tabled.

To boxing people who have heard of the place, the memory of Shelby is precious for many reasons, one of them being that it brought a man of their own profession—namely, Kearns—into singlehanded combat with a state 147,138 square miles in area, producing copper, gold, silver, zinc, lead, manganese, oil, coal, grain, and livestock. No one who was involved in the Shelby affair, including Kearns and Dempsey, is any longer a perfectly reliable authority on the facts of the story, owing to the blurring influence of the autobiographical instinct on boxing memoirs. However, investigation shows that Kearns's performance compared favorably—for tenacity, at least—with those of the predatory railroad barons Jay Gould, Daniel Drew, Commodore Vanderbilt, and James J. Hill. As it happened, it was on Hill's Great Northern Railway, which opened up the north of Montana in the eighteen-eighties, that Kearns rode into the state, with a fiery purpose, and out of it again, with great haste, in 1923. The scope of Kearns's raid has been exaggerated somewhat by his admirers, himself among them, but there is no doubt that it had a profound effect on no fewer than two Montana counties, Toole and Cascade. Furthermore, the name, spirit, and wealth of the whole state

were invoked by those Montanans who struggled with
Kearns first-hand. They stated more than once at the time
that "the honor of all Montana" was at stake. Montana today is perhaps in a sounder financial condition than Kearns,
but that only goes to show the extent of its natural resources. It took an oil strike to draw Kearns to Shelby, in
Toole County, in the first place, and it took another oil
strike, years later, to complete Toole County's recovery
from Kearns.

The raider, who was born John L. McKernan, is now
sixty-five years old. He is still a dapper figure, when dressed
for pleasure, but his hair is thin and a paunch shows at the
conjunction of his pants and sweater when he climbs into
the ring on business, as he did at the meeting of his man
Maxim with Tandberg, in which Maxim won a close decision. That bout netted Kearns and his fighter approximately fifteen hundred dollars. The loser, by the terms of
an arrangement based on his drawing power, got fifteen
thousand dollars. Later, finding good soil in London,
Kearns and Maxim did better. But the spark will never burn
as high in this team as it did in Dempsey and Kearns. The
bout between Dempsey and Tom Gibbons in Shelby, on
July 4, 1923, brought Kearns and Dempsey nearly three
hundred thousand dollars. The loser got nothing whatever.
In those days, Kearns was forty years old and at the height
of his genius.

A good many people in 1923, including writers of newspaper editorials, likened Shelby after the fight to a Belgian
village ravaged by the Huns. They ignored or overlooked
the fact that Shelby, like no Belgian village on record, had
opened the relationship by begging to be taken. Kearns and
Dempsey had never heard of Shelby before its citizens went
to the trouble of raising a hundred thousand dollars to en-
tice them there. In the popular view, Dempsey was the
archfiend of the episode. His reputation as a draft dodger

in the First World War, carefully cultivated by managers
of rival fighters like Fighting Bob Martin, the A.E.F. heavyweight champion, made a strong impression on the public;
during the Shelby crisis, people were quite willing to consider him a profiteer as well as a slacker. They lost sight of
Kearns in Dempsey's shadow. It was only the men directly
concerned with financing the Dempsey-Gibbons match who
realized that Kearns was the brains and backbone of the
visiting party. In language that will not bear repeating, these
men marvelled at Kearns's almost religious attachment to
the principle of collecting all the cash in Montana that was
not nailed down.

It was a booster spirit that got Shelby into trouble—the
frontier booster spirit, which seems to have been a particularly red-blooded and chuckleheaded variety. Up to
1922, Shelby had been a village populated by four or five
hundred cowhands, sheepherders, and dry-dirt farmers. In
1922, oil was struck in the Kevin-Sunburst field, just north
of town. The population rose to over a thousand. It was not
much of a jump superficially; the significant difference was
that all the new citizens had money. Some of them were oil
speculators, some of them were real-estate men from the
West Coast buying up land to sell to oil speculators. A few
were merchants selling standard boom-town merchandise,
much of it liquid, to the oilmen and the real-estate men.
Kearns had not yet seen Shelby with his own eyes when he
first tried to describe it to skeptics in the East a year later,
but his description was not far wrong.

"It's one of those wide-open towns," he said spaciously.
"Red Dog saloon, gambling hells—you know, like you see
in the movies."

It was old Blackfoot country. South of Shelby, the Marias
River wound toward the site of a vanished fur-trading post
on the Missouri. Not far north was the Canadian border.
The Great Northern Railway ran west from Shelby to Gla-

cier Park and the Pacific, east to Duluth and the Twin Cities, south a hundred miles to the nearest real town, Great Falls. In Shelby proper, there were the railroad depot, a few stores, a few houses, a couple of new banks, the Silver Grill Hotel, where fifty extra beds filled the lobby at the height of the boom, and half a dozen saloons.

In one of the saloons, on an evening in January, 1923, a bunch of the boys were whooping it up in a civic-minded way. The party was headed by Mayor James A. Johnson, a large man of fifty-eight who had made a comfortable fortune ranching, and had added to it in the boom through oil leases and the ownership of the First State Bank of Shelby. Sitting around him were men named Zimmerman, Sampson, Dwyer, and Schwartz. It was Sam Sampson, a storekeeper and landowner, who first suggested that the best way to make the nation and the world Shelby-conscious—that being the object of everyone in town who owned property —would be to stage a fight there for the heavyweight championship of the world. Dempsey was champion. The two most talked-of contenders for his title at that time were Harry Wills, a Negro, and Tom Gibbons, a white man from St. Paul. The barroom committee skipped lightly over Wills. Gibbons was its choice on two counts: the color of his pelt and the fact that he was a Northwestern man, from a state with which Montana had close commercial connections. The committee toasted Gibbons, Shelby, and itself. Then Sampson began to send telegrams in all directions. He wired Dempsey and Gibbons and their managers, and received no replies, which was not surprising, in view of Shelby's overwhelming anonymity. He also sent a telegram to Mike Collins, a journalist and boxing matchmaker in Minneapolis. Collins, a friend of Gibbons, agreed to come to Shelby at the committee's expense and study the possibilities.

His reaction on stepping off the train at the Shelby depot was recorded by himself at a later date. "I was startled," he said. Shelby was small and raw beyond the power of a city man's imagination. Mayor Johnson and Sampson led Collins across a few rods of the Great Plains to a saloon, where the Mayor gave Collins the impression that Mose Zimmerman, another committeeman who owned land, was ready to finance the championship fight out of his own pocket. To substantiate this, the Mayor rounded up Zimmerman, who denied indignantly that he was ready to contribute anything but a small, decent, proportionate piece of the total. The Mayor looked sad. Collins walked back to the depot to catch the eight P.M. train for Minneapolis. As things turned out, he was the first of a series of people who started to wash their hands of Shelby by catching a train. They were all called back at the last minute. A Fate straight out of Sophocles had matters in her grip.

Before the eight-o'clock train arrived, Mayor Johnson arranged a mass meeting of citizens in a saloon. Collins was persuaded to address it. He said starkly that Shelby had no boxing arena, no population, and, as far as he could see, no money.

"You would need a hundred thousand dollars before you even talk to Dempsey and Gibbons," he added.

At this point, Shelby startled him for the second time. The Mayor and his friends raised twenty-six thousand dollars on the spot, the contributors receiving vouchers for ringside seats to the fight in exchange. Collins noted that the vouchers were marked July Fourth. The phantom battle already had a date and a ticket sale. This show of *sang-froid* won him over. A short, time afterward, he set out, in the company of a gentleman named Loy J. Molumby, state commander of the American Legion, to stump Montana for the balance of the money. Traveling from town to town in Molumby's private airplane, they brought the total of cash on hand to a hundred and ten thousand dollars in a little more than a week's time. The moment had come, Collins

freely admitted, to let Dempsey and Gibbons in on the
secret. It was now, he said, just a matter of convincing
them that there was such a place as Shelby and showing
them the money.

The two things were achieved in reverse order. It was
after seeing the money that Dempsey and Gibbons—or,
rather, their managers, Kearns and Eddie Kane—brought
themselves to believe in Shelby. The rest of the country,
having seen no money, did not believe in Shelby for some
time to come. At the beginning of May, the boxing critic
of the New York *Tribune,* Jack Lawrence, spoke of a meeting that would take place soon at Madison Square Garden
between the Dempsey and Gibbons parties. "There," he
wrote scornfully, "they will probably hear a counter-proposi-
tion from the lips of Tex Rickard that will waft Shelby,
Montana, back to the pastoral obscurity from which it
emerged so suddenly."

Lawrence was wrong. Kearns and Kane bypassed New
York and Rickard and went to Chicago to inspect the cash
and negotiate the Shelby deal with Molumby and Collins,
who were now the accredited agents of Mayor Johnson's
town. It is apparent that both managers were remarkable
for the grandeur of their vision. Kane showed it by agreeing
to let Dempsey and Kearns have everything the bout drew,
up to three hundred thousand dollars, at the boxoffice in
Shelby, if there was a Shelby, before taking a percentage for
Gibbons. The Gibbons share was to be 50 per cent of the
receipts from three hundred thousand dollars to six hundred
thousand dollars, and 25 per cent of everything above that.
Three hundred thousand dollars was exactly what Kearns
and Dempsey had made from the spectacular million-dollar-
gate fight with Georges Carpentier, which Rickard had promoted two years before on the threshold of New York City.
Kearns was now counting on gouging the same sum from
an infinitesimal cowtown that had no boxing ring, no pro-

fessional promoter, and no large city within five hundred miles. At least, he said he was counting on that. Almost no one in New York believed there would be a fight. Kearns's friends suspected, with characteristic misanthropy, that Doc was up to some sort of practice ruse to keep his hand in and his brain lean and sharp for coming campaigns. Rickard, who did not think much of either Gibbons or Wills as an opponent for Dempsey, having sped Kearns west with a tolerant wink, went on with plans for his own notion of a Dempsey match, with the Argentine Luis Firpo, for autumn delivery.

Kearns, however, was in earnest. It pleased his fancy to undertake this Western adventure on his own. He wanted for once to be free from Eastern entanglements, free from his professional peers. Gibbons and Kane, the parties of the second part, would be amateurs at Shelby in everything but name. At Shelby, every power, privilege, and bargaining weapon would belong to Kearns. If he could carry three hundred thousand dollars out of a town of one thousand population, he would become immortal in his profession. If he couldn't, he had dictated terms that said firmly that all money paid to him and Dempsey in advance was theirs to keep. If they got three hundred thousand dollars, there would be a fight; if they didn't, there would be no fight, and no rebate. Molumby agreed, on behalf of Mayor Johnson, to deliver a second installment of a hundred thousand dollars to Kearns on June 15th, and a third, and last, on July 2nd, two days before the fight. This was Molumby's last major gesture in connection with the Dempsey-Gibbons match. Like half a dozen other Montanans, who tried to learn the boxing business in the next few weeks, he flunked the course.

A slight difficulty occurred in the secondary negotiations between Kearns and Kane. The difficulty was that they had not spoken to each other for four years and had no wish to

start speaking now. Kearns said much later that he could
not remember the reason for the breach, which may or may
not be true; boxing men usually are shy about revealing
the causes of their Grade A feuds—the ones that last anywhere from a year to life. Quartered two floors apart in the
Morrison Hotel in Chicago, Kane and Kearns conferred by
messenger. The messenger was Collins. One question was
who was to referee the fight. It was purely nominal, for
Kearns had already decided on his good friend Jim Dougherty, sometimes known as the Baron of Leiperville, Pennsylvania. After four trips by Collins up and down the hotel's
emergency stairway, Kane accepted Dougherty. He had no
choice. Kearns, as the champion's manager, was in command. Kane, managing the challenger, and a poorly recom-
mended challenger, at that, in the opinion of most critics
—could consider himself lucky to have gained a chance at
the title for Gibbons. That chance was something, although
Gibbons was older and smaller than Dempsey. Beyond it,
there was a possibility of making some money if the fight
was highly successful, which was the dream that Mayor
Johnson had sold to Collins and Collins to Kane. Kane and
Gibbons were gambling, like the men of Shelby and the
men of the rest of Montana who backed them. That explains,
in part, the deep affection Montana came to feel for Gibbons
as the time of the fight drew near.

A few days after the terms were signed, Collins, as
"matchmaker," or supervisor of arrangements, announced
the ticket price scale: from fifty dollars ringside, to twenty
dollars, for the rear seats. There were no seats at the moment, but Mayor Johnson had persuaded Major J. E. Lane, a
local lumber merchant, to build an arena at the edge of
town to accommodate forty thousand people. There was no
money for Major Lane, but the Mayor got him to take a sev-
enty-thousand-dollar chattel mortgage on the arena. Training camps were staked out for both fighters. On May 16th,

Kearns entrained for Montana with a staff of sparring partners for Dempsey, who made his own way there from his
home in Salt Lake City. Kearns was glad to leave the decadent cities of the East, where the newspapers, when they
mentioned Shelby at all, still questioned the reality of the
fight and half questioned the reality of Shelby. He found
Shelby in a holiday mood. The Mayor and his friends had
recovered from the strain of getting up the first hundred
thousand dollars, and had not yet begun to worry about
finding the remaining two hundred thousand. The ticket
sale would take care of that.

Kearns beamed upon these unsophisticated burghers with
boots on their feet and guns in their belts. He addressed
them at a Chamber of Commerce luncheon at the Silver
Grill. With all the sincerity he could muster on short notice,
he told them that Gibbons was a great fighter, "the best
boxer in the world.

"I would not be surprised," Kearns told the meeting lov-
ingly, "if the winner of this contest fought Harry Wills right
here in Shelby on Labor Day. You will be the fight capital
of the nation. We have come here," he added, "at something
of a sacrifice, since we were offered half a million dollars for
the same fight in New York. However, Shelby spoke first,
and Shelby wins out."

Then Kearns took a rapid look at Shelby, whose facilities could all be seen at a glance with the naked eye, and
caught the six o'clock train to Great Falls. All Montana, and
Shelby, in particular, was well pleased with itself at this
point. It is hard to say at just what hour between then and
June 15th, the first day of open crisis, misgivings began to
set in. They must have come soonest to Johnson and Molumby, who were in charge of the ticket sale and the cash-
box. Kearns ostensibly had no notion of how things were
going. When he was told, Montana was stunned by the
change in the manner of the free-and-easy stranger.

Kearns had made his base in Great Falls, partly because it was a town of thirty thousand that offered some freedom of movement, and partly because Dempsey was training there, at Great Falls Park, a mile or so outside the city limits. Before June 15th, Dempsey trained well and seemed happy. The park, in a hollow in the hills of Cascade County, just east of the Missouri River and in sight of the Little and Big Belt Mountains and the Birdtail Divide, was a pleasant place, surrounded by cottonwood trees, that had formerly been a scene of revelry. Dempsey lived and sparred in a roadhouse that prohibition and repeated government raids had closed down. Sometimes the champion fished in the Missouri. He had a pet cow, a Hereford bull, a wolf cub, and a bulldog in camp, as well as two of his brothers, Johnny and Bernie; his trainer, Jerry (the Greek) Luvadis; and his stooge, Joe Benjamin, with whom he played pinochle. His sparring partners ranged from giants like Big Ben Wray, seven feet two inches tall, to small, clever middleweights who could simulate Gibbons' style. Gibbons trained in Shelby. He lived with his wife and children in a house on the great, treeless plain, not far from the arena. If anything more was needed to make Gibbons a favorite and Dempsey unpopular in Shelby after June 15th, Gibbons' choice of training quarters did it. The town saw him and his family every day. Gibbons at that time was thirty-four, six years older than Dempsey. He had had a long and fairly successful career among middleweights and light heavyweights, though the gifted little Harry Greb had beaten him just the year before. He was a polite and colorless man, with a slim waist, a big chest, and a high shock of pompadoured hair.

On June 15th, the day appointed for the payment of the second hundred thousand dollars to Kearns and Dempsey, Kearns went to the Great Falls station to take a train to Shelby. He said later that he was going in all innocence to ask Mayor Johnson for the money, that he did not know that the Mayor and Molumby were at that moment wretchedly chewing cigars in a room in the Park Hotel in Great Falls, having just confessed to George H. Stanton, the leading banker of Great Falls, that the day of reckoning found them approximately 98 per cent short. They asked him what to do. Stanton, like all Montanans, had followed the Shelby adventure closely. As the principal capitalist of that part of the state, he had followed it more closely than most, and he probably had a fair notion of the truth before he heard it from the unhappy promoters. However, he told them it was a hell of a note, and he sent someone to get Kearns off the train. Kearns came to the hotel room, looking hopeful. It was his first business contact with Stanton; it would have been better for Stanton if it had been his last. The promoters explained the situation, or what they could understand of it. They admitted frankly that it confused them. It seemed that a great many tickets that had been mailed out, unbonded, to various parts of the state and country were not yet paid for. It seemed that expenses were unexpectedly large. It appeared that there were sixteen hundred dollars cash on hand for Kearns and Dempsey. Whatever suspicions Kearns may have had before this, the cold facts undoubtedly shocked him. He flew into a rage.

"Why don't *you* take over the promotion and the sale?" suggested Stanton. "From all I can see, you own the fight right now."

"I won't promote!" screamed Kearns. "These guys are the promoters. I'm trying to train a fighter. Let them get our money up or there won't be any fight."

Kearns left the room in a black mood. He went back to the hotel that evening, at Stanton's invitation, and found that most of the money in Great Falls was represented there: Stanton, president of the Stanton Trust & Savings Bank; Dan Tracey, hotel owner; Russell and Arthur Strain, department-store owners; J. W. Speer, lawyer and former judge; and Shirley Ford, vice-president of the Great Falls National Bank. From there on, Kearns was told, the honor of Montana was at stake. The fight would have new promoters. The money would be raised. It *was* raised, within twenty-four hours. At five-fifteen P.M. the next day, June 16th, the press was summoned to see Stanton present Kearns with a check for a hundred thousand dollars, seventeen hours and a quarter after the deadline of midnight, June 15th. Kearns put the check in his pocket and congratulated Montana. "A dead-game state," he said. Stanton accepted his kind words modestly, though it must be said that he gave newspapermen present the impression that he himself had put up seventy-three thousand dollars of the money, which was not strictly true. He had supplied cash in that amount, but it was underwritten almost entirely by Mayor Jim Johnson, of Shelby, with land and oil leases from his own estate. The Strain brothers and the O'Neill brothers, Lou and John, who were oilmen, made up the balance.

While Molumby and Mayor Johnson sat humbly by— the latter quite silent about his contribution to the salvation of Montana's honor—Dan Tracey delivered a tough speech. The Great Falls committee had appointed Tracey head man of the fight. The old promoters, he said, were through as head men. He would protect the interest of his Great Falls friends. He would see that they got every nickel back. He would countersign all checks from now on. He paused, and Kearns advanced to shake him by the hand.

"This reassures me," said Kearns. "I will stick to Shelby and ignore the countless offers I have got from other states for this fight. I am sure," he added thoughtfully, "that we won't have any trouble about the last hundred thousand dollars—due midnight, July 2nd."

Mayor Johnson mopped his brow with a handkerchief.

"This is a great relief," he told the press. "I wasn't cut out to be a boxing promoter."

Molumby had nothing to say. Earlier that day, he had been denounced by an American Legion post in St. Louis for involving the Legion in Dempsey's affairs.

The reign of Tracey as head man lasted eleven days. It was a time of stress and brooding. The backers of the fight knew that since raising the second hundred thousand dollars had been like pulling teeth, the collection of the third hundred thousand would be on the order of a major amputation. The advance sale of tickets brought in no money to speak of. People could not be expected to buy tickets unless they were sure the fight would take place, and the promoters could not persuade the strong-minded Kearns to guarantee a fight before he was sure of the money. The Great Northern canceled a plan to run special trains from the East and the Pacific Coast. The promoters and their friends snarled at Kearns whenever they saw him, and nervously fondled the butts of their guns. Frank Walker, of Butte, Montana, a lawyer and later Postmaster General under Franklin Roosevelt, came to Great Falls to add weight to the heckling of Kearns. Kearns, however, rode his choppy course serenely and nonchalantly, true to his lofty principle of three hundred thousand dollars or no contest.

The strain was much harder on Dempsey than on Dempsey's manager. If Kearns was Public Enemy No. 1 to the financiers of Montana, Dempsey was the people's choice for the part. He was sharply aware of it and of the artillery on the hip of nearly everyone he saw. He said later that he pleaded with Kearns, to no avail, at this time to waive the final payment, to promise a fight, and to take over the box-office management. The champion's state of mind showed in his work. He looked slow and easy to hit in training, and his sparring partners complained of his viciousness when he hit them. On his twenty-eighth birthday, June 24th, seemingly angry at his failure to catch Jack Burke, a middleweight, he knocked down another sparring partner seven times in five rounds, and broke the jaw of the giant Wray, who subsequently took his meals through a tube.

The crises came fast now. On June 26th, Stanton, conferring in Shelby with Tracey and Mayor Johnson, who had been reduced to assistant promoter, was told that the lumber merchant and the contractors were about to foreclose their mortgage on the arena. Stanton stalked angrily to the railroad station, but he was called back into conference, inevitably, at the last minute. Half an hour later, he announced that the creditors had agreed to accept payment on a pro-rata basis from the gate receipts. He said that all was well. Tracey, the tough talker of June 16th, could not bring himself to share this view. The mortgage crisis had broken his spirit. On June 27th, he resigned his job.

"The money that my people put up is nowhere in sight that I can see," he said. "I can't be sure they'll get it back, and I'm through."

Shelby was excited the next day by a telegram received by Mayor Johnson from Minneapolis signed "Louis W. Till," which it assumed to be from Louis Hill, board chairman of the Great Northern, assuring the Mayor that he was "on way with cash and securities so Tom can have chance to put profiteering Dempsey in hospital." The wire turned out to be a hoax. On June 29th, Stanton made a final, desperate move. After consulting with Great Falls leaders on a list of names, and sending telegrams to all parts of the state, he proclaimed that "twenty lifelong friends" had pledged five thousand dollars each to meet the final payment to Kearns and "save the honor of Montana." The announcement was given out now, Stanton said, to dispel doubts that the fight would be held. But the payment to Kearns would not be made until the agreed date of July 2nd, because, he went on sulkily, some of the new sponsors "are disposed to follow the lead taken by the champion's manager and adhere rigidly to the conditions of the contract." It was their opinion, he said, that Kearns "would get out of the fight if he could." Enlarging on the patriotism of his twenty lifelong friends, Stanton said that cancellation of the bout "would have cast reflections on the state that would have been far-reaching in effect." The Northwest, he added, would now save the fight; the Dakotas, Wyoming, Idaho, Washington, Oregon, and Western Canada would send at least fifteen thousand people. The members of the committee would take a loss but "are game enough to see this thing through."

Kearns, ignoring the slurs on his good faith in this manifesto, expressed satisfaction. Dempsey forced a smile and acknowledged the gameness of all Montanans. But on July 2nd, facing the press, with Kearns present, in Great Falls, Stanton revealed that he had been unable to cash the pledges of his lifelong friends. Eight of them had come through as advertised, he said, but in the circumstances he did not feel like keeping their money. He looked defiantly at Kearns. Kearns shrugged. He retired to discuss things with his lieutenant from New York, Dan McKetrick. Then he told Stanton that he would make the "gamble" that had been forced on him. He would take over the fight and the gate receipts with it. From that moment, concern about paying Kearns was outweighed by a vivid fear that Kearns and Dempsey would slip across the border before July Fourth with the money they had already collected, leaving Shelby to whistle for its world-championship fight. There is no evidence that either man contemplated doing this, but practically everyone in Montana was convinced that both of them did contemplate it. Kearns later recalled that Frank Walker, in a state of deep emotion, shook his fist beneath Kearns's nose on July 3rd and warned him not to try to escape.

Shelby had built up to the fight, within its limits. There were concession booths and stands all the way from Main Street to the arena. Entertainers had come from every corner of the state. A tent show called the Hyland-Welty Comedians was playing the town; it starred a certain Patricia Salmon, the toast of the out-of-town reporters, who for fifty dollars a week did three song spots a day, yodeled in front of the curtain, and played the lead in *Which One Shall I Marry?*, *Thorns and Orange Blossoms*, *The Tie that Binds*, and *The Sweetest Girl in Dixie*. An acquaintance of mine from Billings, Montana, drove to Shelby for the fight with his father, an early patriotic ticket-buyer. The sign he remembers best on Main Street was "Aunt Kate's Cathouse." All tourists slept in their automobiles the night of July 3rd. The great Northwestern migration to Shelby had not materialized, but there were enough cars parked on the plain by the arena to show that there was an interest in the fight. Part of the interest was speculative; many people had not bought tickets, but counted on getting in anyway.

Dempsey came from Great Falls in a private railroad car on July Fourth, arriving in the early afternoon. A switch engine pulled his car to a siding near the arena, where a crowd of men instantly surrounded it. "There were no cheers," according to Dempsey. His party, which included a Chicago detective named Mike Trent, and a celebrated hanger-on of the time, "Senator" Wild Bill Lyons, both strongly and ostentatiously armed, took counsel. Some of the crowd were trying to climb aboard. Lyons told the engineer to keep the engine hooked on and to run the car up and down the siding till it was time for Dempsey to get off. When that time came, the crowd pressed close around the champion, but there were no gunshots or blows. "Trying to run out, were you?" called some of the men. A messenger form the ringside reported that it was still too early for Dempsey's entrance, since the program had been delayed. The crowd, however, got solidly behind Dempsey in a physical sense and pushed him firmly to the arena doors, where he waited with half a dozen retainers by a soft-drink stand, listening to comments on his character and lineage.

The reason for the delay was the public's reluctance to pay the official prices for tickets. Kearns had opened the gates in the morning, after surrendering five hundred dollars from the advance sale for the privilege to a crew of federal revenue men who were on hand looking hungrily after their country's interests. At noon, however, there were only fifteen hundred people in the grandstand to watch the first preliminary bout. Thousands milled around outside the gates, many of them shouting, "We'll come in for ten dollars!" These were the aristocrats of the mob. Kearns began to accommodate them at two-thirty, while people inside pushed down from high seats to empty ringside seats, the working press sweltered over typewriters almost too hot to touch, and two bands—the Montana State Elks band on one side of the ring and the Scottish Highlanders of Calgary on the other—alternately administered soothing music. A blind war veteran was singing a ballad in the ring when Kearns finally was overrun by the rest of the crowd outside, which came in free. Dempsey entered at three-thirty-six, thirty-six minutes late. "It was the most hostile crowd a heavyweight champion ever faced," he said a few years later, through a ghost writer, and he was probably right. There was some hissing, he recalled, but mostly "sullen silence." Gibbons made it harder for him by delaying his arrival till three-forty-five and taking ten minutes to have his hands taped in the ring. A few empty bottles came down near Dempsey's corner, tossed by spectators who blamed the champion for the delay. Dodging glassware in the corner with Dempsey were Kearns and Bill Lyons, who wore chaps and a sombrero as well as his arsenal. A number of what Kearns called "my Chicago hard guys" sat watchfully at the ringside just below.

It was a very bad fight. Dempsey, outweighing Gibbons, a hundred and eighty-eight pounds to a hundred and seventy-four, but stale and nervous, could not land his punches squarely. It was widely said later that he would not, out of fear for his safety, but that theory conflicts with the testimony of Dempsey and the opinion of expert eyewitnesses. Gibbons won a few of the early rounds. He opened a cut over Dempsey's eye in the second. Dempsey complained afterward that Kearns, never the most sure-handed of seconds, poured cut medicine inside the eye between rounds, making him half blind until the seventh. From the sixth round on, it was Dempsey's fight, easily. The crowd stopped crying, "Kill him, Tommy!" and cried, "Hang on!" That was all Gibbons tried to do—he had every reason to know he was working for nothing, and Dempsey's strength soon made him sure he couldn't win. Gibbons scored one moral triumph when he survived the twelfth round, a new record against Dempsey, and another when he survived the fifteenth and last, and forced the bout to a decision. The last round was one long clinch; Gibbons wrapped his arms around Dempsey, and the onlookers shouted derisively at the champion and threw cushions. Gibbons made no objection to referee Dougherty's decision for Dempsey. Neither did the crowd. Dempsey got out with the utmost dispatch when the verdict had been given. The Chicago hard guys, led by Detective Trent, hustled him aboard the private car on the siding. At the Shelby station, his car was hooked to a train for Great Falls. He spent the night at the Park Hotel in Great Falls and caught a regular train the next day for Salt Lake City. Both of Dempsey's eyes were discolored when he boarded the Salt Lake train and exchanged a few last words with residents of Great Falls who had come to see him off.

"Don't hurry back!" called his well-wishers.

"I won't, boys," said Dempsey sincerely.

Kearns's departure from Montana was a little more complicated. To this day, he holds to the colorful view that he narrowly escaped injury or death from the guns of the West in getting out with the money. The money, the proceeds of the last day's ticket sale, amounted to about eighty thousand dollars in silver and bills. Kearns and McKetrick counted it in the presence of the federal tax men and stuffed it into a couple of canvas sacks. It is altogether possible that if Kearns had then honored an earlier promise to meet with certain fight fans and Shelby citizens in a saloon to talk things over before saying good-bye, he and the cash would not have left the state intact. The temper of Shelby needed only a sprinkling of ninety-proof rye to boil over. But Kearns, holding to his higher purpose, which was to keep all the money, less tax, broke the date. He and McKetrick made straight from the box-office for a caboose attached to a locomotive that stood waiting in the twilight at the station. The get-away transportation had been chartered with the help of the federal men. As Kearns and McKetrick boarded the caboose, they observed in the street near by the shadowy figure of a small man with a ukulele. This was the late Hype Igoe, a New York sportswriter with a turn for minstrelsy, who, having written his fight piece and lingered in Shelby to take on fuel, was delicately strumming chords for his own entertainment. "This is the New York special, Hype," called Kearns. Igoe accepted the invitation and got aboard, and the special rolled out of Shelby.

Still playing a cautious game, the Kearns party spent the rest of the night in the cellar of a barbershop in Great Falls. Kearns passed up the Salt Lake City express next day, and for five hundred dollars, out of one of the canvas bags, hired a locomotive and coach from the Great Northern's Great Falls agent. He and his friends joined Dempsey the next day.

On July 9th began a series of events that canonized Kearns in the boxing business. The Stanton Trust & Savings Bank of Great Falls closed its doors that day. Stanton insisted that the closing had no connection with the Dempsey-Gibbons fight; he blamed it on post-war conditions in general. However, all other reports from Montana then and later agreed that the public knowledge of Stanton's association with the fight caused a run on the bank, which the banker could not meet because of the temporary withdrawal of seventy-three thousand dollars in cash from his own account to pay Kearns on June 16th. The state bank examiner, L. Q. Skelton, came to Great Falls to take over the bank. He saved himself an extra trip to the neighborhood by taking over Mayor Johnson's First State Bank of Shelby as well, Johnson having stopped payment to depositors on the morning of July 10th.

It was now revealed for the first time that much of the cash paid by Stanton to Kearns had been secured by Johnson with his personal property, which he began making over to Stanton after the fight. On July 11th, the First State Bank of Joplin, Montana, an affiliate of Stanton's bank, closed down. Newspaper reports from Joplin stated that all closings to date were "generally accredited" to the championship bout in Shelby. Boxing people never doubted this for a moment. Kearns and Dempsey have been pointed out ever since as winners over three Montana banks. The better-informed students of the situation, like Kearns, feel that the score should be four, for on August 16th of the same year, almost unnoticed by the press, the First National Bank of Shelby was closed by order of its board of directors, following withdrawals of something like a hundred thousand dollars in the first month after the fight. This left Shelby with, for the time being, no banks at all and practically no assets. The oil boom subsided not long afterward. The arena was torn down and the lumber salvaged by the mortgage holders.

Kearns has related that Mayor Johnson wrote to Dempsey

and himself that summer asking for a loan of twenty-five thousand dollars, and that it was granted and repaid within a year. It is certain that the Mayor was comfortably off when he died in 1938, thanks mainly to another strike in the Kevin-Sunburst oil field, a few years after the first one, which reanimated the town. The career of Patricia Salmon, the tent-show actress, took an opposite course. Her New York press reviews from Shelby in 1923 won her a contract with Florenz Ziegfeld and a season in the *Follies*. It was thought for a time that she, Dempsey, and Kearns (and the U.S. government) were the beneficiaries of the Shelby fight. But Miss Salmon was a one-year wonder. Her star declined as Johnson's rose, and in 1928 she was towed off the floor of Madison Square Garden with a set of swollen feet, after performing consecutively for a hundred and thirty-five hours and forty minutes in a dance marathon that she had hoped would bring her publicity and another job in the theater.

A word should be said about the early unpopularity of Dempsey, for it contributed much to his discomfort at Shelby and to the public's reaction in Montana and elsewhere. Like other entertainers in both world wars, Dempsey, in 1918, did a certain amount of morale-building among war workers. There is evidence that he was popular with sports followers, including Army and Navy men, in 1919, when he won the championship (Willard, the champion, who had also failed to see service, was much less so). The change in Dempsey's case did not set in until after the managers of heavyweights with war records, all of them outclassed as prizefighters by Dempsey, began to play up their wartime service in interviews and advertisements. Dempsey did not speak to Jimmy Bronson, who managed Fighting Bob Martin, for more than twenty-five years after this campaign, though Bronson actually had nothing to do with the wide circulation of a 1918 photograph of Dempsey striking a pose in a shipyard with a workman's tool in his hands and patent leather shoes on his feet.

Dempsey was formally acquitted of draft evasion in 1920. From the time he lost the championship to Gene Tunney, in 1926, he was immensely popular in America and abroad, However, it was plain to anyone who knew him that he never forgot certain aspects of his public life between 1919 and 1926. He was commissioned, as a physical director, in the Coast Guard in the last war. I saw him during preparations for the Okinawa landing in 1945. He had obtained leave to go to Okinawa on a Coast Guard ship, and could hardly control his excitement; in fact, it was almost necessary to gag him to maintain security before the operation began. He went ashore on the Marines' sector of the front shortly after D (or L) Day. He did not stay long, since he served no military purpose there, but it probably helped to compensate him for an hour spent with a sharp-tongued crowd outside the wooden arena at Shelby in 1923. Shelby paid as it went for its attitude toward Dempsey, but, like Kearns, he was not an easy man to satisfy.

The Discovery of Pat O'Dea

This column first appeared in the San Francisco *Chronicle*, September 19, 1934, and is reprinted by permission of that newspaper.

No brains were involved in this "discovery." A friend informed one day that one Charley Mitchell had confided he was Pat O'Dea and would be willing to reveal his identity to just one reporter (me).

Not impressed, since a dozen "Pat O'Deas" had "revealed" themselves since the original disappeared, I was busy with more important items for several weeks before I phoned this particular one and invited him to come and see me at CHRONICLE *expense.*

After two evenings with him I was convinced he was the real, long lost mystery man, and wrote the story.

I choose this story because it more closely approaches national or international importance than anything I have done, and because it was exclusive, so much so it was denied from San Francisco to New York for ten days. Even O'Dea's brother, Andy, said it couldn't be true.

One evening Hank McCormick of Madison (Wis.) assembled several old pals of the real Pat O'Dea, phoned Charles Mitchell in Westwood, and asked questions which only the real O'Dea could have answered (such as what lady did you take out on the night of the Yale game in 1899?). Hank got the right answers and wrote an exclusive confirming mine.

186

Pat was invited back to Wisconsin for a big reunion, helped (with his inspiration) to win an upset football victory, and has been an active San Francisco alumnus of his university ever since (including today).

If there is a further unrevealed story behind the one I wrote, I never believed I had the right to ask Pat for it. I only wish I had done a better writing job the night I did this one.

BILL LEISER

They said he had moved on to the next world—this man who crashed through with football records never surpassed or equaled in the gridiron history of America and then vanished as completely and mysteriously as Aladdin's genii.

It was suggested in the *Literary Digest* of March that he must be resting in the unknown soldier's grave.

But Patrick John O'Dea, football's long lost immortal, is very much alive.

Out of the past he came smiling to sit across the dinner table last night. I could hardly believe it. This man, who once punted the length of the field in the air, this greatest drop kicker and placement kicker the world ever knew, this man who did Red Grange runs as a mere side line to a more spectacular game.

They said I would never meet him. Of him the *Literary Digest*, March 17, reported: "In 1917 when the Australian army was passing through San Francisco, where he was practicing law, (he) joined the Anzacs without informing even his brother, thus leaving the country as unostentatiously as he came. He has not been heard of since. Andy (his brother) is certain he is an unknown soldier."

He was the man who could curve a long punted football as a pitcher curves his throws. He could punt eighty-five yards against your "great" sixty-yarders today. The record says he once lifted the football 110 yards in the wind. In an impossible twenty-mile cross-field gale he place kicked half the length of the gridiron, straight through the bars. He once sidestepped Gil Dobie on the run to drop kick fifty-five yards for a score. There has been no one like him, before or since, in the game.

And he was supposed to have moved on.

Yet there he sat grinning across the table last night, as healthy a specimen as I have seen in my time. He didn't go to war. He didn't disappear into thin air. He merely took up new work in his own way. And, up in Westwood, off in the northeast corner of California, they will be surprised to learn this morning that the Red River statistician they have known for fifteen years as Charles J. Mitchell is actually the long lost Pat O'Dea, one of the greatest athletes of all time.

Everyone who understands anything at all of the history of football knows of Pat O'Dea, the Australian, who came to America in 1896 and, for four years on the University of Wisconsin varsity, displayed a ravishing, kicking, smothering type of football that America never knew before and may never know again.

What's in the record books alone will keep his name alive as long as the game is played. There were heroes, great ones, before 1896, and there have been heroes of the gridiron since 1900, but, to those who saw Midwest football at the end of the last century, the names of Jim Thorpe and Red Grange, even, mean little alongside of Wisconsin's Pat O'Dea.

It was his fame that drove him out of sight. He was in San Francisco, in 1917, well known, too well known, perhaps, everywhere. Always he had to talk football. Always he was helping athletes—he even helped the Stanford crew of 1914. But always he was the man who had been great on the football field, and almost never the man who could talk of new work to be done. He didn't like living in what were to him "mere student days of the past."

With the war, his income from the homeland was knocked down to nothing. He had an opportunity to start in a new field, off where no one knew him—off where he could be just himself and not the man who had kicked footballs for Wisconsin, so off he went to become Charles J. Mitchell of the Red River Lumber Company of Westwood, and he has been there ever since.

No one knew him there. He simply moved in as a stranger. For fifteen years now, Charles J. Mitchell, a secretary-manager of the Westwood Auto Club (and Chamber of Commerce), a director of the Lassen Volcanic Park Association, a leader in the fight for good new roads that are being obtained, and roads open in winter, in that beautiful section, and a statistician for Red River lumber, has been the kind of fighting, astute, well-liked progressive citizen that makes small towns into bigger cities.

"Probably I was wrong," says the very live and smiling Pat. "Mrs. Mitchell, that is, Mrs. O'Dea, always thought I was. But I wanted to get away from what seemed to me to be all in the past. As Pat O'Dea, I seemed very much just an ex-Wisconsin football player.

"I was very happy as Mitchell for a while. Mitchell was my mother's name and Charley that of a cousin I like. Later, I often found it rather unpleasant not to be the man I actually am. So, if you want to write that I'm going to be Pat O'Dea again, for the rest of my life, write it.

"Perhaps I should never have been anything else."

So there he is, his old identity as one of the biggest of all athletes buried behind a fifteen-year-old Charles Mitchell off among five thousand citizens of Westwood, now come back to life again.

He's the kind of man who, perhaps as you and I, simply can't force a real smile before a camera, but what a swell smile he has. And what a stimulating person with whom to talk. And how he can tell you about football.

And what a life he has had, and is still having.

Almost cut down by sharks, as a boy, when he saved a young girl from drowning.

Transferred from the "polite" Australian game to the rough American football of the nineties he adapted himself to become the most spectacular and greatest star of his time.

Almost burned to death, in hot water, with his athletic career barely through.

Then driven by fame to comparative obscurity, and vanishing with a world believing him in an unknown soldier's grave and now coming back as the old Pat O'Dea.

But first, about the football. You don't have to ask him to learn what he did in football. The record books show a Pat O'Dea who outdid Red Grange before Red Grange was born.

Let me pick, here and there, from the old clips, just to give an idea of who was Pat O'Dea.

Against Pop Warner's champion Carlisle Indians, 1896, post season, a night game, and Pat O'Dea's debut. He sent a fifty-yard "punted forward pass" to Judge Ike Carroll who, from an "onside" start, was eligible to and able to fall on the ball at the goal and roll over for the score. The Indians, who never saw the football because it went high over the girders holding the lights, refused to believe what had happened.

Against Minnesota, 1897, his first game against the team that had been treating Wisconsin badly. Got cornered, let the ball loose on the run and drop kicked forty yards through the bars. Dad Moulton, later a Stanford track coach, then a trainer, dropped his water bucket in amazement on the side line. A flabbergasted Minnesota team, from that moment on, was kicked to death, 39-0.

Against Chicago, a "championship game," dropped over two forty-yard field goals and punted Chicago to submission, 28-0, much as Joe Paglia punted California into helplessness last year.

Against Beloit, 1897, a team that was tough, but one in

which O'Dea was supposed to make the team do the work. Team couldn't do it, so O'Dea dropped over two drop kicks, only to get a bawling out from Coach Phil King. (Score, 10-0, field goals counting 5 points each in those days.)

Against Northwestern, 1898, a team supposed to whale the tar out of Wisconsin. O'Dea played with famous "kindergarten" team of those days, which included only one veteran besides Pat. O'Dea had disagreement with alumni representatives, who wanted to bring in more help. Said to have been nettled going into game. Ran two plays, dropped back, took two steps, and let the old drop go sixty-three yards through the bars, the world record. The ball went over the tops of the uprights, and twenty yards on to hit the fence surrounding the field. The game at the finish, 48-0!

Against Beloit, 1899, opening game, and supposed to be mean. O'Dea kicked four field goals and returned a kickoff ninety yards to the goal.

Against Illinois, 1899, another tough one. Twenty-mile gale blowing across the field. Back on his fifty-five-yard stripe, O'Dea prepared for a place kick.

"What are you doing?" asked the referee. (It was after a fair catch.)

"What do you think?" asked O'Dea.

"I think you're crazy, if you're trying to score in this wind."

Bill Juneau held the ball. Pat lined up so as to kick almost for the right-hand corner of the field. One step and he kicked, with the crowd spellbound. The football sailed directly for the corner for a time, then finally, as the wind caught it, swerved back to the left, and floated smack through the middle of the uprights on the goal line, fifty-five yards away—the most impossible stunt ever performed.

Against Yale, 1899, lost 6-0. Asked why Wisconsin lost, O'Dea said because he had missed his man, Richardson of Yale, who made the only score on a long run. Press of the day said two greatest sportsmen of all time were Sir Tom

Lipton and Pat O'Dea, men who could take it when they lost. Press also talked of O'Dea's "best punting ever seen," and weeks later reported information that O'Dea's center with an arm in a cast, couldn't pass the ball back ten yards that day—and also that O'Dea played the game with a broken bone which pierced the skin of a finger on his right hand when he "missed his man."

Against Michigan, 1899, with press commenting freely on proposition that Michigan must stop O'Dea. O'Dea gave them a thirty-five-yard drop kick score to start with, and a long curve punt, which the Michigan safety dropped, allowing Wisconsin man to pick up for touchdown, all in first half. Later, O'Dea was forced out of the only college game in which he did not play the full sixty minutes. Michigan center, as quoted in the old clips, said, "We could have won if we had gotten O'Dea out sooner."

Against Minnesota, 1899. Two plays, then O'Dea carrying the ball. O'Dea cornered by none other than Gil Dobie. O'Dea bluffed a run and Dobie prepared to block, and O'Dea, sidestepping, drop kicked over Dobie, fifty-five yards through the air, through the bars.

That's just a part of it. But you get the idea.

Once, in a tight spot, his little halfback, Paul Trat, had the ball and was in a tangle when a score was needed. O'Dea picked Trat up out of the jam and carried Trat, football and all, over the goal. No, he wasn't so big. A little over six feet, weight one hundred seventy pounds.

Why, O'Dea was supposed to have signals with his ends. He would inform the ends of which way the punted ball would curve after it started down the field. The ends, therefore, had that much advantage on the safety man, who didn't have the information.

I asked Pat O'Dea if it were true that a punted football could be curved.

"Certainly," he answered. He explained how. But I couldn't repeat in detail.

Oh, yes, O'Dea was a hurdle champ, a crack sprinter and a crew stroke besides. But I haven't space for that.

As for punting, seventy-five yards was a cinch for him, any time. He sent the ball just high enough to allow ends to get under it. If his first punt went too far for the ends, the next went much higher. He gave them all they could take, though they never could take all he could give.

Therefore, often, he punted for the goal line, and if the ball went over, in those days, the rival team had to kick off in return from its 25-yard line. That would be a signal for a Wisconsin fair catch, and an O'Dea drop kick for points if points were in demand.

That is, if I read my old prints correctly.

I asked Pat if youngsters today could be taught to curve punts either way.

"Surely," he answered.

"I coached at Notre Dame just after I left Wisconsin. Red Salmon learned quickly. He was examined frequently by rivals, who sometimes insisted that it was really I who was in the game kicking. He had red hair and some tried to tear it off, thinking to expose O'Dea with a wig. He kicked as well as I could."

Yes, Mr. Pat O'Dea believes that it would be entirely possible to teach a half dozen youngsters on each squad to kick as well as he did, or at least, nearly as well.

He learned, you see, in the Australian game, in which they punt forward passes as well as Americans throw them.

He has had a most unusual life.

He was almost cut to pieces by sharks, when he saved a young girl from drowning, when he was sixteen years old, at Fort Phillip Bay in Australia. (He has the Royal Humane Society certificate for that.)

He almost burned to death of hot water when he once

stunned his head in a bath tub. For days there was doubt and once reporters were waiting in the hall for the last word from the doctor. "What are they there for?" asked the deathly sick O'Dea.

"To learn when you're going."

"Go out and make them a bet that they're wasting their time," said Pat. They were.

And now, because of disappearance, he has been suggested as an unknown soldier.

His disappearance was natural enough. Almost every other man who has enjoyed tremendous fame has felt the urge, at times, to get away from it. Pat O'Dea did.

It wasn't exactly the "usual" thing. But there never has been anything usual about Pat O'Dea since, as a boy, he played on amateur Australian game teams before one hundred thousand persons.

Many in San Francisco will know him, and he'll be seeing them again. Frank Guerena, little coxswain of Stanford's old crew, will know him, for O'Dea helped that crew a great deal.

Former Columbia Park boys will know Pat because, twenty-five years ago, when they wanted to go to Australia, he taught them the Australian kicking game, and they went, and split even on their tour.

Fifteen years ago fame drove him away, and changed his name.

Now he's back, Patrick John O'Dea, no longer football's long lost immortal, but a very vigorous, pleasant, smart young fellow, fifty-five years old, who has new work to be done and who's going to be his old self from here on out while he does it.

Case History of a Rookie

This article first appeared in The New York *Times Magazine*, June 3, 1951, and is reprinted by permission of Gilbert Millstein.

I have a number of reasons for selecting the article on Mickey Mantle as representative of the kind of sports story I like to write. (I am not, I should point out, a sportswriter.) To begin with, I have, for many years, found myself increasingly annoyed with what only can be described as the cultural lag or vestigial appendix to be found in stories about sports figures. The writers labored (I use the word advisedly) to perpetuate myths the usefulness of which, it had long since become evident, could not be justified. They were not deterred in their myth-perpetuating even by the damage wrought by Ring Lardner.

In the second place, they retold these legends (I doubt that they need repeating here) in the flatulent, outrageous argot that has become the hallmark of newspaper sportswriting, so that whatever they had to say lost its meaning in a purple fog of what is called "color." The average sportswriters' disrespect or disregard for the English language is egregious.

In the third place, I attempted something that is only occasionally attempted in a story about a sports figure: I portrayed him as a human being functioning in a social milieu,

195

subject to the same pressures (although magnified) to which other human beings are subject, and reacting according to the state of his psychic seismograph. I found drama less in Mantle's biceps, chest expansion, stance at the plate, past record, future prospects and food habits (although these were not ignored) than I did in the fact that here was a very young man who had become the focus of some rather tatty manipulations. The story of those manipulations is, in microcosm, the story of the society in which we live, and, I maintain, infinitely more important than the width, so to speak, of Daedelus' wings.

GILBERT MILLSTEIN

Mickey Charles Mantle, the new nineteen-year-old right fielder for the New York Yankees, is, in the opinion of most sportswriters, the most promising young man to enter big-league baseball since the ascension of Joe Dimaggio, who thinks, without any editorial equivocation at all, that Mantle is the greatest rookie he has ever seen. "Greatest" is a word used sparingly by Dimaggio and then only in its veritable, or non-show business sense. The morning after the Yankees arrived in New York to open the season with the Boston Red Sox, Dan Parker wrote that "if the inking device on the Fordham University seismograph didn't trace a design like a cross-section of Mount Everest set in the middle of the American prairies . . . it's a fraud because . . . Mickey Mantle, the rookie of the aeons, hit New York like fifteen simultaneous earthquakes."

The day after the opening game, which the Yankees won and in which Mantle made one hit, Jimmy Cannon, declining the cataclysmic gambit for the emotional-exhaustion approach, declared: "I'm all out of breath hollering it up for this kid." Casey Stengel, the manager of the Yankees and a notoriously cautious man who is inclined to save his wind

when discussing the future of his charges, said to an in-
quirer: "I'll tell you this—I got sense enough to play him."

Having become a legend before he came of age and a
commercial product of considerable speculative value in less
than six months, Mantle has been subjected to a series of
pressures, both on and off the baseball field, for which nothing in his life, either professionally or privately, had prepared him. In addition to having to learn to become an outfielder, instead of a shortstop, which he used to be, he has
been interviewed and photographed almost daily, invited
out to dinner every night, asked to appear on radio and television programs (which he has done in moderation), questioned closely about the state of his health (he was recently
classed in 4-F by the Army because of a chronic osteomyelitis or bone infection in his left ankle), and approached
even more closely by promoters of one kind or another seek-
ing to make money for him and only incidentally for themselves, they all said.

To some extent this is experienced by every young baseball player, but Mantle is younger than most and, up to this
point, has shown more talent than any of his immediate contemporaries. He was graduated from high school in his home
town of Commerce, Oklahoma—the population of which is
twenty-five hundred—only two years ago. He has played
professional baseball for only two seasons: in 1949, with the
Class D Independence, Kansas, club of the K.O.M. League,
and in 1950 with the Class C Joplin, Missouri, team of the
Western Association. His earnings in those two seasons were
between $175 and $250 a month. As recently as last winter
he was working for $40 a week as an electrician's assistant
in a lead mine in Commerce. When the Yankees signed him
in 1949, for future use, he was paid a little over $1,000, or
roughly $24,000 less and five players fewer than the Yankees
gave for Dimaggio, or $99,000 less than the Pittsburgh Pi-
rates paid last year as a bonus to a pitcher named Paul Pet-

tit. Mantle's wage with the Yankees this year will be about
$7,500, or just $2,500 more than the minimum which must
be paid to a big-league player.

For a "green-pea kid," as rookies are known in the baseball business, Mantle has handled himself with considerable
aplomb on the field and with becoming diffidence, not unmarked by an understandable confusion, off it. His physical
appearance serves to evoke the image, traditional and dear
to Americans, of the clean-living country boy grappling, at
great odds but ultimately in triumph, with the big city and
its perils. He is five feet eleven inches tall and weighs one
hundred eighty-five pounds, all of them symmetrically dis-
tributed. His shoulders are extremely broad and his fore-
arms, wrists and neck unusually heavy even for an athlete.
His hair is a dark blond and he cuts it fairly short. His eyes
are blue and set far apart over a blunt nose. His mouth is
big and sensitive and his teeth are big and white. When he
smiles, even on request, as photographers are continually
asking him to do, he looks a good deal younger than nineteen and just as vulnerable.

It is possible that this image was on Stengel's mind a couple of weeks ago when he discussed Mantle with an acquaintance, although at the time Mantle was batting .316,
had hit four home runs, two of them right-handed and two
left-handed, and was leading the American League in runs
batted in with twenty-six.

"This publicity," Stengel said, "isn't too much good for
him. He's bothered by it. Any kid just coming up would be.
Here he is with all those interviews, trying to enlighten
other people about himself rather than tending to baseball
business. I don't think it's hurt him. I don't think it will, but
if he reads all those press notices he'll ruin his eyesight. And
then people want him to do this and do that, outside work,
things that are not a baseball issue. A ball park is a player's
home. He ought to stay home and use it."

Among the things that are not strictly baseball issues are the financial rewards for endorsements, testimonials and personal appearances, and perquisites of one kind or another that a baseball player may pick up outside the home Stengel likes his men to live in. Their size is limited only by the popular appeal of the player, his ability to bargain or that of the people he permits to bargain for him. This is clearly recognized by the Yankee organization. In a booklet called "Play Ball with the Yankees," which the club has its scouts distribute to likely prospects, it is noted that "Headlines in New York . . . pay off richly in paid testimonials from products using baseball as a means of advertising."

This was pointed out to Mantle, not merely in the booklet but by George Weiss, the general manager of the Yankees, who recalled recently that during spring training he took Mantle aside informally, as he has done other talented young men before, and talked to him in these terms: "Mickey, we like to have our boys protected off the field as well as on. You'll get all kinds of propositions advanced to you. I would suggest that you avoid getting tied up with anybody. The club is at your service without cost." From that point on Mantle's experiences may be said to have been enlightening and they probably will prove profitable eventually, financially as well as intellectually.

The outline of what happened is a little blurred, owing to a natural reticence on the part of some of the participants, but in general the sequence was this: Mantle started out on his own by endorsing a bat, for which he was paid fifty dollars; a baseball glove which brought him two gloves, and a brand of bubble gum, for which he was given a wristwatch. He was also buttonholed by a number of people who wanted to represent him, but he fended off the first comers. On April 15, two days before the Yankees opened in New York, he received a telephone call at the Concourse Plaza Hotel in the Bronx, where he was then living, from a man named Allan Savitt, who had hit upon the stunningly simple device of asking to see Mantle.

Savitt, a small, melancholy individual who wears horn-rimmed glasses, told Mantle that he could get him a deal with an organization that secured testimonials and endorsements from prominent personalities, half of the proceeds for the personality and half for the firm. On April 18 Mantle signed a two-year contract with this outfit, which also pledged itself to cut Savitt in for somewhat less than a third of its share as Mantle's agent. As the days went by it began to dawn on Savitt that he had done himself, to say nothing of Mantle, a great injustice, since it looked as though the young man was a comer in the money-making field.

On April 24 Mantle signed a contract making Savitt his personal representative "in the field of radio, television, personal appearances, stories for books and magazines, and all other fields, exclusive of baseball playing. . . ." Savitt was also to set up a "Mickey Mantle Fan Club" for his client from his Madison Avenue office. For all this he was to get the usual 10 per cent of whatever came in for ten years. The Yankee office found out about both contracts and remonstrated with Mantle about them, although less strenuously about the Savitt instrument than the other. A number of Yankee players represented to Mantle that a fifty-fifty deal was much too stiff, and they also told him that the Yankee office could procure endorsements for him, as it had done for others, without charge.

While the team was in Chicago Mantle was induced to send the endorsement concern a letter of cancellation. Meanwhile, Savitt, who has insisted that as Mantle's personal agent he intended to take nothing covered by the other contract, was making an attempt to buy it back with the intention of destroying it. Between May 15 and May 24 Savitt and a representative of the Yankees met twice, unofficially. Mantle was present only at the first meeting. It was made plain to both Savitt and Mantle that while the Yankees might or might not be able to intervene in the player's personal affairs or those of his agent crucially, they could certainly lean heavily. By last week, although complicated negotiations were still going forward, it looked as though Savitt would still have his client, although not on his original terms, and the other contract would be canceled or bought back. Mantle, at all times, has said he was satisfied with Savitt.

"I just want to lead this boy in the right direction," Savitt confided to an acquaintance during the heat of battle. "I have absolutely no desire to hurt him. I'm not keeping him out late or forcing him into too many outside activities. I'm merely trying to secure things that will bring him money." He said that, above all, it was his desire to "alleviate his headaches—to alleviate a great deal of the responsibilities off his shoulders." Mantle himself was loath to discuss the contracts, but it was evident to a man he talked with that he, too, had reached some general conclusions about life in New York. "People up here," he said, "have funny ideas. Everybody's got a different way of making money up here. Down where we live, all we got is mining and a rubber company. I know they're just trying to make a living and I don't blame them. If I were outside of baseball, I suppose I'd be trying to think of some way to do it, too."

By comparison with what has happened to him since he came to the big leagues, Mantle's life previously might be called bucolic or at least calm. He was born on October 20, 1931, in Spavinaw, Oklahoma, a town of two hundred fifty-five persons. Shortly thereafter, the family moved to Commerce. The boy was named Mickey Charles Mantle by his father, Elvin C. (Mutt) Mantle, now a ground foreman for a lead and zinc mining company. The Charles was for his grandfather, a left-handed pitcher for a semi-professional baseball team, who is now dead, and the Mickey for Mickey

Cochrane, the outstanding catcher for the Philadelphia Athletics, whose real name is Gordon Stanley Cochrane. Mantle has a half-brother, Theodore (his mother had been married before), who was wounded while fighting with the Army in Korea and is in a hospital in Japan; twin brothers, Roy and Ray, 15; another brother, Larry, 10, and a sister, Barbara, 13.

"I always admired Cochrane," the senior Mantle has said, "and I wanted to make Mickey into a ball player ever since he was born, I guess. I put a glove on his hand when he was just a little bitty kid." In addition to this, the father, a right-hander, and the grandfather, a left-hander, pitched to the boy and taught him to bat from either side of the plate, a talent not often developed in ballplayers, and which has since earned young Mantle a typically alliterative sportswriter's identification: "The Sweet Switcher."

At Commerce High School, Mantle played baseball, football and basketball. It was there that he met Merlyn Johnson, the girl he will probably marry when the season is over. The osteomyelitis that kept him out of the Army developed in 1946 when he was kicked above the left ankle in a football game. In high school baseball, he alternately played shortstop and pitched. His marks in school stayed satisfactorily between B and C.

Young Mantle was playing in a kid league in 1949 when an umpire suggested that he have a talk with Johnny Sturm, an old Yankee player who was then managing Joplin. Sturm got in touch with the Yankee office and a scout, or ivory-hunter, named Tom Greenwade saw Mantle play, paid him a shade more than $1,000 to bind him to a Yankee contract and sent him to Independence, where he batted .322 in 87 games. Last year, he came up to Joplin and led the Western Association with .383. In spring training with the Yankees this year, he outran everybody, batted .402, hit nine home runs and knocked in another thirty-one runs, whereupon the

Yankees decided to season him neither at Binghamton nor Kansas City, but to bring him right up.

The job of converting Mantle into an outfielder was turned over to, among others, Tommy Henrich, the Yankees' great right fielder and first baseman, who is now a coach, and Joe Dimaggio, who has literally directed Mantle's steps in the field. "If he's a good ballplayer and I think he is," Henrich said not long ago, "you won't know him in five years. The piece of business he is is there. The sculptor goes to work on him and there he is, a masterpiece."

Another thought crossed Henrich's mind and he stopped for a moment. "You know, in this great big city," he continued, "just base hits won't do the job. Heck, baseball is a form of education. Look at Joe—he got a better education out of baseball than out of college. It's probably the most important thing about the game. Mickey'll acquire a lot of culture out of baseball. An over-all polish."

Among other things, Mantle has acquired an apartment in midtown Manhattan, which he shares with Hank Bauer and Johnny Hopp, and some new clothes. During the Yankees' first home stand he bought two suits, two sport jackets, two pairs of slacks, two pairs of shoes and a half dozen pairs of argyle socks. "This is a lot better living, you know," he told a friend one day while sitting in the Yankee dressing room. "Look around," he said, and pointed at the floor of the lounge, which is covered with an expensive broadloom carpet. "When I first saw this," he went on, "I couldn't believe guys would walk around in spikes on rugs like that there."

Like other minor-league players, Mantle had been accustomed to traveling in buses, dressing out of rusty iron lockers on splintered wooden floors; to cold showers, playing mostly night games under poor lights and eating on a $2.25 daily meal allowance which was never enough. He never saw a club doctor, a trainer or a diathermy machine until he came up to the Yankees, to say nothing of three changes of uni-

form at home and three on the road; unlimited meal allowance, roomettes and compartments on trains, accommodations in the best hotels, and fan mail. A couple of weeks ago
he received some lyrics which hymned him thus:

> Dimaggio recognized his ability for the game
> And predicted he'd make the Hall of Fame.
> At 19, talented and very able,
> Mickey's skill is not a fable,
> His arm is strong, his feet swift;
> To watch him play gives one a lift.

"When you get up here," he said, reasonably enough,
after discussing his new advantages, "you're bound to feel
good about it, and you want to keep getting better and better so you can stay there. Maybe it bothered me a little bit
at first, talking to all those people, but when they quit both-
ering you is when you start worrying."

Marciano Wins
by Knockout in 13th

This article first appeared in the Boston *Globe*, September 24, 1952, and is reprinted by permission of that newspaper.

I suppose this, as far as pretty words go, was not my best job of reporting—but the fact they were put together fast (about twenty-five minutes, thirty at the outside) with an edition to catch, and the tumult incredible all around the press row ... well, it's a job that really satisfied me.

JERRY NASON

The hard and angry right fist of challenger Rocky Marciano beat Jersey Joe Walcott into a senseless lump on the ring canvas in Municipal Stadium tonight, divesting him of the world heavyweight championship after forty-three seconds of fighting in the thirteenth round of a battle which was drenched with blood and drama.

The end came suddenly. It was the only punch thrown by either contestant in the round. When the round started, the old champion, waging the fight of his life, but tiring fast, started to beat a retreat in front of the blood-streaked, beaten face of the Bull of Brockton.

He was on his way to holding his title, the old pappy guy was, and now he was going to protect his lead and beat a hasty and strategic retreat.

So he backed away, in a half circle, and suddenly Marciano lunged for him and Jersey Joe stepped right back into the ropes. There was no place he could go.

He never saw the right glove of the hard-bitten Marciano as it came whirling out of the night. It hit him on the side of the jaw and a splatter of blood shot from an old eye wound.

The champion's face went blank. His mouth hung open and his mouthpiece dribbled slowly from between his lips.

Then he sagged forward and collapsed gently on the ring floor, his forehead on the canvas, supported by his knees and elbows.

The Bull from Brockton stood over him on his shaggy pillars of legs, drenched in his own hot blood on this cool damp night.

The referee, Charlie Daggert, tolled the count, which you could not hear in the tumult which filled the vast stadium.

Right in the middle of his count, at precisely five, Walcott's knees and elbows refused to prop him any longer, and he sort of went down on his face, like a flat tire.

After the formality of counting him out was finished, his handlers rushed in and turned him over on his back and his eyes were closed tight and he was not disturbed by the glare of the ring lights up to which his face was turned.

And the new champion of the world was Rocco Francis Marchegiano of Brockton, Massachusetts, first one born of the Bay State since John Lawrence Sullivan, sixty-two years earlier.

The ring immediately became the scene of astounding happenings. Marciano never had a chance to get back to his own corner.

Perfect strangers from out of the night swarmed in there

with him, and some were jumping over the prone and beaten body of Walcott.

The old champion had put Marciano on the canvas for the count of four in the first round—Marciano, the hard rock, the man who never in his life had been knocked off his feet.

But the old boy put him there in the first minute of the rough, unlovely battle with a left hook which sped like a shot to the side of Rocky's jaw.

Everything Jersey Joe had went into that punch. Marciano buckled all over and suddenly there he was, rolling on the floor, and blinking his eyes.

He took half the count, then staggered to his feet, a puzzled look on his face. A rivulet of blood fell from his nose, but he drove in close and grappled and cleared his head, and then started fighting back. Walcott was out to get him, and early. It was a hard and vicious fight. At the end of three rounds—the fourth and fifth and ninth—they traded savage punches after the bell.

They were both sliced and cut, and battered and bleeding going into the thirteenth round. Walcott had been split wide open above his left eye in the sixth, a round in which the bell undoubtedly permitted him to linger for seven more rounds, for he was being barraged on the ropes, jelly-legged and helpless, under the full fire of Rocky's dreaded fists, when it rang.

From the seventh round on Marciano fought with a gash well up above his hair line from which blood poured down over his face, blinding him intermittently.

In the eighth, a flashing Walcott hook split him beside his left eye, and soon afterward he was sporting a perceptible mouse there as well.

His vision was being troubled as his blinking eyes attested, and Rocky started losing the fight in those rounds, for he could not escape the rally ol' Joe made behind a hit-and-run switch of tactics. Walcott's left hand was living in Rocky's face. And Rocky's shots were getting very wild, indeed.

So, when he went back to the stool at the end of the twelfth round, he knew he was losing the fight, and so did everybody in his corner.

They hadn't seen the cards, but they had been around long enough to know that referee Daggert and the two judges, Zack Clayton and Pete Tomasco, all had Jersey leading in defense of his title by from two to four rounds each.

"Rocky, you win it right away or you don't win at all," Al Weill told him back in the corner.

So Rocky came stalking out for the thirteenth round, and, as it turned out, the last one.

Walcott, knowing in his heart that his aggressive fighting in the early rounds, his willingness to stand and trade punches at no loss of prestige, his late-rounds shift to a crafty boxing campaign had won him the bout, started backing away.

Rocky trudged after him, not too anxious to lead and catch a countering jab, but cautiously waiting for an open shot. With stolid patience Marciano stalked ol' Joe in his retreat across the ring. Then Joe took one backward step too many. He backed into the ropes. His avenue of escape was blocked, his mobility arrested, and like a flash Marciano was upon him.

He leaped like a tiger, drawing back his left glove, a feint which quickly brought the champion's guard low.

And then he launched his right on a wide arch which made a perfect landing on the left side of ol' Joe's jaw.

Rocky said later that he also banged Joe with a short left hook as he was falling forward, but, if he did, nobody on our side of the turbulent press section saw it, or did it matter.

It would have been superfluous. Nothing could have with-stood the shock of the right hand, and Walcott was sense-less the second the punch lodged on his face.

It was a harder right hander than that which sent Joe Louis into oblivion, for all of Marciano's one hundred eighty-four pounds went in behind it. There was light between Rocky's feet and the canvas when he unfurled it.

Thus came the sudden end to a spectacular and bitter, fiercely waged struggle for the championship of the world, and Rocky won it the hard way and he knew it. He said, from his lumpy face, "He's a helluva fighter."

This was a "big fight," although on a more modest scale than in the gaudy days when a sepia superman named Joe Louis made his bid for the crown and a Cadillac convertible, and there was a tenseness around the press rows that crackled.

A man with a big punch had arrived. There had not been a Caucasian ruler of the heavyweights in fifteen years, or since Louis' flashing fists destroyed an earnest but sparsely gifted incumbent named Jimmy Braddock. While a man's color was no longer important, only his competence, you felt that it would be a change-of-pace to have a white boy on top after all these years.

The pigment of their skins cut no sentimental yardgoods, either way, in this huge crowd, which uttered a full-throated roar when, first, Champion Joe Walcott and then Rocky Marciano threaded ringward through the rows of patrons, convoyed by their respective maintenance crews and a fly-ing wedge of local John Laws.

Walcott was bland of face and, for a moment, as the harsh overhead lights struck his craggy features, he looked his 38 years and more. The white sheen of his trunks twinkled like a July 4 sparkler.

His trainer, Dan Florio, a small, nimble man with his

mouth tucked up grimly at the corners, as if it was he who was about to defend the title, fussed petulantly around him.

The champion's manager, Felix Boccicchio, an outspoken fellow who had called Marciano "a plodder" and "the amateur," predicting an unhappy future for the Brocktonian this night, still had enough wind left to respond to the greetings of ringsiders.

In the other corner Rocco Francis Marchegiano stood stolidly on his thick, stumpy legs. He wore trousers into the ring, then shed them. If his pulse was pounding you could not read it in his unflinching, broad, brown face. With his head lowered, he seemed to be concentrating intensely, like a man who has just received a long-distance phone call. He felt sharp as a glass cutter at one hundred eighty-four pounds.

Al Weill was in the ring for this fight, shrewd, clever veteran of boxing's backstage, who had dropped his ridiculous mask and had emerged at last as Marciano's true manager, although in so doing he sacrificed his match-maker's portfolio with the International Boxing Club.

The handler was young and nerve-tortured Allie Colombo, Rocky's lifelong friend, who started with him back down the long trail into the discouraging yesterdays of four years ago.

But of them all, the men who busied themselves around the muscular Marciano—the manager, the seconds, the bucket boys—none was so important unto the event as the smallest of them, Trainer Charlie Goldman.

A gnome of a man, barely five feet tall, it was he who forged Marciano into a heavyweight contender from as crude and unwieldy material as he ever beheld in a gymnasium—and in his forty-third professional match had him up there now facing the champion of the world. It was phenomenal progress. Only Jim Jeffries, Jess Willard and Joe Louis had traveled faster toward the richest prize the ring has to offer.

And you noted that it was to Goldman, little Charlie Goldman, that Marciano was listening. The words of the rest of them, the fidgety, excited words, fell unheeded. But when Goldman spoke, Rocky would nod his head earnestly.

And so the little, familiar tableau ran its course, with the glove lacing, and the announcements and the instructions, and the bustling of the meeting at mid-ring, until, at last, there was nobody up there but Jersey Joe Walcott and Rocky Marciano and the referee.

A sudden hush fell over the Municipal Stadium. Out back there in the night a voice shrilled, "What'll YOU have?" and the crowd chuckled at the witticism because there was no TV being offered the parlor fans, and no radio broadcast either.

Right in the midst of the laughter the bell rang.

If the script called for Marciano to come forth with a rush like a shaggy bull, eager to reach this elder statesman whose remarkable mobility and cleverness made him a miracle champion after twenty-two years in the ring, Rocky did not disappoint them.

But ol' Jersey Joe confused him by not running. Everybody said Joe would run, making Rocky miss and flick the challenger's face full of left jabs.

But Walcott crossed them up. He'd back off two steps and wait, throwing the loving embrace of a python around Rocky's arms and rendering him helpless.

Rocky would break away, miss again, and get clipped briskly as the champion stood his ground. And then he belted Rocky to the floor with that left hook.

Walcott was shooting the works, and a left hook to the body was his key punch, and for three or four rounds he made Rocky wince with the fury of it.

But Marciano started to come in the fifth, and in the sixth he stormed into Joe, battered him at mid-round with three lefts and two hard rights to the head, and had him, finally, on the ropes, weary and wobbly, up for the kill, when the bell rang.

So Rocky had to postpone the ending for seven rounds. But what an ending . . .

My Wild Irish Gold

This article first appeared in MAN'S DAY, March 1953, and is reprinted by permission of that magazine.

Enclosed you will find a magazine story that is a favorite of mine although it was read by practically no one. Unfortunately, the magazine was one of the Hillman publications that ran for two months and was crossed off as a tax loss. Its editor, Johnny Ross, did attract good writers, however, such as Pegler, Mauldin, de Seversky, etc., because it paid good money. Believe me, sir, the magazine business is every bit as daffy as Hollywood.

This story, incidentally, was pretty well cut up by the editors, but I had so much fun getting it—in Dublin—that it will always be a favorite with me. Oddly enough, the facts in it are not generally known by Americans although they support the Irish Sweeps loyally.

TOM O'REILLY

Over the years about one thousand Americans have had their numbers come up in the Irish Hospitals' Sweepstakes. Their wonderfully amazed expressions with those toothy smiles caused by sudden riches have amused newsreel viewers all over the world and they remind me of a little girl being given her first doll. Only Sweeps winners aren't little girls— just great big lucky clucks with small touches of larceny in their high, adventurous hearts.

Actually, the thing I love most about the Irish Sweeps is not the money (I'll never frown if I encounter some) but the fact that the real roar around the entire proposition is a gargantuan joke on the British. Did you ever take a close look at this side-saddled set-up or did you buy your ticket between the martinis? Well, climb into your best nine A.M. executive attitude and I'll present a few quick facts.

An Irish Sweeps chance costs one Celtic pound. That adds up to about $2.80 in U.S.A. tickets and if you've led a blameless life you might just be lucky enough to win 50,000 Irish pounds which happily equal $140,000 authentic Wall Street passes. Between your $2.80 and that $140,000 lies one of the grandest stories in this world. When you raise the curtain on this touch of irony, you find that the entire Irish Sweepstake operation depends on the seemingly starchy British.

Comparatively few Americans realize that all the Irish Sweeps—and there have been seventy in the past twenty years—are lotteries dependent upon three or four big horse races staged in England. These are the Grand National Steeplechase, run near Liverpool in the spring; June's Epsom Downs "darby" as they call it, never having been to Kentucky; and either the Cambridgeshire or the Cesarewitch, in the fall.

The English, quite properly excited behind those correctly frozen facades, run their pretty horses around their great big tracks and the Irish profit to the tune of millions of pounds without paying one Celtic, harp-stamped shilling to the British Government. That is because Sweeps tickets are illegal tender in perfidious Albion just as they are in America. The great Irish Sweep, Kevin m'lad, is illegal in

the country that makes it all possible. Indeed, the whole
situation might well result in an amendment of Dean Swift's
classic advice to Irishmen—"Burn everything that comes
from England except the coal"—to read "and the horse-race
results."

Now the first thing any American wants to know about
Irish Sweeps tickets is how they get to the United States
and are they authentic or counterfeit? Years ago a bunch of
cuties—probably from Chicago—printed a pile of no-good
ducats and sold them to those honest, dead game, little old
ladies who call the Irish their "kissin' kin" and enjoy dreaming once a year with a Sweeps ticket. Well, it was a dirty
trick but the fellows running the Sweeps shined up their
shillelaghs and fixed that one fast. They called on some
Dublin engravers and printers who are real artists and today
an Irish Hospitals' Sweepstakes ticket is as beautiful a job
as any one hundred dollar bill ever foaled by the United
States mint. The shadings of the pretty colleen on the ticket
(she is always an employee of the Hospitals' Trust) are absolutely perfect and unmistakable. A counterfeit would be
as obvious as a rhinestone in Tiffany's window.

How do the tickets get here? Simple. They are mailed.
Every once in a while you will read about a large batch of
tickets, "valued at $1,000,000," being nabbed by the Cus-
toms officials inspecting a boat or airplane. Well, those
things only happen to fellows trying to take too big a swallow of the Irishman's ale. Ninety per cent of the Irish Sweeps
tickets sold in this country arrive here in the family letters
from Aunt Bridget to her niece with the roving eye named
Sheila. Figure it out for yourself. When a football team from
County Kerry came over here to play at Yankee Stadium, in
the thirties, fully eighty thousand people turned out for the
event and everyone of them had kinfolk back on the Emer-
ald Isle.

According to tradition the Irish are supposed to be a

whimsical, dreamy, moon-struck sort of folk who, as the poet said, "are the men that God made mad. For all their wars are merry and all their songs are sad." Now did it ever occur to you that the tiny, modest little business of running seventy Sweepstakes during the past twenty years adds up to a tidy and somewhat comforting figure on the cash register? The last time I looked the dear, impractical, whimsical Celts who run the Sweeps had handled some hundred million pounds. They had paid out prize money, given their government its share in stamp duty, contributed to their hospitals and employed around ten thousand people to run this quaint little game. Whatever was left—a tidy sum to be sure—went to the promoters. Well, I wish I could be dreamy that way. What kind of sleeping pills do they use?

I have been buying Sweeps tickets for well over sixteen years, and when you pay out that long and don't win something, it sort of rankles. You start to think of a way to get even. Well, I finally found the answer. By George, I'll go *live* in one of those heavenly Edens called an Irish Hospital. They're not going to counterfoil me. One Sweepstake alone —the Cambridgeshire in 1949—handled 1,504,637 pounds with the hospitals getting 225,695 pounds. In a country where the hospitals are picking up a kitty like that on the English races three times a year I couldn't imagine a nicer place for an old man to get sick. In fact it made me fashionably pale just to think of it.

Sweepstakes dreams are somewhat extravagant, of course, and I had an idea that perhaps I would hit senility in silk pajamas, reclining on a golden bed with room enough to practice my harp lessons while gorgeous colleens, ignoring Hollywood's vulgar advances, attended me with trays of caviar and syringes of champagne and we all tossed the dark meat out windows for County Meath's famed Ward Union Stag Hounds.

Now when a man visits Dublin, unless he has the misfortune of being run down by one of those double-decked busses hurrying with Easter Monday crowds to the Fairy- house race course, he is likely to see the offices of the Hos- pitals' Trust Ltd. before entering an actual hospital. This gorgeous air castle, of modern design, is a one-story dream factory covering twelve acres. Seeing it among the city's graceful old Georgian houses has the same effect as though one had stepped off Manhattan's Queensboro Bridge, with its Victorian iron curlicues, into the lobby of the United Nations' glass and marble Secretariat building. It is one of the two great industrial show places pointed out for every visitor to Dublin, a city of five hundred thousand. The other rube rendezvous is the great Guinness Brewery, on the banks of the Liffey River.

It should also be pointed out here that world encyclo- pedias and almanacs, which purport to outline Ireland's principle industries, studiously ignore the Sweeps, and Irish consulate officials in New York and other American cities are under strict orders not to discuss this delicate dido. Yet one day in Dublin will convince you that the manufacture and sale of Sweepstakes tickets is rivalled only by farming as the nation's greatest industry. Sweepstakes books are en- countered on every hotel desk and shop counter, behind all bars, and even among those grizzled opportunists who tool horse-drawn equipages from the steamer pier and some- times get you to the hotel you would like to live in. You see the seller of a winning ticket also gets a prize.

This pretty pony pentagon has a fine waiting room with deep rugs, comfortable arm chairs, handy writing desks and a heavy refectory table all of which are lighted by the sun through beautiful French windows opening out on a spa- cious green lawn. The remainder of the building consists of private offices and one vast hall capable of seating four thousand clerks working under a four-acre ridged roof, with one side of each ridge constructed of glass, to provide a north light, while the other is soundproofed to deaden noise. The floors, of teak over concrete, are designed to keep mice from destroying the precious records. Kept in the latest photographic style, these records—listing dates of sales and addresses of ticket owners and sellers in over one hundred and fifty countries from Abyssinia to Zanzibar—fill thousands of filing cabinets protected by a modern, ocean-liner fire alarm system which, on detecting smoke in any part of the building immediately flashes a warning of the location on a large electric signal board. Five printing companies are kept busy throughout the year turning out tickets, draw sheets, advertising cards and promotional literature. Approximately 2000 people work permanently in the building with the number doubled at each Sweepstakes drawing.

It might be interesting to note at this point that one recent and typical Sweeps paid out 190,000 pounds in wages and salaries, 50,000 pounds for postage and telephones, and 37,000 pounds for stationery and printing. When such sundries as legal expenses, advertising, rents, insurance, etc. has been paid, the amount of money spread around Dublin added up to well over 1,000,000 pounds. That happens with, as you can imagine, considerable fanfare, three times a year. How whimsical can you get?

Now one of the more amusing angles to this whole Blarney Stone bingo game is the fact that a Jewish gentleman was the cause of it all. This gentleman's name is Captain Spencer Freeman, formerly of the British Army and a native of Wales. While crowding sixty, and without any pay, he helped steer the British Air Ministry through the buzz bombs, the fires, the raids and the whole works, winding up decorated as a Commander of the British Empire. If you think there are any cheap guys running this Irish Sweepstakes deal you're mistaken as a burp at a harp recital.

In the late twenties, Captain Freeman practiced up for this cutie Celtic caper by operating several small sweeps in

Switzerland and Lichtenstein, where a fellow can make a few honorable mistakes because skiers are accustomed to tripping. Then in '29, when sober old Wall Street was catching brokers from windows, he hit Ireland with the idea of the ages. The Irish hospitals needed money. In the words of Dr. John Corcoran, past president of the Irish Medical Society, "They were forever struggling against financial despair, with the wolf at one door and the wounded at the other." Freeman joined with a local man named Dick Duggan, mentioned money and horses to a struggling Irish hospital and the Sweeps were off and running.

With the horse-loving Celts the Sweeps were an instant success. Duggan and Freeman got in touch with a gentleman named John McGrath who arranged the legalization of the Sweepstakes idea by the Irish parliament quicker than you could say "McGuillicuddy." What McGrath doesn't know about Irish politics hasn't even been suspected. An exceptionally large sixty-one-year-old man with a leonine head and keen blue eyes, McGrath commanded the Fourth Dublin Brigade in the 1916 rebellion and was also the head of Irish Underground intelligence. If his customer's feet are in the clouds this man's definitely are on the ground.

McGrath was instrumental in laying the groundwork for the great Shannon River power plants that brought electrification to Ireland. In '29 when the power plants were completed, McGrath turned to the Sweeps. His name has much to do with the fact that the Sweeps have a sacred standing in Ireland comparable to that of baseball in the United States. And that is rather remarkable when you recall Doctor Johnson's classic observation that "The Irish are a fair people; they never speak well of one another."

When the money you pay for a Sweeps ticket reaches Ireland it is scrutinized by no less than five public committees before being split up between the prize winners, the hospitals, the government, the populace and the promoters. You will notice on each ticket two names. One is that of Joe McGrath and the other handle belongs to Viscount Powerscourt. M'Lord heads the Hospital Committee of over forty representative citizens who select the hospital fund trustees and prize fund trustees (everybody's watching), hire auditors and generally supervise the entire operation.

Any detailed explanation of all the machinations of the five committees that handle your Sweepstakes money would only bore you. Did you ever read the statistics of a mining company? Let's just say that these committees are manned by fine fellows and nobody is starving.

So everybody is happy, or reasonably so, the hospitals, the government, the promoters—even the plunging public who always hope for the next time—except perhaps the mathematician who figured the chances of a player winning the first prize were about 400,000 to 1.

Ah, but faith, 'tis a darlin' game, for the glory of the Ould Sod and you wouldn't be after fussin' over the odds!

Passing of the First Floor Back

This article first appeared in *COLLIER'S*, July 31, 1943, and is reprinted by permission of Dan Parker.

Why did I write "Passing of the First Floor Back"? Because my smooth-talking literary agent, Mark Hanna (who can write better than most of his trained seals), bamboozled COLLIER'S *into buying it, and, of course, because I needed the money. It is a representative piece because of the mediocrity that permeates it, down to the last misplaced comma. Aside from that, I wrote it because a stroke of genius, earmarked for fellow sportswriter Leonard Cohen, my grouse-shooting companion, hit me that day by mistake.*

DAN PARKER

One of the war casualties not reported on official lists is the National Sports Alliance, the world's least exclusive club and most unfraternal fraternity. The barnlike headquarters of this famous fight managers' debating and berating society, located above a garage on Jacobs' Beach, was only a towel's throw from Madison Square Garden. Not long ago, it was padlocked for lack of (a) interest, (b) principal and (c) members. Thus, unwept, unhonored and unsung, the

221

decade's greatest single cause for confusion (next to Adolf
Hitler) returned to the vile dust from whence it sprung.

"There's two National Sports Alliances," explained Al
"Weskitt" Weill, who all but busted a gut trying to save the
ship. "One's the National Sports Alliance, Inc., and the
other, the National Sports Alliance, Red Ink. We used to be
the other but now we ain't nothin' no more. Defunk, you
might say. The war kilt us."

Jacobs' Beach, world-famous habitat of the genus *admin-
istrator pugni* is now a long, lonesome road. Most of the
good fighters are in the Armed Forces. The work-or-fight
regulations have sent fight managers scurrying to defense
plants where, for the first time in their dronelike lives, they
are soiling their soft hands with honest toil. Only a few of
the boys are left.

It was with the loftiest ideals that the National Sports
Alliance was organized several years ago. There already existed a benevolent organization for taking care of indigent
(known in the profession as "indignant") fighters and managers, called the National Sports Alliance, Inc. As Mr. Weill
pointed out with characteristic subtlety, the only "Inc." con-
nected with the new fistic fraternity was the bottle of red
ink with which Phil Rosen, treasurer, kept its accounts.

The Alliance was off to a good start with the election of a
president, a vice-president and a secretary. But when the
office of treasurer came up for consideration, every manager
in the hall reached for his wallet and watch and fastened a
dirty look on his neighbor. Fight managers know one another too well to have a ballot for treasurer come out otherwise than one vote cast for each member present.

Lou Diamond, the Honest Brakeman, might have been
suggested for the job. Lou has a reputation throughout the
fight racket for uncompromising honesty because in all his
years as a brakeman, no freight cars were ever reported
missing from his trains. But Lou was in Florida, and the

election was being held on Jacobs' Beach. So it looked as if the show would end in a permanent deadlock.

Then someone thought of Phil Rosen. Phil ran a cigar store across the street, had never heisted a safe, padded a swindle sheet or nabbed a lollipop from an infant. He was declared treasurer by acclamation without being permitted to say a word in self-defense, and during the life of the National Sports Alliance, he was custodian of the club's assets—the bottles of red ink.

There must have been money in the treasury at first, though, because when Charley Cook, the president, announced at one of the earlier and scantily attended sessions of the Alliance that he couldn't call the meeting to order because there was no quorum, Al Weill himself got up and made a motion that the chairman be permitted to draw upon the treasury up to twenty dollars to buy one.

The idea behind the organization—probably the greatest flight of fancy ever taken by the human mind—was that fight managers needed protection from anyone except one another. "Consolidate and demand" was the motto of the managers as they got down to business. Their slant on the matter was that promoters and fighters were always conspiring to do them wrong.

"Our battle cry will be 'One for all and all for one,'" said Charley Cook, as he opened the meeting called to shape the Alliance's policies.

Despite Dan Morgan's cynicism, "that within a month it will be 'Everyone for *their* self!'" the managers enthusiastically drew up the following program of action:

No manager was to steal another's fighter.

Stray fighters who showed up in managers' nets were to be returned to their rightful owners.

Fight promoters were to be compelled to pay bigger purses.

Managers were not to engage in cutthroat competition.

Managers with more than three fighters were to "spread

the wealth" of their surplus cauliflower to less fortunate brethren.

No manager was to speak disparagingly of another manager, but the sky was the limit on promoters, fighters and boxing writers.

At first the Alliance met every week. The session would get under way at eight P.M. and would last until long after midnight. But, much as fight managers like to hear themselves talk, they soon tired of a good thing and decided to meet only once a month.

When the meeting was called to order, the Bill of Rights was suspended, not to mention those sections of the penal code having to do with libel and slander. A discussion might get under way on whether to admit foreign fight managers to membership, and before the boys in the back of the hall could holler "Sit down, yuh bum, yuh!" the speaker would be heckled by brutally frank references to long-concealed episodes in his private life. Four-letter words buzzed around the place like flies. No epithet was barred if it could be pronounced. Yet at the end of a four-hour soiree of slander, the members who had been bombarding one another most heavily with billingsgate would walk out, arm in arm, as if nothing had happened.

To meet expenses, the Alliance had—or thought it had—two sources of revenue besides dues, which somehow or other weren't counted upon. These were the commission on two pay telephones and a ten-cents-an-hour "couvert" for card players.

If a manager could shame the sergeant at arms out of trying to collect the ten-cent fee for playing pinochle, he would. Otherwise, he'd pay it grudgingly. Thus, the income from that source was scantier than Margie Hart's costume.

The pay telephone would have yielded a good revenue because fight managers use the long-distance phone with a cavalier disregard for expense. However, a pay station in the hands of a crowd of fight managers who not only know all the old angles but invent new ones was like a side of beef in a wolf pack.

There were three slots in the coin box, but only the one for nickels was used. The boys found out quickly enough that this particular bit of telephone equipment had an idiosyncrasy. By dropping a nickel and simultaneously hitting the coin box a sharp rap, they could make it sound like a quarter to the listening operator.

The Alliance's share of the phone receipts thus fell far short of expectations, but all members understood why that was and they asked no questions.

There were other reasons for the meager revenue from the coin phones, and one of them was the cause of the classic feud between Al Weill and Eddie Walker, known, respectively, to the trade as The Vest and The Gimp. Walker was managing Chalky Wright, but the superannuated colored boxer hadn't yet won the featherweight title; so The Gimp wasn't in the chips. The need for economy in his business dealings was acute, therefore, and that explains why Eddie's office was in the nearest phone booth. The Vest, on the other hand, had collected plenty of gravy, and other managers envied his suite of offices in the Gaiety Theater Building, complete with mahogany desk and three brass cuspidors. Such was the Vest's opulence, in fact, that he had two telephones—only one of which was a pay station.

One day in the Sports Alliance clubroom, owl-faced Mushky McGee, Weill's social secretary, proudly displayed a key to the Weill suite which The Vest had given him in lieu of a raise.

"Let's see that," commanded Walker, taking the key.

On some subterfuge, he ducked out of the clubrooms with it and had two extra keys made. One he kept, and the other he gave to his partner, big, good-natured Eddie Mead (Henry Armstrong's manager), who died last summer.

For months after this, Weill battled with the telephone company for overcharging him. His bills doubled, then tripled. He was charged with calls that he never remembered making—calls to Los Angeles, Chicago, New Orleans, Miami and even Havana. He protested in vain to the telephone company. They demanded immediate payment of the bills under threat of having his phones removed, and as no fight manager can exist without a phone, Al had no recourse but to pay up.

Then one night the mystery was solved. Returning from a fight in Philadelphia about two A.M., Weill decided to stop off at his office. A light shining through the frosted glass door awakened forebodings in the breast of The Vest. Bursting into the office, Weill found Walker, his legs stretched out on the polished mahogany desk, leisurely conversing with someone on the other end of a long-distance telephone hookup, which later investigation revealed to have been in Houston, Texas.

"Take off your coat and defend yourself!" screamed Weill. "This is accessory before the fact!"

Walker calmly completed his conversation, hung up, doffed his coat and squared off. With no witnesses and without services of referee or judges, the two managers set about breaking Rule No. 6 of the Fight Managers' Union and the early morning peace of Broadway. Looking like a woodcut of two old English bruisers, they struck grotesque poses and lumbered around the office, wheezing, puffing and waiting for openings. The first opening occurred in Weill's belt, which broke under the strain, causing his trousers to slip.

"Wait a minute!" he commanded, holding up his hand and his pants simultaneously. Walker, always the gentleman, stepped back. Weill made repairs. Then the fight was resumed until there was a recurrence of the trousers-dropping episode. Again the weary Walker gallantly allowed The Vest to pull himself together. This went on until both were winded and decided to finish their fight some other time. Not a blow had been struck.

Whenever the phone rang at the Sports Alliance headquarters, the reaction was the same as if someone hollered, "Who lost this C note?" There was a mad scramble for the booth, and the one who got there first usually landed a job for one of his fighters. The call would invariably be from an out-of-town promoter who wanted to use a certain manager's fighter.

The swifty who won the race would say, "You want Kid Murphy for Holyoke next Monday night? Too bad. He broke his hand in the gym yesterday and won't fight for three months. But don't worry. I got just the boy you want. A great club fighter! I'm givin' you foist call on his soivices." Invariably, the manager on the phone talked the promoter into giving his ham the assignment intended for someone else's fighter.

The night Charley Cook ran for re-election against Jimmie Johnston was probably the most memorable in the history of the Alliance. The Cook-Johnston race wasn't the cause of the excitement, as Charley was returned to office by a good majority. It was the knockdown, drag-out battle between Meyer Ackerman (Meyer the Philosopher) and Maurie Waxman (the Bullshawickey) that converted the clubroom into a replica of a voting booth in Boss Tweed's day.

The entrance to the Sports Alliance quarters was blocked by agents of the rival candidates for the secretary's job, which paid the munificent sum of three hundred dollars per annum if and when caught. It was worth a member's life to run the gantlet.

Sandwich men patrolled the sidewalk wearing such signs as: "Meyer is Our Desire," "Get the Axman for Waxman" and "Don't Be a Slacker, Man. Vote, Already, for Ackerman!"

Candidate Waxman, an excitable fellow given to suspicion, nervously paced the sidewalk, scenting plots against
him and watching for repeaters.

Ackerman, however, took it all philosophically. "So I lose,
what's the difference? So I don't win!"

When the ballot boxes were closed at ten P.M., it was
found that there was a deadlock for the office of secretary.
A conference was called and it was decided to keep the ballot box open for another hour to receive votes only for this
office.

A hasty check revealed the names of all those who hadn't
voted. Agents were dispatched to all the neighborhood
hangouts (pronounced hang-gouts) of fight managers with
instructions to shanghai the laggards, if necessary, to get
them to vote. Shortly thereafter, Jimmie Johnston corralled
a group of his henchmen and led them on halters to the voting booth, where they all cast Ackerman ballots and voted
Meyer the Philosopher into office.

Meyer accepted the honor philosophically. Shifting his
cigar to the other side of his mouth, he shrugged his shoulders and said, "So I win. So what? So the world still re-
volves on its axis."

At the beginning of the organization, some of the fight
managers were all for dropping out when they learned that
the first rule was to be, "Thou shalt not steal thy neighbor's
fighter."

The Alliance hadn't been functioning only a few weeks
when up stood Frank Bachman one meeting night and
charged that Cold Deck Hymie Caplin was tampering with
his fighter, Lew Jenkins.

"Your fighter?" interrupted a heckler. "You mean Fred
Browning's fighter!"

Browning, a Dallas man, indeed had Jenkins under contract, but hadn't been working at the trade of managing
him, so Frank had stepped in. Despite this extenuating cir-

cumstance, Cold Deck Hymie wasn't one to let the matter drop there.

"May I jump off the top of the Chrysler Building and get hit on the head with a baseball bat as I shoot by every floor, if I'm trying to swipe Bachman's fighter!" Caplin shouted. "I'm his standard bearer. Him and me are old friends. Bachman's one guy I wouldn't steal a fighter off of. A trolley car should grow in my stomach if I do!"

The next week, Caplin started making Lew Jenkins' matches; and that's how Rule No. 1 of the Sports Alliance went out the window. The only satisfaction Bachman ever got was when Jenkins, who had won the lightweight title, hit the skids and petered out.

The rule forbidding managers to underbid one another was the next to take a licking. Telegraphic offers were either intercepted or read surreptitiously over the shoulders of the recipient, and the wires then burned with cut-rate offers. It got so bad that some of the shrewder managers had their telegrams sent in code. All this caused the organization to slump.

The cause of brotherly love wasn't advanced much, either, while Dynamite George Smith was around. George makes a career of collecting pet hates. When the Alliance was started, he published a calendar featuring an official list of his enemies, graded by the star system in the order in which he hated them. Promoter Mike Jacobs was the only five-star man on Smith's lists for some time, and a few pet enemies made four-star rating. As for the pikers who rated only one star, they received the Sam Goldwyn treatment from George. He didn't even ignore them. Smith's ratings were sought eagerly by fight managers, most of whom considered it a rare honor to be included in the list. In fact, "Zoonk" Zerkin, noting that his name was missing, asked, "George, what did I ever do that you should snoot me like this?"

One of the final attempts to revive interest in Alliance

meetings was the idea of having self-service beefsteak parties. One was held, but so many members incurred fork-stab wounds that the scheme was abandoned.

When the war broke out, the affairs of the National Sports Alliance went from worse to awful. There weren't enough fighters around for the small clubs to survive. The managers gradually drifted away from the fold on West Forty-ninth Street. Then, one night, when the few remaining members of the Alliance who had been hanging around the clubrooms in hope of intercepting a pay-dirt phone call left the place, the owner, despairing of ever collecting his rent, trudged up the flight of stairs leading from Jacobs' Beach, clamped on a heavy padlock—and the National Sports Alliance (Red Ink) was but an unpleasant memory.

Are Wrestlers People?

This article is reprinted from *ESQUIRE*, January 1934, copyright by Esquire, Inc., 1933.

The only reason I can think of for picking the piece entitled "Are Wrestlers People?" is that I think it is funny. I can't explain why.

Some years ago the fashion editor of one of the monthly magazines paged a lot of people for their opinions of a dress created by Dior or some such character. I was among them. They sent me a photograph and a little blank on which to express my opinion of the dress.

I wrote: "I think this is a real pretty dress." And I got first prize.

WESTBROOK PEGLER

Often, as I have sat at the ringside, watching great, hairy lumps of living meat spank, throttle and wring one another, it has occurred to me to wonder whether wrestlers love and are loved and whether they really suffer. Or are they, like the fishworm, incapable of emotion and insensible to pain?

Perhaps I am wrong in assuming that the fishworm has neither sentiments nor senses but I do assume as much because it spares my conscience on those rare occasions—the last one was in 1926—when I string him on the hook. I did have a twinge of misgiving some time ago when I read in a sporting-goods catalogue of a device for luring the fishworm from his hole in the ground. This was an electrical apparatus, something like a tuning-fork, which, being jabbed in the ground near the worm-hole, uttered a faint mooing note and brought the male, or bull, worm charging out of the soil with his neck arched and his pulses pounding in his veins.

It suggested that the fishworm might have depths after all and that we might all be mistaken in our easy belief that because he does not quack, bark or snarl, he doesn't know he is being ill-treated. Maybe he is just reticent. There are New Englanders like that but we call them canny.

It would be very unchivalrous, I think, to impose upon the most beautiful sentiment of all in any of God's creatures with the siren call of love to seduce him to his doom. This, moreover, is quite aside from the moral aspect of the matter. Sex is something which Nature has implanted in all of us and in its proper relation to life is a very beautiful thing. But I would call it most immoral to inflame the fishworm's passion by artificial means even though we did not string him on a hook but merely left him there, bothered, bewildered and breathing hard.

The wrestler is a strange organism. It has certain characteristics which must test the conviction of the most confirmed Fundamentalist, suggesting that 'way, 'way back in some rocky cave all of us were wrestlers. It walks on its hind legs, it can be trained to speak and understand and Mr. Jack Curley, the promoter of wrestling shows, once had one in his herd which could cook a good dinner. However it cooked only one dinner for Mr. Curley.

He was entertaining a party of friends at his home in Great Neck, Long Island, that night and his wrestler had

cooked pheasant for them. During the meal, Mr. Curley remarked to the lady sitting next to him that his cook was a
wrestler.

"Oh, I would like to see it," the lady said and Mr. Curley,
clapping his hands, cried, "Wrestler! Come heren sie!"

That was Mr. Curley's way of addressing this wrestler. It
was a German. When he wanted the wrestler to go downstairs he said, "Wrestler! Downstairsen sie" and when he
wanted it to go upstairs he said, "Wrestler! Upstairsen sie."
The ablative, you know.

So when the lady said she would like to see the wrestler
which had cooked the dinner, Mr. Curley clapped his hands
and called, "Wrestler! Come heren sie!"

The kitchen door opened and the wrestler entered. It was
wearing a pair of wool wrestling trunks and sneakers. Its
hide and the fur on its chest were moist.

"Wrestler," said Mr. Curley, "dinner is very good tonight."

"Jah?" said the wrestler, puckering its face in an appreci-
ative grin and blinking its knobby ears. "Fine. But boy is it
hot in that kitchen. Look how the sweat runs off of me."

Many a night at the ringside I have heard laymen sitting
in the forward rows explain to their ladies that the punishment which wrestlers inflict on one another really does not
hurt them as they are used to it and cannot feel, anyway.
This is of a piece with the assumption that the fishworm
cannot feel. I am not sure that it is true.

The fishworm wiggles and squirms when it is put upon
the hook and the wrestler trumpets terribly and whooshes
and writhes when it is being twisted in the ring. This may
only mean that some vague intuition, such as turtles possess, is telling the wrestler not to go over on its back. Yet the
wrestler is so amenable to training that it is comparatively
easy to teach it to recognize a signal and, in violation of a
strong natural instinct, to roll over on its back momentarily
after thirty or forty minutes of wrestling, while the referee

gives its adversary a slap on the shoulder signifying that it has won the contest.

The word contest, of course, is merely a trade term. Most of the minor politicians who constitute the various prizefight commissions and supervise wrestling do not authorize its use in connection with wrestling bouts. They insist upon calling them exhibitions and the newspaper boys who cover them call them mockeries or make-believes and refer to that thirty or forty minutes of action which precedes the fall as the squirm.

Wrestling is the one hazardous occupation in the sport department of journalism because wrestlers are vindictive in a dumb way and one never can tell when one of them will pick up another and throw it at a correspondent sitting at the ringside. Moreover, after one has seen a few squirms one has seen them all and consequently one is likely to doze off during that time when the wrestlers are putting on the squirm. One learns to gauge these catnaps and come out of it just in time for the signal.

But the wrestler may resent this as an affront to its art and retaliate by heaving two hundred fifty pounds of moist and rather smelly weight, usually foreign matter, into the journalist's lap. I have seen as many as six journalists mown down by one wrestler thrown in this manner and had a very exciting evening myself once when I made a mistake at the ringside.

One wrestler was sitting on top of another and, with the dumb concentration of a trick baboon untying a shoelace, was twisting a large, bare foot.

"Hey, wrestler!" I cried, in honest error, for they were badly tangled up, "you are twisting your own foot."

At that the wrestler let out a loud howl of "Ow-oo," thinking that if it was twisting its own foot it must be hurting itself, and let go. But it happened to be the other wrestler's foot after all and when the first one let go the other one jumped up.

This enraged the wrestler which had been twisting the foot and six times that evening it threw the other one at me with intent to inflict great bodily harm. But, fortunately, though it had plenty of swift, its control was bad. So nothing happened to me, although the New York *World-Telegram* was hit twice and the New York *Times's* typewriter was smashed.

The fact that wrestlers utter sounds of apparent anguish does not necessarily prove that they really feel pain. They are trained to that, too. In former times they wrestled without sound effects and these were introduced in recent years by Mr. Curley who hired an expert in bird-calls and animal cries to instruct the members of his herd. At first the wrestlers made some ludicrous mistakes and one sometimes heard a wrestler twittering gayly when it was supposed to bleat piteously.

As to whether they love and are loved I just have no way of knowing. Maybe so, though. Hippopotamuses do.

The Old Gentleman

This article first appeared in COLLIER'S, June 23, 1934, and is reprinted by permission of Quentin Reynolds.

As I recall, I went to the Kentucky Derby with an old friend, Bill Corum—then and now sports columnist for the New York JOURNAL-AMERICAN. *He loved horses; I wasn't too much interested. We both lost betting on the Derby and I suggested to Corum that if I could find an article for* COL-LIER'S *(for whom I was then working), they would pay my expenses (plus paying for the article).*

Bill suggested we go to see Man o' War, then around seventeen or so. Bill knew everyone in racing circles and we were well received at the place outside Lexington where the horse was kept. With the help of the knowledgeable Corum, I saw the horse through his eyes and did the story. It was that simple.

QUENTIN REYNOLDS

Big Red was munching grass in a Kentucky pasture, but when Bobby Harbut said softly, "How yo' feel today, sugah?" Big Red looked up. The Kentucky sun touched him and it burnished the chestnut of his coat until it shone softly golden. The long line of his neck was smooth and his legs were slim and to look at him you'd never know that he was just an old gentleman whose active career was now but a glorious memory.

"Stand up straight, Red." The Negro boy's voice was soft. "Show off fo' the gentleman."

Big Red seemed to take a deep breath. Now he stood up straight, with his head held high. There he stood, calm, majestic, every inch a champion—and how he knew it! Horses know things like that. Seventeen years old he was, but this horse is ageless. His hair is a bit longer than it was back in 1920 when he was the wonder horse, but otherwise he is unchanged.

"Jes' lookut that hoss," the Negro kid said, and there was awe in his voice. "Ain't he grand? All hoss, he is."

Bobby Harbut knows a lot about Man o' War. Bobby wakes the old gentleman up every morning at six o'clock and Bobby puts a saddle on him. When Big Red (he's never been anything else to those who know him) was racing he had a habit of trying to run from under the saddle. It was as though he were saying, "I don't need a saddle or a whip or a boy to ride me. Just put me on that track and let me run." Big Red still has that habit.

"It ain't that he's a mean hoss," Bobby said, with a look of concern in his eye lest you misunderstood. "He's jes' naturally spirited. He sees that there saddle, he knows he's gwine t'run and he gets all excited."

Well, Bobby puts that saddle on him and then Bobby leads him out of his barn and across the road to Sam Riddle's private track. Willie Harbut, who is Bobby's father, gives the kid a boost into the saddle and Bobby strokes the softness of Big Red's neck and Bobby whispers in Big Red's ear—just as Loftus and Kummer once did in the days when Man o' War was making the best horses in the country look like a bunch of goats.

Now, the mornings in Kentucky are cold and there is always a breeze that brings the insinuating scent of the blue grass to you and you forget your age—whether you are a horse or a man. Big Red is a race horse again as soon as he steps on that track. Maybe he feels vaguely puzzled because of the absence of crowds and because, except for the impudent chirping of birds, there is silence. But he feels like running in the morning and as you see him lengthening out, sticking his head forward; as you watch his mane streaming in the breeze; as you see little Bobby Harbut pulling him in, holding him down to a steady gallop—why, the clock turns back and you're seeing Big Red as a two-year-old again.

Man o' War was a great-looking yearling back in 1918, and nobody thought that Sam Riddle paid too much when he gave August Belmont five thousand dollars for him at the Saratoga sale that year. Still, that was a high price for a youngster even in those days of ready cash. But Sam Hildreth, probably the greatest of all modern trainers, told Riddle that he liked the looks of this horse. He told Riddle that Man o' War had a full sister Masda whose speed was absolutely incredible.

"I timed Masda," Hildreth said, "and when I looked at my watch I couldn't believe it."

Family may not count for much when it comes to humans but it counts a lot where horses are concerned. Maybe it's because horses have greater hearts than humans have or maybe it's because they have an instinctive pride in their lineage—a pride that makes them do their best all the time. You seldom hear of a horse that doesn't try his best in a race. Jockeys, trainers—they are seldom as honest as the horses they handle, though as a class they are as honest as most humans.

Man o' War is a son of Fair Play and Mahubah, two pretty fair parents for a youngster to have. As a two-year-old, Man o' War started ten times and met defeat but once. We'll talk about that one later. It was as a three-year-old that he really established his greatness, though he had established his class before. Many a horse looks like a world-beater as a two-year-old, only to find the pace too fast as a three-year-old horse. But not this big chestnut.

He did everything they asked him to do, and they asked a lot of him. Starting with the Preakness, he won eleven straight races and he was challenged only once. That was in the Dwyer Stakes at Aqueduct, when Harry Payne Whitney's John P. Grier forced Big Red to a driving finish. John P. Grier was trained by the astute Jimmy Rowe and he was ready for Big Red. He ran his race, too, and broke his heart, but he was against something bigger than mere horseflesh.

He stayed with Big Red for most of the distance—until Big Red became annoyed. Then he turned it on to finish two lengths in front. Big Red always broke the hearts of those gallant but outclassed opponents. There is no use enumerating the victories won by Man o' War during 1920. He was king of the horse world and that covers it. In all he won purses totaling $249,465, which puts him twelfth on the list of big money winners. But most horsemen put him first in the list of great horses.

Watch him gallop around that track and you can't help but think of those days and you long for a wishing stone that works. Eight miles he goes every morning and his hoofs beat out a thunderous roar on the dirt.

Little Bobby has to keep pulling him in and Bobby whispers, "Easy, Big Red; we're jes' gallopin', we ain't racin'."

When he's finished, Bobby and his father lead him back to his barn and always Big Red looks at Bobby reproachfully as though to say, "Listen, youngster, why don't you let me run? I'm not so old, youngster. I got lots of running left in me."

Now there are those who might say that this is just the querulous whine of an old gentleman who ought to know better, but that isn't true of Big Red. You see, Big Red doesn't know that he's old. He doesn't feel old and then there's the magic of that Kentucky sun and the spell of that blue-grass-perfumed breeze. I'm sure that Big Red wonders sometimes why it is that they don't wake him at dawn, put a blanket on him and ship him off to Saratoga or Pimlico or Belmont Park or even Churchill Downs. Especially Churchill Downs. That Kentucky Derby is one race they never let Man o' War win. They pointed him for the Preakness the year he was a three-year-old and that came a week after the Derby. Paul Jones, son of Sea King and May Florence, won the Derby that year. He won it in 2:09. Big Red could have walked the mile and a quarter in faster time than that. Paul Jones was a fine gelding. But Man o' War was a great horse —not just a fine horse.

No, they don't let Big Red go to the wars any more and he seems to accept the fact philosophically enough. He's just a stud horse now, but so great is he that his owner gets five thousand dollars for his services. They send him to the stud twenty-five times a year, which means that he more than earns his keep. Now he lets his sons and his daughters and their sons and daughters carry on his name. During his earlier years in the stud the get of Man o' War proved to be sensational. American Flag was the first of his progeny to earn fame. The next year it was Crusader; who in 1926 was the greatest money winner of the year. Mata Hari, that beautiful filly who led the last Kentucky Derby field for three quarters of the distance, is a granddaughter of Big Red.

Big Red lives in a barn that Sam Riddle built especially for him. There are four stalls in the barn and three pals of Big Red live there with him. Mars and Crusader are two of his favorite sons. Each is eleven years old. Both of them are owned by Sam Riddle. Then there is the seventeen-year-old-Golden Broom, owned by Mrs. Walter Jeffords, Mr. Riddle's daughter.

I wonder if Big Red ever thinks of a certain afternoon in August, 1919, when he looks at Golden Broom. That was the only afternoon in his racing career that Big Red's number didn't go up on the board first. Upset, to whom he conceded fifteen pounds, beat him that day and Golden Broom was another starter. Well, horsemen will tell you that bad racing luck beat Big Red that day—not Upset. There was an assistant starter working at Saratoga that afternoon. He didn't get the horses away together. Big Red was actually facing the other way when the barrier was sprung.

Golden Broom was a streak away from the barrier. A great sprinter, Golden Broom. Upset, too, got away fast and they were both well on their way when Johnny Loftus turned the big fellow around and got him started. Nobody can say that Big Red didn't run his heart out trying to make up those lengths which separated him from the field. He caught Golden Broom and the rest of them all right and ten lengths from home the big fellow's head was nodding at Upset's saddle girth. The crowd wasn't screaming encouragement to the big fellow. The crowd was praying for him. He almost made it, too, and he was only a whisker behind at the finish. But he was behind. They said that it was a bad ride by Loftus that beat Big Red. Let it go at that. Big Red got revenge a year later when he walked right away from Upset in the Preakness.

It is hard to believe, looking at Golden Broom now, that he ever raced with such a one as Big Red. Each of the four horses has a separate pasture. Golden Broom looks like a tired old man. When they lead him into the field he leans against the wooden bars which enclose it and promptly falls asleep. You never saw such a horse for sleeping as that Golden Broom, but as little Bobby says, "He was a good hoss, mister, but they ain't but one champeen."

Bobby knows. It is he who washes and rubs down Big Red after his morning workout. It is he who mixes the six pounds of oats, "hand of bran" and bunch of carrots that Big Red eats every day. It is he who talks to Big Red and it is Bobby who quiets him when visitors excite him. Big Red is a fine host. During the past year thirty thousand people visited him.

One defeat could never dim the memory of his twenty glorious victories. There have been great horses in this country. There were those two marvelous horses of the early twentieth century—Sysonby and Colin, both owned by James R. Keene. There was the magnificent gelding Exterminator, which raced through six seasons to win $252,596 in purses. There were Luke Blackburn and Hindoo, kings of racing during the 1880's. Domino, Salvator and Artful were great, and Equipoise deserves to be listed in this august company.

Was Big Red greater than those? Who can tell? Is one sunset more beautiful than another? Was a moonlit night fifty years ago more bewitching than a moonlit night this month?

But I'll take the old gentleman when he was out there with his eyes flashing and his nostrils quivering and those steely, sinewy legs trembling just a bit. I'll take him when he was kicking mud into the eyes of the best horses of his day. Whether he was greater than the ancient kings we do not know. But he was greatest of our time and you'd know it if you traveled out to Kentucky and saw him standing in the middle of a pasture with the sun burnishing the chestnut of his coat until it shone softly golden.

Yes, he's just an old gentleman now but those old Kentucky gentlemen know how to grow old gracefully, and they never lose the proud look which is their birthright.

I'll Be Back,
Says Ben Hogan

This article first appeared in *SPORT*, September 1949, and is reprinted by permission of that magazine.

Of all the athletes I've ever known or watched, none commanded more of my personal admiration than Ben Hogan. In my opinion, he is the most determined athlete—and, very possibly, the most skillful—who ever lived. No one ever has possessed so much competitive spirit. His comeback from a near-fatal accident bordered on the miraculous.

This article on Ben is my favorite because it outlined the grievous injuries he suffered in that automobile-bus accident and the vastness of the problem confronting him: a return to the top; and because, I think, some of my own confidence in him shone through the paragraphs. I tried to indicate, without appearing utterly irrational, that Ben Hogan could come back. The fact that he did, in brilliant fashion, increased my sentimental feeling for this article, this small bit of the Hogan history.

BILL RIVES

Ben Hogan and his lovely wife, Valerie, rode along silently that morning last February. Ben was at the wheel, his eyes trying to pierce the mid-morning fog that lay damp and thick over the desolate stretch of country east of El Paso.

Their silence was not a signal of concern, or sullen anger, or temporary incompatibility. There simply wasn't much to talk about.

If Ben had been a struggling young golfer, there would have been excited conversation, for he was riding the crest again. In the few months before, he had won the National Open with a record-breaking score of 276; he had stored away the championship cups of the PGA and the Western Open; and though the winter tour was but a few weeks old, he had won almost four thousand dollars to take the money-winning lead among the pros. Now he was after the Masters title, one of the biggest of them all.

Certainly that was something to talk about. But it was nothing new for the Hogans. Long ago, they had stopped talking about Ben's chances on the tournament tour. It would have been ridiculous. One might just as well ask if Joe Louis would have a chance against Maxie Rosenbloom.

So when they talked, they talked about things other than golf. Their handsome new home in Fort Worth, for example; they looked forward with childlike anticipation toward the day when they would spend all their off-tournament time there.

In a sense, the Fort Worth home was a monument, a monument to the hard-won success of a poor West Texas blacksmith. Valerie, Ben's childhood sweetheart, shared in that often bitter struggle to the top; like Ben, she had a big stake in that house in Westover Hills.

But, at the moment, they did not talk of home, or of golf, or of anything else. They sat silently, with the warm comfort that comes from being near the one you love.

Suddenly, their reverie was broken.

Four bright lights abreast loomed before them. An on-coming passenger bus had pulled out to pass a truck.

Hogan yanked the steering wheel to the right, but a collision was unavoidable. Instinctively, he flung himself in front of Valerie.

That split-second act saved both their lives. Had he remained in the driver's position, Ben most certainly would have been killed instantly; if he had not taken the major portion of the blow which fell where his wife was sitting, she could not have survived the injuries he received.

The car was collapsed as the bus struck it; a forty-five-hundred-dollar automobile, it was later sold for salvage for six hundred dollars, after being put on display in a Fort Worth department store.

Where Ben had been sitting, the steering wheel was driven through the seat. Only six inches of free space separated the back rest of the seat and the dashboard panel. The car's frame was smashed to the ground.

Valerie was only slightly hurt but Hogan's body was crushed. They were in a lonely, thinly populated territory of West Texas, thirty miles from the nearest town, Van Horn.

In the excitement, no one called an ambulance immediately; everybody assumed someone else had done it. Hogan lay critically hurt, conscious and in great pain, for an hour and a half before an ambulance finally appeared. It was four hours before he was carried, more dead than alive, into the Hotel Dieu, a hospital at El Paso, one hundred and twenty miles west of the accident scene.

His left collarbone, his pelvis, his left ankle and several ribs were broken. But his constitution, hardened and strengthened by years of golf, absorbed the fierce injuries and kept his heart pumping. The doctors said he would recover.

But a month later, blood clots, which can be swiftly lethal, began to form, and Hogan soon was wrestling with Death. Doctors told him later that he never got a break; virtually every possible complication set in. But Ben had fought bad breaks before and, miraculously, he lived.

Now, in his convalescent period, the little battler is constantly subjected to the general assumption, all over the country, that he is through; washed up. The word is out— Ben Hogan, one of the greatest golfers in history, will never play golf again, or if he does, he'll be lucky to hack around in 90 strokes. He'll never be able to reproduce his championship form. He's cooked, like a goose.

Golf writers are whispering it all over the country; some have said so in print. Followers of golf, who know the rigorous physical demands of the game, shake their heads in sympathy and say, "It's too bad about Ben. The poor little guy had to hit from the heels when he was at full strength; what can he do now? His accident finished him off."

Maybe so and maybe no. Hogan has been a fighter all his life and he refuses to be counted out until the battle is over.

Who can safely say that Ben Hogan is through? The doctors who treated him cannot, and under the circumstances, they probably are the best judges.

I have known Ben Hogan personally for years. With the zealous, detailed attention of a golf writer and the admiration of a duffer, I have watched his climb from the caddie ranks to golf's pinnacle.

Since his accident, I have spent many hours with him. He has discussed his golfing future frankly with me. I watched him tremble with eagerness and uncertainty as he putted for the first time following the cruel blow that almost laid him in his grave.

SPORT Magazine asked me to get the real low-down on the case of Ben Hogan. Put an end to these rumors; let's have the truth, the editors said. Will Hogan ever play again?

Only the passage of time will bring the full answer to that question. Many factors are involved. But of them all, this single, stark fact looms as large as any—

If determination and courage will put Ben Hogan back at the forefront of golf, then he will return there. For Ben Hogan is no ordinary man; his mind and his heart have contributed as much to his phenomenal golfing as his physical skill and coordination.

In all the conjecture about Hogan's future, little consideration has been given to his clear grit and his wild, almost irrational, resolution.

Ben Hogan is determined to return to golf. He has told me many times, in recent weeks, of this resolve. He spoke quietly and without visible emotion, but the intensive rush of his words, the glow in his eyes, gave away the depth of his feelings.

We sat for hours, on numerous occasions, in his home and in the clubhouse of the Colonial Country Club in Fort Worth. Every time, he had a putter in his hands; he carries it with him wherever he goes.

I was not content with one interview, because I could not believe that anyone who had suffered the physical injuries that Hogan received could be sincere about playing golf again. Like other persons over the country, I felt that Ben Hogan never would play again.

But I've changed my mind. Time and time again, in our conversations, I brought up the subject of his golfing future. I was probing for the slightest indication that he was whistling in the dark; that he was only kidding himself and that he knew it, in spite of his bold and brave words.

But never did Hogan give the slightest indication that in his heart, he knew he was through.

"I'm more determined than ever," he said. "You know, when I started out, I had a tough time. I was a scrawny, little kid without any money. Most people thought I was too little and too frail to play championship golf. I didn't have a perfected game to use against the big-name players.

"I starved and worked and practiced, and many times it

seemed that I couldn't possibly make the grade. But I hung on."

When Hogan began touring with the pros, he had only two things in his favor—a great love for golf and an intense determination to play it well. In the first issue of SPORT, back in September, 1946, Kerr Petrie wrote that Hogan was violating the eight-hour-day rule because he practiced so much.

"I have always had to practice," Hogan said. "I'm not a born golfer; I'm a made golfer. I worked hard to become a championship golfer, and I worked hard to stay one. I'll work hard to become one again, too."

Once in 1932, in his early tournament days, Ben lived for three days on fifteen cents worth of oranges. In 1935, he and Valerie were married and started out on the tournament trail with fourteen hundred dollars which Ben had scraped together over two years of self-denial.

They started out in Canada in the spring and by the time they reached Oakland, California, summer had passed and the bankroll was down to eighty-six dollars. Someone stole the rear wheels off their car; after repairs, they had fourteen dollars left.

"But I wouldn't give up, even then," Hogan said. "I won $368 in that tournament and from that day to this, I've never had to worry about my next meal."

Ben wasn't bragging when he said that. He isn't the bragging kind; he merely was reciting the facts of his case history and emphasizing the determination he possessed as a young golfer. He never has lost it.

Valerie agrees with Ben in his decision to play golf again. She has stuck by him through times good and bad; she has starved with him on tours and she has smiled at him as he was presented handsome checks.

She knows that years ago, he dedicated his life to golf.

She knows too, that he could never rest easy if he didn't give it another try.

"Ben," she told him, "whenever you're ready to play, I'll be on the first tee, pulling for you."

Valerie understands; sitting long hours by his hospital bed, she saw his love for golf clearer than ever.

In his many delirious moments, Ben would try to raise up in bed and wave the gallery back on the right or left side; he would grip an imaginary club and work his hands as though he were waggling a driver. Always, in his subconscious, there was golf.

But, while Hogan didn't know it at the time, Death was at his side. After a month of slow and painful recuperation, it appeared that Ben was out of the rough and on the green —safely on the road back to health.

In his rational periods, he and Valerie talked happily about their return home.

But complications came. Phlebitis, which inflames the veins and obstructs circulation, struck him in the left leg. Three days later, a blood clot tore into his right lung.

"It was like someone had stuck a knife into my chest and was grinding and twisting it, deeper and deeper," Hogan said.

Ten days later, another one appeared. Hogan's doctors held a hurried consultation; a delicate operation, in which the chances to survive are 1 to 3, was necessary. Dr. Alton Ochsner, a noted New Orleans surgeon, was reached by telephone. He caught the first plane for El Paso and reached Hogan's bedside, a few hours later, as the golfer's life was going slowly out of his resisting body.

Hogan now bears a ten-inch scar across his abdomen, where Dr. Ochsner went into his circulatory system and tied off the Vena cava inferior, one of two large veins close to the backbone. The Vena cava inferior brings the flow of blood upward, from the lower part of the body, into the heart.

The specialist did that to prevent the possibility that a third and fatal clot might rush, tearing and cutting, through Hogan's blood stream.

With the Vena cava tied off, smaller veins had to be forced into extra duty, to carry an additional load of blood. Therefore, long, tight elastic stockings were placed around Hogan's legs to increase pressure on the veins. This treatment also brought a new, acute form of agony; his legs felt constantly as though they were going to sleep. Sharp shooting pains darted through them continuously.

All this time—from the time of the accident until he left the hospital eight weeks later—Valerie was by his side, growing gaunt and hollow-eyed and losing weight with worry.

When they finally left the hospital to go to Fort Worth, she slept like a log on the train. Ben lay awake, nervous and eager over the fact that at last, he was going home. The next day he kidded her, complaining that she was a heck of a poor nurse.

"Ben," she said quietly, "it's the first night I've slept since you've been hurt."

Life has taken on a new meaning for Ben Hogan. His fight to live has made him sharply aware of the joys of activities which most of us take for granted.

"You can't imagine," he said, "how wonderful it is just to be able to talk to people."

The support of the public, as he lay dying, was a source of inspiration. "I never realized," he murmured, "just how swell the American public can be."

In Hogan's competitive career, he has been called "The Frigid Midget," a player without nerves or feeling, a callous, tough customer.

"Because I concentrate so thoroughly when I play," he

said, "a lot of people think I'm aloof and distant and cold-blooded. But I'm not a Bob Hope or a happy-go-lucky Jimmy Demaret. I have to concentrate when I play and I believe that if concentration is needed in order to make good shots, then that is what the public expects. I believe that is what they pay for. Whatever color or showmanship I have comes through my golf shots.

"Since my accident, I have received so many gifts and good wishes that I have been overwhelmed. From all over the country, presents and cheering words have poured in. One stranger wrote me eleven times, urging me to keep my chin up, to recover and to come back and play again. If I can do it, I won't let him down.

"I received cheese from Wisconsin, dates from Arizona, fruit from Florida, cherries from Oregon, books, candy and other gifts from all over this nation."

From his home state's PGA came a handsome plaque inscribed "Our respect and admiration to our pal, Ben Hogan, a champion of champions. The Texas PGA."

On the eve of the Masters tournament, the entire field of players and officials posed for a picture which was mounted in a beautiful frame and sent to him inscribed: "To our friend, Ben Hogan. On the eve of the 1949 Masters tournament, we send you our heartfelt good wishes for a speedy and complete recovery." Later, they sent a humidor, engraved with all their names.

Hogan is an utter realist; he doesn't indulge in any romantic or fanciful ideas when he talks about his return to golf.

"I don't know what my chances are," he said. "All I know is, I'm going to give it everything I've got. My recovery is going to be slow but that can't be helped."

At the moment, Hogan can't even walk, much less play, eighteen holes. About nine holes is all he can walk.

If Hogan returns to top form, it won't be the first time an

athlete has conquered physical troubles. Craig Wood won the 1941 National Open with his back heavily taped; Ed Furgol has a shriveled left arm and yet he plays fine golf; Denny Shute once had an operation on his left wrist and people immediately said he was through (but he wasn't); Sam Snead has had, and still may have, sacroilliac trouble.

There remains the question of his age.

"Ben," I asked him, "what about that? You're thirty-seven now. Suppose it was a year or two before you got back into good physical condition. Just for the sake of discussion, let's say that when you return, you'll be as sound as a dollar. But you'll be almost forty years old. What about that?"

"Age makes no difference," he said quickly. "If a man has the desire, he can play. The trouble with most men is that they lose that desire after they get around forty years old; they'd rather sit in the clubhouse than to get out and practice."

(This might be a good place to point out that when Wood won the Open, he was thirty-nine. The oldest man to win it was Ted Ray; he was forty-three years old when he won at Inverness in 1920.)

"Why, less than two years ago," Hogan said, "I discovered something to improve my swing. I began playing better than ever. And I was thirty-five years old; that's considered old for an athlete.

"I can't tell you what I found out; I won't even tell Valerie."

He grinned. "But I'll tell you this—it's the greatest invention since the self-starter."

Hogan said that the effectiveness of his game will depend upon "a lot of things."

Because of his collarbone break, he may have to alter his swing; he may have to change his stance; he may have to sacrifice a little distance in favor of accuracy. His nervous system may be so upset that he won't be able to sink those long putts. He may become a quaking wreck after his long layoff; it took him six months to get back on his game after military service, and then he was healthy and strong and had nothing to blame but the long period of golfing inactivity.

But you can't write off Ben Hogan; you can't toll ten over him until he's had his chance.

Golf is Ben Hogan's life. He speaks of it in reverent terms. He believes that it gave him a priceless opportunity: the chance to travel the country over; to mingle with the highborn and the so-called common man and to learn that in essence, they are one and the same; to achieve success, and to have fun while earning a living.

In return, Hogan has tried his best to uphold the dignity of golf and to contribute something to its technical perfection. At all times, he has tried his best to give the spectators full value for their gallery fees.

It is not hard to believe Hogan's sincerity, therefore, when he says:

"Why, ever since my accident, I've never even thought of doing anything else except returning to the tournaments."

If Ben Hogan fails, it will not be because he did not put forth every possible effort; if he fails, it will be because he hasn't the strength; it will be because his accident robbed him of the physical attributes a championship golfer needs.

Failure, of course, would bring him great sorrow. There's no denying that; no man ever loved golf more than Ben Hogan. To have it taken away would be a calamity.

But if he fails, he'll fail with honor and he'll not complain.

If he never hits a golf ball again, Ben Hogan will pass his days in peace and happiness, once he has conquered the sharp pain of failure. He'll be happy simply because he's alive.

Those of us who have never been close to Death cannot understand what he means. But Ben Hogan assures me there is joy in breathing, in living without pain, in talking to friends and in being with the ones you love.

The Defensive Platoon

This column first appeared in the San Francisco *Chronicle*, November 24, 1951, and is reprinted by permission of that newspaper.

I selected this because it won first prize in Best Sports Stories for 1952, in the news division. It was written at the stadium immediately after the game. Though the platoon system is not with the colleges any longer, I believe this story represents the topical thinking of the particular era. It was the first popularized effort to take the defensive game into the press box. In a sense, I like to think it stands as a memento of College Football, 1951.

ART ROSENBAUM

Were you asking for the names of the gentlemen who scored the touchdowns?

Sorry, dear sir and madam, but you won't find them here. They went that-away, to be readily identified in other scripters' versions of this upsetting Big Game.

I was a specialist today. I represented the press box's own platoon system. In this case, the Defensive Platoon.

Other typists followed the ball. Me? I had a cleat in my face, a knee in my ribs and a helmet in my tummy. I was with the poor fellow at the bottom of the pile.

Touchdowns? Take 'em away.

The following account concerns itself with the men who handfought their way through a phalanx of blockers to smash down a straight-arming runner; of crashing ends and submarining guards; of that necessary evil of the grid, the lowly lineman.

Yes, California's Bears at once proved and disproved the critics' judgment of them. In preseason, it was stated that only legislation would prevent the bold Bear from entering the Rose Bowl. Then misfortune moved in. By season's end, the Bear was considered to have lost his early season snarl. Today he played just like the Bear that was—especially on defense.

When was the last time Stanford failed to score in the first three quarters? When was Stanford limited to a single touchdown?

The answers to both questions would be, "Never." And in recognition of their sterling efforts, we suggest the following workhorses step forward to take deep, deserving bows:

Ed Bartlett, Dwight Ely, Steve Glick, Pete Mering and George Pelonis.

They represent the fierce end-to-end line in California's 5-3-2-1 defense, a line that made it easy for the three linebackers to lay a few finishing tackles on their work. Stanford was not traveling very far on the ground today, and the furious fivesome deserve the back-claps.

Of course, Les Richter was present. He was the man who called the defensive signals, and he had an approving pat on the back of the lap for any man who followed instructions perfectly.

Richter, on those occasions when he was healthy and active, seemed to have his defenses pegged to meet Stanford Quarterback Gary Kerkorian's mind.

"Every time I thought they'd stay in a certain defense,"

complained Gary later, "they shifted on me. And when I thought they'd shift, they stayed put."

Here's an instance:

All day long, Bartlett had been crashing from his left end position. In the third period, Richter had been hurt. Stanford was moving. Suddenly Bartlett drifted wide and when a pitchout arrived in Stanford Halfback Harry Hugasian's arms, Bartlett arrived on the same timetable. The eight-yard loss ruined Stanford's scoring chance.

Of course, some of you disbelievers will say the best defense is possession of the ball, an eminently successful department for the bold Bears today. But we of the defense rise to a point of order. How would they have gotten the ball in the first place if we (Cal) hadn't taken it away?

Stanford had thirty-three running plays. California enjoyed seventy rushing attempts.

The game was won on the ground.

It's true Stanford tried the sky 31 times, whereas Cal went upstairs just 10. But there was desperation in some of those Indian passes, all explainable by going back to the source—that charging Bear defensive line.

And speaking of passes, this was a day of satisfaction for Dick LemMon, the left defensive halfback. Last year a Kerkorian to Boyd Benson pass had tied the Big Game for Stanford. The throw was over LemMon. Dick had been under some criticism this season as a possible puncture in the Bear air defense.

But LemMon was "Mr. Ack-Ack" himself today. On those occasions when linebacker Hal Norris didn't dent Stanford's Bill McColl at the line of scrimmage, LemMon was draping himself all over the agile All-America at the point of the pass.

LemMon literally knocked himself out on one situation when it appeared McColl had caught the ball after it was batted about near the corner. LemMon came up woozy and the officials declared it incomplete.

Another who helped was sure-fire tackling Dick Lee at right half, who personally stopped a Stanford march early in the third when he (1) outfaked Bob Mathias to nail what appeared to be a long run (2) hauled down Kerkorian on a bootleg after a seven-yard run that might have stretched to seventy, and then broke up Kerk's pass intended for tall Sam Morley. Stanford was forced to punt.

The experts also gave more than a nod to the linebacking of freshman Matt Hazeltine. In Cal's 5-3 accordion setup, the outside linebackers often move on the line, in a sort of standing crouch, prepared to charge or to drift. Hazeltine, under orders from Richter, was often noted through press-box binoculars as the guy who was there first after the lineman's initial impact.

Although Stanford backs wore their helmets tight, Freshman Matt was in their hair all day. A pest.

Don Robison, the surprise choice for safety, and Richter were also on the offense, but we'll skip that. If you'll notice, Richter was even removed from the offensive unit after a while. His ponderous impact was more important in the middle linebacker role. He was definitely Double A today.

Was Stanford's defense that bad? Not really. Remember, California's speed backs have averaged thirty-two points per game during the season. Remember also that in this case Stanford's attack simply could not jell against stern Bear frontal assault, and the burden was therefore on the Stanford defense. California rolled up 316 yards on the ground, but that's par for the course on seventy plays. Only three touchdowns were scored. . . . Oops, sorry, there's that word again. I wasn't going to mention touchdown.

Maybe it's just as well for Stanford that Johnny Olszewski was operating on one wheel.

Stanford opened with a seven-box defense, or 7-2-2. Cal moved against it. Later the seven-diamond, or 7-1-2-1, was used, and this was better.

Right Guard Leon King was knifing across the line, and when a pass situation evolved, he was in the general area. But when Cal trapped or returned with a slant to the weak side, that hole was huge. To King's credit he widened later, as did the Stanford tackles, Bob Latham and Al Kirkland, and Stanford's defense after the first touchdown shock was definitely improved. Jess Cone, at right guard, also helped.

Stanford's line played it straight originally, but soon fell into a sag. The ends were even with the ball, but the middle men played off the line in an attempt to ruin Cal's blocking angles. Line coach Herm Meister of California said later the Bear staff had anticipated this "sag" from other Stanford defenses against the "T."

Stanford experimented. Cone replaced King. Skip Crist was a linebacker for Ted Tanner. Later Chuck Hokanson took Latham's job at tackle. At best, the assignment wasn't easy.

I'd nominate Rob Eadie and Hart Cook as the most effective Stanford linemen.

You can have your long passes and dashing runs. We of the defense, who revel in the crush and thunder of a resounding tackle, have other ideas. In the second quarter, for instance, Cal's Sammy Williams was inserted at defensive left half. Stanford's Kerkorian chose to bootleg, and was keel-hauled overboard by a jarring thigh tackle.

A few moments later Richter "shot the gap," as we in defensive circles express it, and gave Card Ron Cook a bouncing ride in reverse.

Of course we defenceers hate leather, and we aren't interested in the ball. But if Kerkorian insisted on fumbling, then why shouldn't a deserving lineman like Steve Glick take possession?

Deep in the second period, Hazeltine was jammed into the line, but at the last split second dropped back and slid over to smash down Stanford's Bob Meyers, who had taken a pass from Kerkorian. Total gain: 3 yards.

Lee was all over the place as Stanford began its third-quarter effort. Then Linebacker "Skip" Crist had an inning. He shot the gap to nail Robison with a yard, then drove Billy Mais out of bounds on a bootleg, forcing the Bears to punt.

Did we mention that Chuck Essegian, the other Stanford linebacker was in on everything? Consider it mentioned.

Here's a funny one. Robison had punted eleven yards and eight yards. His next effort was high and far, best of the day. Mathias fumbled and tackle Don Curran recovered for California. Actually, Stanford's Latham had rolled into the kicker and a penalty would have been in order if Cal had chosen. But, because Latham had charged so hard, Robison was forced to rush his kick. He rushed it for his best effort of the afternoon.

So there was California on Stanford's 10. The score was only 14-0 then, and the Stanford defense rose up. King and Eadie stopped Robison with one. Latham knocked down a pass but Cal was penalized for illegal use of hands. Eadie and Latham cornered Mais with a 12-yard scolding.

King refused to commit himself on an obvious trap, with Johnny O. carrying. Olszewski found himself wrapped in King's grasp for no gain. A march that had started on Stanford's 10 ended on Stanford's 36, and embarrassed Cal had to punt.

The team of LemMon and Lee was at its best in the late going, when Stanford heard the message from the tower and decided to take to the air.

End Paul Andrew also had a hand in this situation when he clutched Kerkorian's shirt on a pass attempt and Kerk was deposited earthward for a nine-yard deficit.

Have I mentioned that California punt coverage was excellent? Strictly defensive stuff.

Personally, I liked Stanford to win, 35-30. It could have happened, if it hadn't been for the defenses. Remember how the Stanford defense rose up to force Richter into a field goal attempt. Had he negotiated same, the Bears would have led, 17-0. Also remember that the defense rammed him on his third conversion try, which failed. On that basis, two touchdowns and the field goal would have built Cal's total to 30 points.

As for Stanford, I visioned five touchdowns. The Cal defense gave the poor Indian four less.

It was a day for the defense, Your Honor.

My case rests.

The Delinquent Juvenile Horse

This article first appeared in The Louisville *Courier-Journal*, May 6, 1956, and is reprinted by permission of that newspaper.

I liked this story probably because I liked the horse and the race he ran, and I enjoyed writing about him. There is something very fascinating about great horses and their reaction to the efforts of top trainers and jockeys to fit them to harness. This rascal ran because he liked to run, and ran only when he felt like it in spite of all the work by his handlers.

EARL RUBY

Needles, the juvenile delinquent from Florida who hates to work and apparently likes nothing better than to beat the tar out of nice young colts who mind their teachers, has done it again.

Carrying Dave Erb on his shoulders like a bouncing orange ad for the Sunshine State, the winter book champion spotted fifteen competitors twenty-four lengths in the Kentucky Derby yesterday afternoon. Then he put his ears back and began picking them off two and three at a time.

Pounding like Ponder around the last turn he was throwing dirt into the faces of all except Fabius—and was beginning to cut the ground out from under the dark brown son of Citation.

Sweat streaming off his rump and lathering under his legs, he strained to the last big inch of his tremendous stride.

Thousands of roaring fans in the steepled stands saw the bounding orange gradually eclipse the fluttering ball of red on the rail, then suddenly pass it as if blown by Hurricane Hazel to win by more than half-a-length in one of the most fantastic runnings of the Kentucky Derby.

Bugle Call—Needles and Fabius were among early arrivals in the paddock. Other starters joined them one by one, nervous and excited.

Needles looked bored.

The bugle sounded and attendants jumped to attention. The parade to the track began. The band struck up *My Old Kentucky Home* as Career Boy, the No. 1 horse, stepped onto the track.

They circled up the track in front of the clubhouse. Then back down past the grandstand a quarter of a mile to the starting gate. Attendants on ponies had to hold many of them as they shied at the noise of the crowd and flash of cameras.

Needles sauntered along with the rest until they passed the starting gate. Then decided to thunder with it. He stopped. Jockey Erb, who had seen him do this innumerable times on morning workouts, looked around helplessly.

His pony boy wheeled and started over for him. Needles decided reluctantly to move on.

Erb turned him around and guided him directly into No. 1 stall. (He had No. 1 post position, though his number was 3.) This apparently was exactly what he wanted. He stood quietly loafing while the others danced their pre-race jitters away.

They're Off! The gate really was two gates, joined together to accommodate the large field, and triggered electrically by one button held by Starter Ruby White on his high perch on the left.

Three minutes after Needles entered his stall the gates flew open. All seventeen came out like a cavalry charge. It was as near-perfect a start for so many horses as ever has been seen here. Also near-bedlam, as jockeys screamed and one hundred thousand spectators roared.

Terrang, fleet winner of the Santa Anita Derby known for his early speed, quickly dashed to the front. Right behind him were Fabius, Ben A. Jones and Head Man, also known for quick getaways.

Down past the stands for the first time they whirled ahead of the horde.

"Where's Needles?" cried a woman standing on a chair in the rear of the press box.

"Here he comes," shouted a masculine voice back of a giant set of binoculars. "Next to last."

There was a crash and the lady was on the floor.

Ben A. Jones, the horse named for the trainer, sprinted into the lead as the large field swept toward the first turn. Terrang and Fabius quickly overran him as they pounded along the back stretch. Head Man held to third. And No Regrets, California Derby champion trained by Louisville's Dick Waggoner, moved into fourth.

Needles was sixteenth, twenty-four lengths back.

Jockey Erb decided it was now or never. He gave Needles his head and clucked to him. . . .

"Let's go, boy," he cried.

Nothing happened. . . . "What the hell, I thought," he laughed later. "I was scared stiff. Then he started running."

"I saw a hole and we went for it."

He passed Jean Baptiste, Black Emperor and Career Boy as if they were standing still . . . then Count Chic, who also had started a move that earned fourth place.

He was coming around the far turn now. Past Pintor Lea.

Past Come On Red, which also was moving up from a sad fourteenth to finish a thrilling third.

Another stride and he was passing Countermand, Besomer and Invalidate.

Around into the head of the stretch he raced. A quarter of a mile to go and seventh. Three lengths off Fabius, who had shaken off Terrang to take the lead on the turn.

No Regrets moved up to second, hung, then gave up the chase. Terrang, third, tired and dropped back.

Needles passed these, Head Man and two more winded sprinters. He was in the stretch now and going after the flying devil-red silks ahead.

Then came the eclipse and the wire.

Then the Dead End Kid shuffled into the winner's circle and suffered a blanket of roses to be draped across his steaming shoulders.

Cobb

This column first appeared in the Detroit *News*, August 30, 1955, and is reprinted by permission of that newspaper.

In the last forty-five years I have written some fourteen thousand columns and while some were undoubtedly better than others, I could not select one as my favorite.

I am sending you the Cobb column because it is of more recent vintage and concerns an athlete whom Grantland Rice always referred to as the "greatest competitor in the history of sports."

There certainly was no greater competitor than Cobb nor was there probably ever another as fierce.

He was undoubtedly the most colorful and controversial figure of his time and there will not likely ever be another like him.

This column was intended to explain Cobb; to show what made him click.

H. G. SALSINGER

MEMORANDUM: Fifty years ago today the name "Cobb" appeared in a box score for the first time. It appeared in 3,032 more box scores before it vanished twenty-four years later.

266

Brilliant and unorthodox, a fiery genius and the game's outstanding individualist, Cobb made baseball history for more than two decades. He dominated the game.

He gained pre-eminence not because he was the fastest baserunner, nor the best base stealer, nor the fleetest fielder, nor the leading hitter but because he had the nimblest brain that baseball has known.

He had the ability to perceive a situation and take advantage of it before his opponents became aware of it. He was a keener student of the game than his contemporaries and understood the game better than they did. More than that, he understood them better than they understood themselves. He knew their mechanical faults and weaknesses but he also knew their strength.

He was baseball's greatest player because he outthought opponents, kept a play ahead of them. He was not the greatest fielder, since there were several better. He was not the greatest place hitter since Wee Willie Keeler was admittedly better. He was not the greatest slugger since a dozen or more players could hit the ball farther. He was not the fastest man in the game since several others were just as fast and a few probably faster. His wide edge over the field was mental. He thought quicker than any rival and he put his mechanical skill to better use than they did. Many of his hits were attributed to superior speed, but the explanation does not hold since several other players were as fast but they did not cause fielders to overhurry the way Cobb did. They did not upset infields the way Cobb did.

In running bases, Cobb's lightning brain worked faster than his legs. Branch Rickey, who managed the St. Louis Browns when Cobb was at the peak of his career, commented one day:

"He has brains in his feet."

He continually crossed up infielders. He would break unexpectedly and fail to break when they expected him to run.

Every move he made was carefully planned. Going into a base he knew what the infielder would do. He developed different slides, including the hook, the fallaway and fadeaway. He would go straight into a bag or to the outside or inside. He would purposely slide wide, past the bag, then hook the outside corner with his toe.

He was not a natural hitter when he entered organized baseball and he could not get a loud foul off a lefthander. By the time he became established as the league's top player he could hit lefthanders better than righthanders.

He could not slide at the start of his career but became the most expert slider in the game.

He studied infielders, outfielders, pitchers and catchers and made mental note of their individual playing habits. Nothing escaped him. The mechanical moves of an infielder, the peculiarities of an outfielder, the unconscious giveaway signs of a pitcher or catcher were all known to Cobb.

He used no mystic powers, had no occult gifts. Some of his plays looked downright stupid but they were anything but that. He would let himself be caught flatfooted between bases. Then the rundown started. Nine out of ten times Cobb would advance. He had a simple explanation:

"All you've got to do is make them keep on throwing the ball. Sooner or later somebody will make a wild throw."

Someone generally did.

Cobb upset batteries and infields. He was responsible for more wild throws than any other man who played the game. He constantly harried pitchers, saying:

"When I'm up there at the plate I know the pitcher is under a lot more pressure than I am, especially in a close game. I've got a psychological advantage over him."

He scored from first on singles, streaked from first to third, or scored from second on sacrifice bunts and infield outs.

The delayed steal was one of his favorites. He would turn

first base on an outfield single, come to a stop, and when the outfielder pulled back his arm to lob the ball to the infield, Cobb was off. He knew the outfielder would have to change position to make a fast throw to second.

He was so far ahead of the field that comparisons seem odious. When he retired in 1928, after twenty-four years of big league competition, he left behind enough records to convince even the most skeptical of his rightful place at the head of the all-time ranking.

Cobb was probably the greatest competitor any sport has known, the fiercest. He was at his best when the pressure was on. He gloried in the clutch. His most brilliant plays generally came when the odds were heavily against him. He was one of the poorest losers in sport and his bitter dread of defeat made him a spectacular winner. He could endure anything but failure. There was no amount of drudgery that he would not undertake to reach his goal.

He is baseball's lonely figure sitting on the Olympian heights.

There has been only one Tyrus Raymond Cobb and the game never will see his like again for the pattern of play has changed and not for the better either.

His is the story of a mighty brain and the driving force of genius that made him great when other men, superior in physical strength and natural ability and speed, remained mediocre.

Boxing's Dirty Business Must Be
Cleaned Up Now

This article first appeared in *SPORTS ILLUSTRATED*, November 1, 1954, and is reprinted by permission of Budd Schulberg.

I've been a fight fan all my life. I was brought up on Ace Hudkins and Fidel LaBarba and Jackie Fields. I don't know of any sport that goes deeper. It is both ennobling and debasing. When it is good it is so very good. And when it's bad—

I hesitated before choosing a negative piece to represent me in this book. I thought of the rousing contests I had tried to catch the feeling of—Marciano and Moore; Basilio and Demarco. But my love of boxing is qualified by my resentment of the influences that corrupt it. The blight of that corruption spread over the Gavilan-Saxton fiasco in Blinky Palermo's Philadelphia. I got sore. I hope my report for SPORTS ILLUSTRATED *still sounds that way.*

BUDD SCHULBERG

Johnny Saxton may be an orphan, but no one can say he lacks for cousins in Philadelphia. Anybody who can clown his way through fifteen listless rounds and still be rewarded

with a world's championship must have a covey of doting
relatives in the Friendly City. I am still checking on the
lineal connections between the new "champion" and his
benefactors, Referee Pete Pantaleo and Judges Jim Mina
and Nat Lopinson, all of whom gave the defending champion, Kid Gavilan, the treatment a GOP candidate expects
in Mississippi. They voted the straight Saxton-Palermo ticket.
The three officials, if not blood relatives of the hitless wonder, have at the very least a touching sentimental attachment for the Riverdale foundling who plays Cinderella to
Manager Blinky Palermo's unshaven Fairy Godmother.

Blinky's champion "fights," as they used to say, "out of
Philadelphia." He can't move far enough out to satisfy the
nearly eight thousand fans who suffered through the grue-
some, gluesome twosome between him and fading Kid Gavilan in Convention Hall the other evening. Blinky Palermo,
a numbers man who traffics in fighters (Ike Williams, Billy
Fox, Clarence Henry, Dan Bucceroni, Coley Wallace, etc.),
operates out of Philadelphia. One of boxing's top-ranking
ambassadors of ill will, a field in which there is always stiff
competition, Blinky is frequently identified as "The Philadelphia Sportsman." It has become a sort of private joke, especially suitable to those papers who would rather not spell
spade s-p-a-d-e. In 1951 a federal district court found Blinky
guilty of contempt for refusing to answer questions before
a rackets grand jury. Contempt is also the word for Blinky's
attitude toward boxing fans in foisting Saxton, the human
grannyknot, on them as Kid Gavilan's successor.

Johnny may never have known what it is to have a real
brother but he has certainly found the next best thing in
Honest Pete Pantaleo, another Philadelphia sportsman, who
handled the fight with such tender concern for Saxton's welfare that it is difficult for me to understand why there
should have been such bitter criticism of him in the press.
Extending a helping hand to an orphan boy trying to make

something of himself is certainly a praiseworthy gesture. Statues of Pantaleo may yet be found in orphanages throughout America. A fitting inscription, to be engraved at the base of the noble bronze head of Pantaleo, might read as follows:

"For service to one of our own, above and beyond the call of duty, in donating the welterweight championship of the world to Johnny Saxton. Disregarding his own safety and placing himself in the greatest jeopardy by inviting the wrath of 7,909 onlookers and millions of irate TViewers across the nation, Pantaleo nevertheless persevered and proved the courage of his convictions by awarding Saxton even those rounds in which he failed to throw a single punch. Hail Pantaleo, boxing's Patron Saint of Orphans!"

The cost of this charitable project will surely be underwritten by Blinky himself. It is the least he owes Honest Pete. The debt can never be paid in full.

Not to be forgotten while we hand out these skunk-cabbage bouquets is the role of Commissioner Frank Wiener, who made quite a show of rushing to and fro, exhorting the "fighters" to cease their loving embraces and affectionate staring at each other. Wiener had already distinguished himself by announcing before the weighin that if Gavilan came in over the official weight limit, Saxton could still win the title by winning the fight. If the Kid won, the Commissioner went on to explain, the title would be declared vacant. You and I, who aren't so courant with these things, may wonder why, if Gavilan was to be asked to turn in his title, it should be handed on a silver platter to Blinky's boy, who ranked fifth in the division, below the logical contender, Carmen Basilio. The only explanation that comes readily to mind is that it was Be Kind to Saxton (and Palermo) Week and Commissioner Weiner was getting things started early.

Not since the days when Schmeling was winning his

heavyweight title when reclining on his back after an al-
leged low blow from Jack Sharkey, or when Carnera was
receiving his crown from the benevolent Sharkey, not since
those sleazy days when talking pictures and smelly fights
were in flower—well, I guess what I am trying to say is that
Saxton can now share with Carnera the booby prize for
being the most undeserving and unwelcome champion in
modern history.

The bloodless and—except for Gavilan's earnest final round
—nearly hitless mazurka was actually a fitting climax to a
prolonged shell game that really began over a year ago
when Carmen Basilio knocked Gavilan down and came
within a lash of depriving him of the title that had made
him the assistant Presidente de Cuba. The Kid rallied to win
but the smart boys looked at each other and decided that
another good fighter was showing signs of wear and tear, no
disgrace after more than a decade of active campaigning
against Ike Williams, Ray Robinson, Billy Graham, Johnny
Bratton, Tony Janiro, Tommy Bell, Paddy Young—the best
of the welterweights and middleweights throughout the
forties and early fifties. When your champion begins to have
trouble making the weight and his best is a year or two behind him, you look for the fattest money match over the
weight. So the Kid made a pass at Bobo Olson's middleweight title, which not only produced a pleasant pay night
for Gavilan, Manager Angel Lopez & Co., but postponed
the agony of paring down to 147 from an aging natural
weight of 155. Then, when you can no longer escape the
ordeal, you naturally look for the most money combined
with the easiest opponent who can pass muster as an approved contender.

Bypassing Carmen Basilio, who had been waiting nearly
a year for the rematch he had earned, Angel Lopez, who
does the Gavilan business, made a private deal with Blinky
Palermo whereby Blinky would guarantee Angel forty thou-

sand dollars if the Kid would put his title up for grabs, and with Saxton how else could you describe it? It seemed strange that there should be no provision for a rematch, a customary protection for champions.

I put this down on the raised-eyebrow page of my little black suspicion book. Was it an omen? Was Gavilan so confident of winning that he disdained the usual return-match clause? Or was he getting ready to abandon the welterweight class? The Pennsylvania commission explained that it did not permit a return-match guarantee in a title fight. But after the what-shall-we-call-it, when Gavilan flew into a dressing-room rage and cried robbery, Lopez insisted that there had been a return-match guarantee after all. A secret agreement between him and Blinky. Seems as if there were as many secret agreements surrounding this fight as there were around the Treaty of Versailles. But Commissioner Christenberry cracked his whip for Basilio, somewhat belatedly, and said Saxton would have to meet the free-swinging Syracuse No. 1 boy within ninety days if he wanted to be recognized as champion in New York.

Was Gavilan really jobbed out of his title, as he so tearfully claimed, and was it a Carbo-Palermo double play? Paul John (Frankie) Carbo (not unacquainted with murder and commonly described as the undercover owner of Gavilan and dozens of other high-ranking fighters) had worked with Blinky before. They have been pointed out as the background figures the night Blinky's Billy Fox "knocked out" Jake LaMotta, said to carry the Carbo colors in the grand stakes. Christenberry, in a survey of boxing that will bear rereading, described Blinky as "next to Carbo the most notorious character in the combine." Why did Carbo and Palermo have dinner together at Dempsey's Restaurant a few nights before the Gavilan-Saxton? And what was Paul John, alias Frankie, celebrating in a Philadelphia hotel after the Gavilan-Saxton?

These were some of the inevitable, unanswered questions as the song was ended but the aroma lingered on.

The fight itself was not fixed, in the opinion of this trusting soul. I can't get into the tail-chaser about who won which rounds because after the second I started scoring it with an N for nothin' happened. Saxton is a nothing-happen fighter who has perpetrated this sort of thing throughout his curious career. Two of his Garden fights were thrown out as no contests, although the Minelli mess somehow went into the record books as a KO for Saxton. Like this most recent fight, and the kazatzky before it with Johnny Bratton the only beating was the one inflicted on the spectators.

Gavilan was an aging twenty-eight, weakened from weight making, rusty from a six-month layoff, rarely using his injured right hand and frustrated by a well conditioned and accomplished spoiler. The Cuban was no longer the flashy Keed who fought in theatrical but effective spurts, incredibly hard to hurt and almost always good to watch. In recent years the spurts were shorter, the coasting periods longer. Came a night when the good fighter couldn't fight, especially in there with a stiff who wouldn't fight. Kid couldn't; Johnny wouldn't—that's the story if you only had money enough for a four-word telegram. The fix didn't have to be in. The fates have put the fix in, helped along by the wiles of Mr. Blinky and the Gavilan piecemen when they conspired to match a no-longer-boring-in Kid with an always-boring Saxton.

If Pantaleo had been a real referee instead of what he was, he would have bounced them both out of the ring after eight rounds and advised the abused paying customers to ask for their money back. Gavilan didn't earn his forty Gs and Saxton didn't earn his championship of the world. If it had to be judged as a fight I would have called it for Gavilan because 1) you can have more fun in Havana than you can in Philadelphia and 2) Gavilan has been pretty great and deserves better than to blow his title in a home-town, sleight-of-hand and 3) the Kid came on to win the last round in something like his old style, shaking Saxton up and providing the only real action in the fight. All the rest of the action was handled by the books, who were swamped with Saxton money throughout the day.

I don't know about the other ruling bodies but the Schulberg Boxing Commission, which headquarters in New Hope, Pennsylvania but has no working agreement with Frank Weiner, refuses to recognize Saxton as champion. It saw with its own eyes such welterweight worthies as Jackie Fields, Young Jack Thompson, Young Corbett III, Jimmy McLarnin, Barney Ross, Henry Armstrong, Fritzie Zivic, Ray Robinson—yes, and Kid Gavilan. In deference to these real champions, we declare the title vacant.

The Gavilan-Saxton turkey trot deserves a thorough airing. In fact, it may be time to ask again, as responsible sportswriters have been asking so long, whether boxing is going to be a legitimate sport or a dirty business? Jim Norris, the personable president of the IBC, as an honorable man and a true fight fan should welcome an investigation of the dark underside of boxing. It can destroy the sport as the Black Sox conspiracy might have ruined baseball if an effective commission had not been set up to protect our pastime from its inside jobbers. To say this is not to attack boxing but to attack the boxing racket.

The boxing managers have their guild, the IBC is a powerful network of promoters from New York to San Francisco; even the veteran boxers are getting together. Maybe it's time to launch the Association for the Protection of the Poor Put-Upon Fight Fan. The APPPFF. The middle P's don't stand for Palermo or Pantaleo. Won't stand for them, in fact.

Cheap at Half the Price

This column first appeared in the New York *Herald Tribune*, May 16, 1953. Copyright 1953, New York Herald Tribune Inc.

The column, "Cheap at Half the Price," is a sample of work done in haste under pressure of deadline. For the HERALD TRIBUNE's *first edition in New York, I must have a column in by six* P.M. *After a big fight that doesn't begin until after ten o'clock, I substitute a new column for the late editions. It's a matter of collecting facts and thoughts in the midst of turmoil, putting together nine hundred or a thousand words at top speed in the crowded press rows, trying to offer intelligible if not intelligent comment without duplicating the product of the colleague who is writing the news story. It doesn't make for deathless literature, but it beats working.*

RED SMITH

J. J. Walcott, the odd gentleman from Jersey who has mocked the calendar for something like forty years, made a mockery of the heavyweight championship of the world tonight in two minutes twenty-five seconds. He also made a hooting, disgusted, short-changed gathering in Chicago Stadium understand why there has been so much confusion about his real age. He can't count his years; he can't even count to ten.

Rocky Marciano, making his first defense of the title he won from Walcott last September, threw one respectable punch. It was a right uppercut to the expression, and it knocked Walcott to the floor. There old Joe sat like a darkly brooding Buddha, thinking slow and beautiful thoughts while ten seconds drained away and he made no effort whatever to get up.

That's all there was. Last autumn's wildly wonderful battle, one of the finest, closest, and most exciting of all heavyweight title fights, was replayed as one of the most sordid of all time.

Walcott was guaranteed a quarter of a million dollars for this night's work. If its finish guarantees his departure from boxing, the price was not too great.

After twenty-three recorded years as a professional fist fighter, the former champion went out in a total disgrace that no excuses can relieve. If he was truly knocked out by the only real punch of the bout, then he didn't belong in the ring. If he was not knocked senseless and did hear the count of the referee, Frank Sikora, then it was a disgrace because it was apparent through the last several seconds that he was not going to get up, or even to try. If he did not hear the count, then he was befuddled by Marciano's blow or else his hearing is no better than might be expected at his age, for the toll of seconds was clearly audible in the press rows half the width of the ring away.

In any case, there could be no justification for the complaints which he and his proprietor, Felix Bocchicchio, made to the referee, or the subsequent shouting in their dressing room, where Walcott's lawyer, Angelo Mallandre, declared he would protest to the Illinois State Athletic Commission.

It was unmistakably a count of ten, and Walcott remained

unmistakably on his hunkers throughout, and the Marquis of Queensbury rules unmistakably define this as a knockout.

Walcott compounded his own disgrace by putting up no part of a fight during the brief seconds preceding his sit-down strike. From the opening bell he backed away and grabbed as the champion moved in on him. Once, coming out of a clinch, he brought his right up to Marciano's face; once he dropped a looping punch that landed on the back of Rocky's head, and two or three times he pawed at the champion's celebrated nose with a long, timid jab.

He backed to a point near his own corner, where the ropes were on his right and Marciano's left. Rocky threw a left hook, which some observers thought was blocked, although Walcott said later that it landed. The uppercut followed and Walcott sprawled on his back, rocked to a sitting position, and remained there.

Unfortunately for the reputation of a fine young puncher, Marciano will receive little credit for his successful defense. He was willing and even eager to fight, but it even takes two to tango.

While the customers jeered and cops and ushers cleared the ring of a half-dozen strangers who piled in, presumably in confidence that here was one former heavyweight champion whom they could whip, Walcott departed with only one possession intact. He still had his record of never getting off the floor in eight championship fights.

It had not looked like a killing punch and Walcott did not seem badly hurt. He sat in a kind of round-shouldered hunch, heels wide apart on the canvas, knees bent, the posture of a child playing jacks. By the time the count reached eight, it was clear he would not get up before the toll was completed. He didn't stir until the referee had cried "Nine," and he was not off the floor until well after "Ten."

"I was robbed in New York the first time we boxed Joe

Louis," Mr. Bocchicchio announced with simple dignity in
the dressing room, "but I never saw no robbery like this."
   He could, just possibly, have been thinking of that quarter of a million cold quid.

All Jeff Had Was
His Fists

This article first appeared in *ARGOSY* magazine, December 1954. Copyright, 1954, by Popular Publications, Inc.

James J. Jeffries always has been my favorite athlete. An unwilling hero, a badly misunderstood man, he has been largely forgotten by fight writers, or, when remembered, pictured as a hulking oaf who lacked all the class of a champion. I knew big Jeff fairly well in his latter years and learned he was a very fine humanitarian, a greatly loved individual by the many he helped, as well as a keen commentator on the ills of boxing.

Jeffries was Dempsey without personality, they said. Yet my story, honestly researched, shows that there was a great deal to him. Perhaps he was the most substantial all-around "man," as to character, who ever held the title.

AL STUMP

Honest Martin Dowling's roadhouse on Coney Island—at eight o'clock of a murderously hot June night in 1899. Tonight the baroque appeal of Dowling's is enhanced by a drunk-taken mob of tourists, gamblers, Broadway sports, theatrical big names, whores, fixers and ticket-sharps. They fill the main barroom but don't get past the stairwell, where a husky guard stands watch.

Upstairs is Jim Jeffries, who in a couple of hours and three blocks away at the Seaside Sporting Club will fight Bob Fitzsimmons for the heavyweight championship of the world. Dowling's place is in an uproar.

"Gahdammit!" yells Dowling, a beefy man in a splotched apron. "Gah*damm*it, keep it a little quiet! Jeff is supposed to be resting."

Working his way through the festive scene comes Dick Toner, who is called "the Rat," a former rough-and-tumble brawler now operating a pest-extinguishing service in New York when he isn't advising fighters. Toner is passed by the guard to the second floor. There he hears a sound of lusty snoring behind a closed door.

"He's sleeping?" Toner asks, surprised.

Billy Delaney, a bald midget of a man, manager of James J. Jeffries, is nervous. "He can sleep anywhere, but he'll be sore if I wake him. But, Dick, it's only a little while till fight time."

Including Delaney, who is loyal but slow on the uptake, the closest confidant of the challenger from California is Toner, a fellow with his eye to many fistic peepholes and, quite accurately, the only Easterner whom Jeffries feels he can trust. "I'll get him up," says Toner.

Inside, Jeffries is sprawled naked on the bed. A slight breeze through the open window riffles the thick hair on his shoulders and upper back. He grunts and sits up at Toner's shake—the preacher's son who at only twenty-four has dropped Jim Corbett in a training-camp session, drawn with Gus Ruhlin and Joe Choynski, knocked out Slaughterhouse Hank Baker and beaten Sailor Tom Sharkey. Right away he wants to know, "How are the odds now?"

"Still better than three to one on Fitzsimmons. Jesse Lew-isohn, the financier, just bet twenty thousand dollars on Fitz."

Jeffries says nothing as he gets into his ring tights. He pulls an old brown, store-bought suit over them. He looks like a big, rumpled bear. "I'm glad we got our bet down, Rat," he tells Toner. "Now we'll see."

Earlier that afternoon, at the same odds, Jeffries has sent Toner out to wager five thousand dollars—on Fitzsimmons to keep his world title. He is that unsure of his ability to beat the protective ring thrown around the champion in the East. Word is whispered, in fact, that the fight is rigged for Fitz to win.

Now, in Jeffries' dressing room, Fitzsimmons comes in with Referee George Siler to discuss the matter of breaking from the clinches. Jeff, stretched quietly on the rubbing table, listens a bit while they wrangle, then jumps up and says, "Here, let me show you what I call a clean break."

Suddenly, grabbing Fitz, he clinches. Then with a pow-erful surge, he throws the champion away from him. Fitz sails backward into a wall, his small knob head rattling the plaster. "See what I mean?" Jeff asks innocently.

"You sonofabitch," roars Fitzsimmons, recovering and rushing at Jeffries. Handlers have to haul him from the room.

It is a fight. Not the classic bloodletting described in most boxing history books, not in a class with a Jeffries-Jim Cor-bett match to come later, but still a thing to remember for what it proves. Fitz comes out straight up, slashing with both hands, tigerishly sure he'll win. Jeffries is crouched. The punches bounce off his shoulders and the top of his head. He looks awkward, unsure. Then—thirty seconds be-fore the second round ends—a thick left arm with two hun-dred and ten pounds of weight behind it spears out to split Fitzsimmons' lips and knock him down.

He is up after a one-count. He is hurt, and staggering. Jeffries cocks his right, but holds it, and lets the champion clinch out the round.

"Lordy, Lordy, you had him and let him get away!" wails Bill Delaney in the corner.

In the fifth, Fitzsimmons gets in his best blow, a right to the eye that cuts to the bone. While Jeffries paws at the blood, Fitz throws his crusher, the solar-plexus punch which has won him the title from Corbett, and stands back for the big man to fall. But Jeffries only winces and walks to his corner at the bell.

In the tenth, power tells again. Fitz overswings a right and Jeffries hooks to the heart. Foam spurts from the lips of Fitzsimmons as he goes down. Referee Siler makes a slow-motion count and is even slower getting out of the way when Fitzsimmons gets up at "seven." But he's finished and everybody knows it.

In the eleventh, it is a pitiful sight. Nobody has ever handled the freckled champion, yet now all it takes to set him up is a short left to the chin. Fitz jerks spasmodically. His eyes roll.

James Jackson Jeffries knocks him out and takes the championship by merely reaching out his right and pushing his man over.

All he's had on his side has been his fists.

That was all Jim Jeffries ever needed. The quiet, plodding, inexorable Jeffries won his fights one way and all by himself. As pure fist-slinger, the unbeatable ring animal, he remains after fifty years an object of authentic wonder. Quite possibly he was the greatest heavyweight of all time.

Weighing two hundred twenty pounds, and six feet two at his peak, he broke three of Tom Sharkey's ribs and ruined the Sailor in the most riotous fight ever held. Joe Goddard, the Australian Iron Man, was a hospital case after meeting

Jeffries. Gus Ruhlin, the Akron Giant, threw in the sponge after five knockdowns. Jim Corbett and Fitzsimmons had two tries apiece at the man of concrete, and the record reads: four KOs. He needed only ten professional bouts to reach the title and he held it from 1899 to 1905 through the "Golden Age" of the dreadnought division—an era when all the above, plus Peter Jackson, Joe Jeannette, Sam Langford, Joe Choynski, Jim McVey, Kid McCoy and Peter Maher were in action—and moreover he did it without a defeat or ever being knocked off his feet. The Jeffries record is unique.

When he retired at the age of thirty, the Grizzly Bear was still undefeated champion, a butcher with no more meat on the shelf. There simply was no one left to challenge him.

Yet to his dying day, which came at the age of seventy-seven in 1953, he never was appreciated as were the men he beat. The legend builders passed him by so that he lived out his last years almost publicly forgotten. And they buried old Jeff good and deep for a reason he never denied. He hated being champion.

"I wasn't swell enough for them," he said one day a few years ago. "I couldn't give them a show. Maybe Sullivan and Corbett could do it, but all I ever got out of it was embarrassment. They wanted to put me on exhibition like a prize pig and when they found out that wouldn't go, they tried to swindle me out of the title."

Jeff's expression was unforgiving as he talked. He was no bent, cackling antiquarian, but massive, deep-voiced and keen-memoried right to the end. He had retired, years earlier, to the old Jeffries family home in Burbank, California, and he retired rich. He was the rare ex-champion among the old-line heavyweights who wasn't laid in his grave a pauper. He won more than a half-million dollars fighting and at the reading of the Jeffries' will in 1953 there was more than that in his poke. He owned stocks, bonds, farm acreage and real estate worth eight hundred thousand dollars. The fight game never could turn Jeff into a preening exhibitionist—just as it couldn't defraud him of his gains.

"I may be an old blister now," he'd say comfortably, "but I wound up having the world by the tail. Had fun, son, a lot of fun, *after* I got rid of the title."

The fighter who hated being champion was born in Carroll, Ohio, on April 15, 1875. Old Man Jeffries, the father, was a Methodist preacher turned itinerant revivalist. He had a large, hungry family and was, in a word, improvident. In 1881 he moved west to the pueblo of Los Angeles, settled on a dirt farm of twenty acres, scratched out a bare living and put his four sons to work early.

When he was fifteen, young Jim was swinging a sledge alongside men in the Lacey Boiler Works. At seventeen he held his journeyman boilermaker's card and a little later he hiked fifty miles to get a job in the copper mines at Temecula, California. The miners were slabfisted Croats with a fiendish idea of fun. They stripped all newcomers, made them run a gantlet of swinging pick-handles, then tied them hand-and-foot and dangled the screaming pilgrims over a five-hundred-foot open shaft by a rope.

Young Jeffries ran the gantlet. But at eighteen he weighed one hundred ninety pounds and stood six feet, a boy who had piloted a plow from the time he was eight. He walked back up the line and asked the biggest miner to step out. "I'll wrestle you," he challenged. "The loser gets the rope."

It was a catch-as-catch-can brawl at first that turned into an eye-gouging, groin-kicking contest and then into a fight with fists. It went nearly an hour with only brief rests. In the end, Jim was still standing—the miner was on the ground, a wreck. Temecula suddenly developed a large respect for the kid. And a saloonkeeper-matchmaker named Charley Murray, who had an interest in the mines, had an idea. In

Los Angeles a Negro heavyweight named Hank Griffin had compiled an unbeaten record. "You can make a couple of hundred fighting Griffin," said Murray. "Just leave the arrangements to me."

Murray filled the Los Angeles Athletic Club for the match. With only a few weeks of boxing lessons from Billy Gallagher, a local middleweight, Jeffries was outclassed and, for thirteen rounds, brutally beaten. His nose was broken and one eye closed when he came out for the fourteenth. "Throw in the towel, white boy," taunted Griffin, who was unmarked. "I ain't hit you hard yet."

Carelessly, Griffin extended his jaw. Jeffries struck with his left. It knocked Griffin into the ropes and as he rebounded, young Jim instinctively stuck out his right hand and let Griffin meet it.

They carried Griffin out.

Old Man Jeffries raised so much hell about Jeff's fighting that he only worked in the gym the next three years. But finally, when he was twenty-one, he hooked on as a sparmate for Gallagher. "Shifty Billy" took him to San Francisco, won a purse and left without paying Jeff. Stranded and broke, he spent a week sleeping in poolrooms. Then he drifted into Groom and Ulrich's Bar, which was San Francisco fight headquarters. The talk was that nobody in the vicinity could stand up to Danny Long, a two-hundred-ten-pound cop who held the West Coast heavyweight crown.

"For a square meal," Jeff offered, "I'm willing to go up against Long."

He looked so much like what he was—a simple countryman with a bowl haircut, suit too tight, naïve earnestness sticking out all over him—that Matchmaker Groom broke out laughing. "Why, you rube, Long would kill you."

Jeff persisted. "Well," he said, "they ought to pay to see that."

A few weeks later, Jeff walked out at the bell and took

Long's best punch on the chin. He kept coming, pushing awkward blows to the head. In the second, Jeff centered a left hook on his beard that dropped the cop for the count. As he fell on his face, the burly farmer turned to Groom, popeyed in the first row. "Pay me," he said.

Groom had to hand him seven hundred fifty dollars—the promised winner's end of a one thousand dollar purse—and Jim Jeffries knew then that he would be a fighter. It was so easy it was ridiculous.

Back again in Los Angeles, Jeff met and liked Billy Delaney, who was a good trainer, if no great shakes as a manager. They shook hands on a deal—a fifty-fifty split of everything Jeff could win. Delaney's initial brainstorm was typically ambitious—Jeff would catch on as a sparring partner for the world's champion, Corbett, then preparing to fight Fitzsimmons at Shaw's Springs, Nevada.

"It never crossed Billy's mind—or mine—that I had no business fooling with Corbett," Jeff said years later. "Why I didn't know enough then to get out of the way of my own feet.' '

Out of the ring and in white tie, James J. Corbett could charm the pince-nez off a Nob Hill dowager. At Shaw's Springs, however, he had turned fight-camp nasty—a Corbett habit.

"This is Jeffries, come to give us a hand," introduced Charley White, Corbett's handler. "They say he can hit like a horse."

Corbett looked down his aristocratic nose at the large bumpkin. "No doubt," sneered Corbett. "They made sure of it by sending us the horse."

There would come a time, in 1904, when Gentleman Jim would stand, hat in hand, and ask Jeffries to take *him* on as an employe but now Corbett was enjoying the world's biggest love affair with Corbett, and all sparmates were expected to bow low. Two days later, in the privacy of a walled-in handball court, they squared off. Exactly what happened has many versions. It made sports-page gossip for years. One "eyewitness" wrote that "unknown Jim Jeffries knocked down Corbett with a single blow." Another had the Gentleman kayoed. Before he died, Jeffries revealed the truth.

"Nobody warned me Corbett was mean. I figured he'd just box and take it easy. But the first time I led my right, he smashed in my mouth. It broke a tooth and I went wild. I grabbed him and threw him into the ring corner and when he bounced out I took a swing and knocked him right back again. Sure, he went down. He was hurt plenty. Delaney grabbed me. Charley White began cussing and striking at me. Corbett covered up fast. He laughed and said we'd had enough for the day. I said, 'You damn well have, Corbett!' "

Jeff wasn't kicked out of camp. But after that, he was kept out of Corbett's sight. On St. Patrick's Day of 1897, one month later, when Fitzsimmons removed Corbett's belt at Carson City with a fourteen-round knockout, nobody noticed Jeff, sitting in a bleacher seat.

"That night, riding a train to Oakland, I told Delaney I could whip either of them," Jeff would say. "He said, sure I could, but I'd better see a doctor first. In Nevada I'd been spitting blood."

It was pneumonia. It almost killed him.

On the Coast, Delaney nursed him back to health. Doctor bills wiped out their small savings, and a championship, or anything like it, never seemed farther away until Jeffries met Joe Choynski.

Choynski was then the game's Number One spoiler, not quite a champion, but a veteran of three hundred brawls. The two fought at Woodward's Pavilion on San Francisco Bay on November 30, 1897.

Jeffries went the full twenty rounds. And he scored the

only knockdown, finished the strongest, and Referee Eddie Graney called it a draw.

Jeff always believed he learned to fight that night. Choynski taught him not to move as a stand-up target. He developed the "Jeffries crouch"—it became a national fad—with left arm extended like a swinging beam, head tucked in, belly covered. It was the best offense-defense the heavyweight division knew. Soon afterward, it was to earn him a bout with the famed Sailor Tom Sharkey. He won in twenty rounds. He knocked out Peter Jackson, Joe Goddard, Van Buskirk and Hank Baker. And, with Fitzsimmons ducking a Corbett rematch, it took him East in 1899 to the fight on Coney Island when he broke eastern gamblers and became champion.

After all that, you'd have thought that Jim Jeffries would have enjoyed his title. But the championship was ashes in his mouth.

The trouble was, Jeff only could fight. Fans could adore Sullivan for his drinking and boasting, admire Corbett's elegance, become outraged at Jack Johnson's affairs with white women. Beside them Jeffries was a clod.

Many attempts were made to build him up. In 1901 William A. Brady, the "Ziegfield of boxing," put him in a stage play, *The Man from the West*, designed to remove the onus. The play flopped. It had to be withdrawn when audiences booed the champion.

At one time Jeffries threw it all over. He disappeared into the wilds of Arizona, lived with Indians for a time and hunted and fished, the hobbies he liked best. He was brought back by Brady for a London tour. At the Royal Aquarium, he met all comers, with one hundred fifty dollars offered to any Britisher who could stay four rounds. Jeff knocked out two dozen men so fast that the box office dried up. No show, no fans.

Brady, desperate, brought forth a two-hundred-fifty-pounder called the Welsh Terror, building up the match so flamboyantly that King Edward and party announced they would attend. "Carry this big stiff, Jim, and let him win the purse," said Brady. "We'll be in with the Limeys then for a rematch."

"Nix to you," said Jeffries, his favorite expression. He belted the Welsh Terror once and they picked him out of the ringside seats.

The real Jeffries character never was revealed in his fighting time. He was a man of deep conscience. When San Francisco was leveled by the 1906 quake, he drove a buggy along Hill and Fifth Streets in Los Angeles each night, selling newspapers at a dollar a copy. Then he rode a relief train to the Bay with food, clothes and medical supplies. He worked for a month in the missions with the injured. He was big-hearted in all things. Frank Gotch, the wrestler, fell ill. Jeff paid his bills, then organized a touring Jeffries-Gotch Athletic Show which netted thirty thousand dollars for Gotch.

In 1903, Jeff heard that Bob Fitzsimmons had tried suicide. Fitz had lost everything after a second Jeffries match. He sent for Fitz.

"Tell me straight," said Jeffries. "Did you have something on the wraps in San Francisco?"

In a rematch a year earlier, Fitzsimmons for seven rounds had sliced Jeffries' face to ribbons. He almost blinded the big man in one eye. In the eighth round, Jeffries hooked a left to the liver. Fitzsimmons fell, paralyzed. When he got up, counted out, he threw his gloves and his bandages to the crowd, crying, "That does it! I'll never fight again!" Jeffries never did get to see what was on those bandages—he always suspected they had been treated.

Now, embarrassed, Fitz admitted that his corner man, George Dawson, had soaked the wraps in collodion. Dried out, they were like rocks.

"All right," said Jeffries, "that is that." He never alluded to it again and put Fitzsimmons to work as his sparmate on a ten-thousand-dollar guarantee; he was still helping out the broken old battler until Fitzsimmons' death in 1917.

That was another one of Jeff's handicaps. He was too gentle a human being and, in the ring, he never really developed the "killer" instinct. The flaw, if that is what you want to call it, first came to light in Jeffries' fight with Peter Jackson.

The clever Australian remains one of the all-time glove fighters, but against Jeff in 1898 he was slowed by age. In the third round, a short left draped him, half-unconscious, on the ropes. Only vast pride kept the old campaigner hanging there, feet limp on the canvas.

Jeff stepped back, dropping his hands. "Hit him again!" screamed Billy Delaney, his shrewd, bald-headed trainer.

The referee gestured coldly. "He ain't on the floor."

Jeffries couldn't do it. He lifted Peter Jackson off the ropes and stretched him on the canvas.

"Now count him out," he growled at the official, "and be fast about it."

The two fights Jeffries is best remembered for came against Tom Sharkey and Jim Corbett. In his first title defense, he met Sharkey at Coney Island.

Entering the ring, they found a bank of four hundred arc lights overhead to illuminate the first motion pictures of an indoor heavyweight title bout. Jeffries had a thick thatch of black hair. So scorching was the heat that both men lost almost all their hair in the following months.

At the bell, Sharkey ran out and swung an uppercut that caught Jeffries flush on the chin. It rocked him to his heels. In the second round, a Jeffries blast lifted Sharkey into midair and spread him on the mat. He came back without a count. The fight went that way for twenty-five rounds of toe-to-toe slugging. Neither would retreat. Jeffries cracked an elbow and bled from a dozen face gashes. Sharkey's forehead split open; one ear was torn loose and flopped down. In the seventeenth, the Sailor straightened the champ with an uppercut and then struck a hard, a perfectly timed left hook to the jib. "Now fall, damn you!" howled Sharkey.

Jeffries shook his head. His next punch broke three of Sharkey's ribs. The next instant, the crippled Sharkey was swarming over his man, rocking Jeff with the assault of a madman.

"I was sure one of us would be killed, it was that kind of a brannigan . . . the worst I ever was in," testified Jeff. "No braver man than Sharkey ever lived."

They were still standing, throwing leather, at the end. The decision, by a wide margin, went to Jeffries. Sharkey went to the hospital, a physical wreck. Police held Jeff for two days until it was clear that his victim wouldn't die. But the beating finished Sharkey. He was forced to retire not long after.

The crafty Jim Corbett now made a move to get back his crown. He was thirty-five, but months of secret training had brought him to perfect fighting trim. "You don't dare put him in with a real boxer," Corbett taunted the Jeffries crowd. "All he's done is lick sluggers."

There was a tendency for his advisers to hedge, but Jeff had been hungry for Corbett ever since the incident at Shaw's Springs. "Anyway, a champion should never draw the line," he said simply.

As Corbett expected, the match developed into a repetition of his John L. Sullivan pigsticking. By the twenty-second round, the dancing, swooping Gentleman was far ahead on points. Jeff's face was an open wound. One eye was sealed shut. The most skillful boxer of them all had slipped every punch but one. A mistake in the nineteenth round cost him a knockdown, but Corbett was unhurt, and his fists were shooting out like twin rapiers.

"He's making you play his game!" groaned Bill Brady between rounds. "You've got to cut out boxing and wade in there and smack him."

Jim Jeffries had a distinct memory of the fateful twenty-third. "There was a thunderstorm going on outside, rattling the building. Still, it was nothing to what Corbett was doing to me. Right after the bell, that devil slid in, jabbed my bad eye and started to throw his right. That was all I needed. I hit him two punches in one—something I never see these modern pugs do. First I clipped him with the straight left. Then I turned my hand and put my weight behind a left hook that traveled maybe four inches."

Corbett buckled at the waist and sprawled on his face— stone-cold.

For the next five years, Jeffries terrorized the division in a manner that not even Dempsey and the young Louis approached. In January 1905, he quit to take up the peaceful life of a California rancher and businessman. In more than sixty fights he had never known defeat. At thirty, there was nothing left for him to do.

Too bad the story doesn't end there. The final chapter is well-known as one of the ring's starkest tragedies. Retired, Jeff grew fat and lazy on his Burbank acres. He opened a Los Angeles bar and grill, ate and drank what he wanted, fished and hunted and by 1909 weighed nearly three hundred pounds. Meanwhile, the country was crying for a "white hope" to unhorse Jack Johnson, the most unpopular titleholder of all time. Johnson had won the title from Tommy Burns after Jeff's abdication. "Little Artha's" loose moral code shortly had the U.S. public in an uproar.

For a long time Jeff laughed off the pleas that he make a comeback. But in five years the pressure was tremendous. "They kept at me until I was half crazy," he related. "Even in the churches they were sermonizing that I was a skunk for not defending the white race's honor."

On July 4, 1910, six years after his last real fight, undertrained and short of wind, Jeff reluctantly entered the ring against Johnson in Reno. He was thirty-five; Johnson, twenty-six. Jeff's brother, John, broke down and wept when his efforts to get Tex Rickard to call off the affair failed. There was no question in the Jeffries camp that it was a suicidal mission. Two days before the fight, a dysentery attack left Jeff pale and weak.

Even then, it took Johnson fifteen rounds to put Jeffries off his feet, for the first time in his life. He got up at nine. He went down again, a giant shorn of his power, got up and stumbled forward. Then it was over, with Jeff's seconds leaping into the ring and leading him away.

"That's my only regret," he looked back four decades. "That wasn't Jeff in there with Johnson. Just a fat man making a big fool of himself."

Tex Rickard paid Jeff $192,000, his biggest purse, for the humiliation. He went back to Burbank and the shadows drew around him. Shortly after he had won the title from Fitzsimmons, Jeff married his Frieda and they remained devoted for thirty-seven years. His family life was rich and full, yet it was easy to see an unrest in him. The fight *game* he frankly despised—*fighting* he loved. He opened "Jeffries Barn," a free center where any young athlete with ambition could come and learn from the master. He developed numerous good amateurs because, as Jeff said, "The amateur fighter is the real thing—he doesn't do it just for the money." On the side, Jeff anonymously gave to many charities.

In 1941 Frieda was killed by an auto while crossing a street in Los Angeles and Jeff never stopped grieving. After that he ventured outside just once. In 1944, Dan Tobey, the announcer, organized an Army-camp tour by fight greats.

When Jim Jeffries was introduced, soldier fans had to be told who he was.

His grave is on a sunny slope, beside Frieda Jeffries, in Inglewood Park Cemetery, Inglewood, California.

Mother of a Champion

This article first appeared in HARPER'S magazine, February 1929, and is reprinted by permission of John R. Tunis.

Running back over the past few years I discover I have been described in print as an "agitator," a "bellyacher," a "grouch," a "liar," and a "serpent," besides being characterized as "wrong-headed," "tiresome," "petulant," "insincere," "jaundiced," "violent," "venomous," and "cowardly." Among other sins, it appears I "have had a run-in with officials of the Polo Association," and that I "have forfeited the respect of all honorable sportsmen."

This article was the cause of some of this applause. Although F. P. A. in his column in the old New York World *termed it "the best sports story since R. Lardner's 'Champion,'" others were less flattering. One critic called the article "a sensational, spiteful and thoroughly unwarranted attack which the writer had neither the courage nor the factual material to make in the open like a man." However, the last word went to an editorial commentator in the San Diego* Union, *who remarked:*

"The conservatives who are outraged by this article can be consoled by the realization that it is good for them."

I selected "Mother of a Champion" because it depicts a phase of American life as prevalent today as it was when the piece was written years ago. It came from watching big-time sport, and the boys and girls who make it up. The champion is just about every American feminine titleholder of the past thirty years. In the United States, being a good loser is not as important as being a winner, for in sport as in war, America is only interested in victory.

JOHN R. TUNIS

She sat before a most inadequate mirror in the dressing room, an unsophisticated girl of twenty-one preparing to take her part in the great drama that was soon to begin outside. In the corner of the room sat her mother buried in a wicker armchair covered with faded cretonne, murmuring nothings—affectionate and anxious nothings; but nothings, nevertheless—to which her daughter paid no attention. The business of appearing before the public as a world-famous athlete is a serious business, not to be undertaken lightly or indiscreetly.

From the array of bottles, tubes, and glass jars with glass stoppers on the narrow table she took cold cream out of a square receptacle marked "Cleansing" and spread it carefully over her face. With the aid of a towel she rubbed it off with careful, adept movements. Then she took another kind of cream from another jar labeled "Tissue," massaging it in with practiced fingers. Next she seized a bottle bearing the magic word "Astringent" on a paper label, and dashed the pinkish fluid all over her countenance. Finally came the really important part of her makeup. For just a second she glanced bewilderingly over the regiment of bottles and jars which lined the table, and with a quick gesture selected one bearing the entrancing name "Florentine Lemon Skin Food." The skin food made from the lemons of Florence she delicately smoothed in a thin layer about her cheeks and chin; next from a square box of "Florentine Flower Powder, Span-

ish Rachel Shade" she suffused her tortured face in flesh-
colored chalk. A careful and scientific application of lipstick,
a longish session with a pencil along the eyebrows; at last
she was ready. No more, it is true, so unsophisticated-look-
ing at close view. But, after all, what of that?

Her mother, meanwhile, had been growing impatient.

"They're waiting for you out there, Florence . . . hadn't
you better hurry? . . . Goodness sakes, you didn't use to take
so much trouble with all those powders and things when you
first started . . . I remember back in twenty-two . . ."

"Oh, cut out that Civil War stuff, mother. You make me
tired with your everlasting . . ."

A knock at the door interrupted the conversation. "Are
you ready, Miss Farley? Your opponent's waiting for you."

"All ready," sang out the Champion in the tone which
made the newspapers describe her as "Happy Florence Farley, the Girl with the Laughing Voice."

"Com*ming*, com*ming*. Come along, mother dear." And she
emerged from the dressing room with her arm about her
mother's waist. Inseparable, those two!

In the narrow hallway outside they were soon parted by
the crowd that pressed and eddied about them. Schoolgirl
autograph collectors demanded the champion's signature,
not realizing that champions never signed albums before a
match. After a match, yes, before a match, never! More than
one title had been lost through writer's cramp. It was just
this attention to detail which had brought Florence Farley
to the position she now occupied.

Someone seized her arm; an invitation for the weekend
was bellowed through the din and confusion.

"To Southampton? Oooohh, how lovely. I'd just adore to
come. But, really, I hardly know. You'll have to ask Mother;
you see, she just won't let me go anywhere without her."

A burst of applause rippled through the crowd as she
stepped outside the door of the clubhouse. The photogra-

phers hurried to their points of vantage, the officials came eagerly forward to greet her, the crowd indicated its approval. The Champion was going into action to defend her title.

Throughout Florence Farley's career her mother has consistently remained in the background; the general public who follow sports is, as a rule, unaware of her existence. But if any one person can be said to be responsible for the astounding success of Florence Farley in the world of amateur games, certainly Mrs. Farley should have most of the credit.

Plainville, New York, is an hour and six minutes from the Grand Central Station. It has two banks, a country club, and a population of commuters who take the eight-one to town every morning and return by the five-ten every evening. They are met at the station by their wives, plump ladies dressed in unbecoming but fashionable hats who drive three-thousand-dollar sedans on which the husbands spend their lives trying to earn the monthly installments. When Jim Farley moved out to Plainville in order that six-year-old Florence could have a yard to run in and air to breathe, he was lucky to have enough money left, after paying the first installment on the purchase price and the interest six months in advance on the first and second mortgages, to be able to buy a second-hand Ford. If you knew Plainville you would realize that people who drive second-hand Fords are hardly likely to be adopted by the social leaders of the town.

Not that Jim Farley cared. But his wife cared very much indeed. It hurt her that Jim was in the cotton-goods business and prospering indifferently, while the husbands of the ladies who drove the three-thousand-dollar sedans were in radio or real estate or stock and bonds or something that was prospering. It hurt most of all that she and Jim never were asked to join the Country Club. To be sure they had no money to join the Country Club, they did not desire to join the Country Club; yet the fact that they were unasked was difficult to swallow. In Plainville either you belonged to the Country Club or you did not. The Farleys did not.

Curiously enough it was Florence who was to solve this problem for her worried mother; it was Florence who was the first of the Farleys to establish herself at the Club. At the age of eleven this long-legged child was such a capable little sportswoman that she was continually being asked to go up on the hill to play with the Patterson children or the Davis girls, all older but by no means her equal. From taking on and defeating the Pattersons and the Davises, it was but a step to being asked to engage some older players. At last one sunny afternoon in midsummer Mrs. Farley was officially invited up to see Florence play with Mrs. Jenkins, a player at one time of national repute. Knowing nothing at all of games or sport, Mrs. Farley sat upon the porch of the clubhouse a silent and aloof figure, until the moment when her offspring came up the path to the steps, her face red but her manner triumphant, her pigtails damp with perspiration, but her bearing that of a conqueror. Behind her labored the clumsy Mrs. Jenkins, tired, panting, exhausted; Mrs. Jenkins who never knew Mrs. Farley when the latter's Ford was parked behind her new magnificent limousine each night for the five-ten. That particular afternoon, however, she was unusually cordial.

"Give that child of yours time, Mrs. Farley, and she'll be a great player some day. I know what I'm telling you, too."

Mrs. Farley smiled serenely and put her arm around Florence's moist back. In her victorious daughter she was beginning to see an opening to the Country Club and to Plainville society.

At the end of several years Florence Farley was a name to conjure with in Plainville; if you could defeat the Farley child your ability needed no further discussion. You were immediately put down as a very useful player. In fact, so well known did Florence become about town that it was practically necessary, as Mrs. Farley explained to Jim one night, for them to have a new car, and a closed one at that. When Jim mumbled that he couldn't afford to while cotton was selling so low it wasn't worth picking off the bushes, his wife reminded him that for Florence's sake they couldn't afford not to. This settled the argument.

It was fortunate that they did have that closed car when the Pattersons suggested that they all go over to Jamestown where Lucile Patterson and Florence could play in the junior tournament being held for the first time at the Jamestown Country Club. After much planning and consulting, the eight-mile trip across country was undertaken. Lucile was put out of the play by eleven o'clock in the morning. Mrs. Patterson remembered a luncheon engagement and hurried away shortly afterward, leaving her daughter to return with Mrs. Farley and Florence and the Cup at seven-ten. By the time they got home the news had spread all about Plainville; Jim Farley, who had to walk home from the station, heard it the moment he stepped off the train. Three people called out to him the good news as he walked up Pleasant Street; in fact, the whole town was aware of the feat of his child. He had supper waiting for them when they returned, tired but happy.

"A damned good performance for the kid," he said, as he kissed her with delight. "Good child."

Nor was Mrs. Farley any less pleased than her husband. But had they known that their troubles were starting, they might have been more sober in their happiness. Two weeks later Mr. George P. Clements, the president of the Club, called upon the Farleys one evening to extend his congratulations. In the course of the conversation he also exposed plans under way for adventures in more distant fields.

"We were thinking, that is, a number of us were thinking,

of sending Florence down to compete in the National Junior
Championships at Hot Springs next summer."

"Ooohh," interjaculated Florence impulsively. "Ooohh,
Mother, wouldn't that be wonderful?" To her Hot Springs
was as far away as Russia. Or Fairyland. But she stopped
short when she observed the distress upon her parent's usually placid countenance.

"I'm sorry, Mr. Clements, but who could go down with
her? Of course, the trip would be dandy, and I'd just love
for her to go, but I couldn't think of letting her go that far
with just a lot of girls."

"Certainly not, Mrs. Farley, certainly not. We intend to
have you both go."

Then Mrs. Farley *was* shocked. "Why, Mr. Clements!
Both of us! It would last a week. That would cost, that
would cost . . . why a hundred dollars!"

The President of the Country Club was unmoved. Quietly
he agreed that it would.

"Yes, yes, p'raps. But you see it's this way, Mrs. Farley.
They's a number of us prominent men about town been
watching your little girl now for some time. We've all of us
noticed the progress she's made and we're anxious to encourage it. Wanna encourage sport among the youngsters.
Fine thing, athletics. Teaches 'em to be, you know, manly,
fair play, all that sort of thing. And then besides"—here he
leaned slightly toward Jim Farley as though a mere woman
could hardly understand the details of business—"And then,
besides, it's mighty good properganda for the town, mighty
good properganda to have a little girl like Florence get her
name in the papers occasionally. Why, they's any number of
folks never heard of Plainville until she won that title the
other day over to Jamestown. I understand the week after
that we got a lot of inquiries for the new real estate development back of Johnson's woods; hadn't had any prospects for
that property for two years. Now Mr. Simmonds, the presi-

dent of the Trust Company, you know he's influential in the
Chamber of Commerce too, well, he thinks he, that is we, I
mean they could find ways and means to get you and Florence down to Hot Springs without it costing you or Mr. Farley one red cent. Not one cent. Do you see?" And he paused
for a moment to allow the combined munificence of the
Chamber of Commerce and the President of the Trust Company to take effect. It took effect immediately.

. Mrs. Farley saw. She saw for the moment even more than
Mr. Clements did. And the sight dazzled her somewhat. Mr.
Clements, thinking that she was dazzled only by the pros-
pect of a trip to Hot Springs, pressed home the argument.

"And a first-rate vacation, too, Mrs. Farley. Not but what
I'm sure our little girl here wouldn't bring us back some
more glory, heh, heh, heh. . . ."

The little girl was not so sure as he was. But a trip to Hot
Springs! . . . They went next summer as planned.

It was at Hot Springs during the Junior Championships
that they first met Duncan Fletcher, the Vice-President of
the Eastern Association, and a power in sport. Duncan
Fletcher was a suave young man with a million dollars from
his father, and clothes and manners from a New York tailor.
His one ambition in school and college had been to become
a champion; early in his career it became evident that he
had neither the persistence nor the patience; accordingly
he gave up this desire and decided that, if he could not be a
champion, at least he would be the friend of champions. His
eye was fixed ultimately upon the presidency of the National
Association; little by little he had climbed from being a
mere delegate from his own club to being a sectional delegate, then a director, and finally one of the two vice-presi-
dents of the Eastern Association. His next step was a minor
office in the National Association; he was a hand-shaker par
excellence, knew everyone, made himself known to everyone; and under the circumstances it was not surprising that

he happened to bump into Florence and her mother the
morning after they arrived. What surprised them, and also
flattered them slightly, was the fact that he knew all their
history.

Ten minutes of conversation with Mrs. Farley convinced
Duncan Fletcher that he was in luck. They had arrived in
the rain the previous night without hotel accommodations,
their reservations having been carelessly made in the name
of Mrs. Hurley. Players were all accommodated ("special
rate to players and their families at the Alhambra during the
tournament," page 8, circular of the championships) in the
Annex. The Annex was directly over the kitchen; sleep was
impossible there after five A.M. No one had spoken to them,
practice was difficult to obtain, a cold west wind was blowing and, in short, Mrs. Farley was ready to return home. In
fact, a time-table with trains marked was in her hand when
Duncan Fletcher addressed them. During those next few
moments of crisis the Vice-President of the Eastern Association was at his best; he displayed that marvelous executive
ability which was to win him such a prominent place in the
world of sport. A quarter of an hour later he had secured a
suite for them in the main building at no extra cost, obtained tape and bound up Florence's blistered hand with
care and skill, seen that they had a good table in the dining
room, and installed a dozen roses in their sitting room.
Naturally, mother and daughter were charmed by his attention and a flattery not too obtuse.

The championship lasted six days, during which Duncan
Fletcher was an ever-present help in time of trouble. On the
last afternoon, the afternoon of the finals, when Florence returned to the clubhouse with her National Junior Championship, flushed, happy, triumphant, she was presented
with a bouquet of roses, tied in satin ribbon, more roses than
she could carry. The runner-up who was badly beaten, was
also presented with an enormous bunch which she laid

aside, remarking, "I'd have preferred a better score and fewer flowers."

Luckily the Vice-President of the Eastern Association did not hear this catty remark. He was at the moment telling Florence's mother that he knew from the start that the child had it in her. This was the exact truth. Nor was his delight in her victory in the least disingenuous, his enthusiasm one bit forced. Mr. Duncan Fletcher knew a good thing when he saw one.

Some eight months later Plainville was honored by a visit from the Vice-President of the Eastern Association. This visit, which took place in the living room of the Farley home, was attended by Mr. Farley (reduced to silence and marveling at his wife's wonderful ability to get things for Florence without paying for them), that good lady, and Florence herself, just a bit dazed at the prospect unfolding itself before her. Naturally, Mr. Clements as the President of Florence's home club was also present, rubbing his hands in delight and importance. Ever since her picture had appeared in the Sunday Rotogravure Section as, "Suburban Miss Who Wins Title, Happy Florence Farley of Plainville, N. Y., at Hot Springs," Mr. Clements had had the Chamber of Commerce behind him to a man.

Mr. Fletcher, however, saw visions of the future in fresh woods and pastures new. He imagined himself, without too much effort, described as the "man who discovered Florence Farley." In fact, immediately after her victory in the Junior Championships Mr. Fletcher explained to all the newspaper men who came to his dinner—"just a small, informal affair, boys"—that he had found her in a country town outside New York and, recognizing her ability at once with his keen tactical eye, had sent her down to Hot Springs on his own initiative. He has told this story so often now and it has been

printed so much that he believes it himself. So does everyone else, including Mrs. Farley and Florence.

"Well, Mrs. Farley, of course you know best; but it seems
to me that in a way you really owe it to Florence to give up
this next summer to her and let her play in the National
Championships. Frankly, I don't think I've ever seen such a
promising youngster, not since Miss Benton at any rate. If
she does well this summer I'm almost sure, in fact, I can almost guarantee that she will be sent abroad next year by the
Association."

Mrs. Farley's mind was dancing, dancing, but her face
was calm and undisturbed. "Well, I hardly know whether
we could arrange to devote a whole summer to it, practicing
and so forth. And then there's Florence's singing. She has
made so much progress in the past six months I sort of hate
to interrupt all that. And Mr. Farley's vacation, he likes to
have us go to the camp with him; don't you, Jim?"

Mr. Farley gulped, swallowed hard as the eyes of the
room were upon him, some almost resentfully it seemed,
and nodded. He could not speak.

"Why, Jim Farley would be the proudest man in this
whole country if his little girl was to win the national title,
wouldn't you, Jim?" interposed Mr. Clements in an over-
powering voice. "As for the singing, she can study while
she's abroad next summer. Certainly, study mornings,
y'know. A few weeks under Lebaudy or Obendorfer is
worth ten years from some hack over this side." Mr. Fletcher
voiced his opinions about musical education with conviction. "Honestly, Mrs. Farley, if you don't take advantage of
this opportunity you'll regret it all your life."

Mrs. Farley was impressed; but she was not a lady to take
steps without being sure of things. Accordingly she remarked
tentatively, "But so much money, Mr. Fletcher, all this time
practicing, and then going way out there to Omaha for the
National Championships—"

"Not a word about money," said Mr. Fletcher with the air
of a person who is waving aside a subject slightly obscene.
"Not a word. You see the Eastern Association has a special
fund for just such purposes. We send you and Florence west
about a month before the tournament begins, to get accli-
mated, and then on the way you'll stop off at one or two invitation affairs, select affairs in the bigger places. You'll meet
some mighty nice people, Mrs. Farley, just the best kind of
people in Chicago and St. Louis."

So Mrs. Farley and Florence went west. Of all their campaigns they still look on this as the happiest; for the little
girl in pigtails found everything so new and strange, found
everyone so cordial and hospitable, found conditions for
playing so perfect that she enjoyed herself enormously, more
in fact than she was ever to enjoy herself in the future when
the duties and responsibilities of being a champion were always with her. Her game also progressed; she suffered one
or two defeats at the hands of local players in minor tournaments, just enough to make her work hard at strengthening
her weak points. She practiced assiduously, asked advice
from older players, and by the time the Championships
rolled around was playing better than she had ever played
in her life.

Now her mother had a task to restrain that eager, impetu-
ous child. Her duty it was to see that Florence played
enough and not too much, that she ate the proper food, that
she went to bed early and got up early, that she took every
morning the exercises the doctor had prescribed for those
recalcitrant muscles, in short, that she lived the life which
would mean victory. Each day for weeks before the tournament Mrs. Farley walked over to the club with Florence, sat
there when she was practicing, took her back to the hotel,
first making sure that she was well wrapped up against a
possible cold. And gradually, little though she knew about
sports, Mrs. Farley began to note the improvement in her

daughter's game. Little by little it was borne in upon her
that this child of hers had the makings of a champion. Perhaps, after all, Florence had best give up the idea of a singing career. Was she not destined for greater things?

Meanwhile Mr. Duncan Fletcher had not neglected to
keep the press informed of the progress of "My little proté-
gée," as he used to call Florence on every possible occasion.
But even the newspapermen were unprepared for her suc-
cesses in that tournament. She went through the first three
days with ease, defeated her opponents without difficulty,
and on the next to last day put out a former national titleholder. Mrs. Wing, it was true, was no longer in the top
class; she was still good enough to make trouble for most
players. That afternoon lived long in Mrs. Farley's memory;
the crowd deserting the other contestants to watch her pic-
turesque child in pigtails, the murmurs and rumors and reports flying about the clubhouse, the whisper from someone
behind her that Mrs. Wing had just been badly beaten by
"that infant from New York." And the afternoon lived with
her for another reason.

He caught her while she was waiting for Florence to dress
after the match. Yes, she was Mrs. Farley. His card said he
was Mr. Raymond K. Noble, Western Manager for the *Daily
Mail* Syndicate. He had been ordered by his New York office to see Mrs. Farley because the manager in the main
office saw in Florence a future national champion. Would
she care to write for the *Daily Mail* Syndicate?

Mrs. Farley was shocked. Florence write? She couldn't
spell c-a-t; composition was her weakest subject. And her
writing was terrible, just simply terrible. Now if Mr. Noble
had asked her to sing. . . . That gentleman smiled ever so
slightly, and explained that his company was not interested
in singers. He also explained that in most editorial offices
there were trained reporters who did much of the actual

writing and could send proofs to Florence "for correction."
He also explained that he did not himself believe that Florence was well known enough to the sporting public to begin
writing immediately; but that next year if she won the title
it was possible that the *Daily Mail* might find room for her
in its pages. With great delicacy he offered Mrs. Farley a
check for five hundred dollars, and explained that to save
her trouble personally he had drawn up a contract which
she need merely sign as Florence's guardian. Mrs. Farley
took the contract and looked at it a minute. Two years before she would have signed anything on Florence's behalf
for fifty dollars. But she had been learning things. She was
not entirely unprepared for this. As it was, she replied that
she would be glad to take the contract back to her hotel,
study it, and let him know her wishes in the matter. For in
the background she had a vision of the astute Mr. Fletcher
coming to her aid.

Inside of the hour Mr. Fletcher was actually reading the
contract in her bedroom in the hotel. What a splendid fellow! What a help he was, so able and competent! With a superb gesture he read it, tore it in two, and tossed it to the
floor. Mrs. Farley was impressed as he intended, and thanked
herself more than ever that she had been cautious. Could
Florence write and still maintain her amateur standing? Oh,
yes, yes indeed. But that contract? Never! Sign no contract
which tied one up at a salary of only three thousand a year
for five years. That was Mr. Fletcher's advice. He explained
that the manager was correct in asserting that most athletic
stars had help and assistance in their literary endeavors. He
departed, assuring Mrs. Farley that other contracts would
not be long in presenting themselves. Mrs. Farley was learning rapidly. When Florence the next afternoon went brilliantly down to defeat before the best woman player in the
country, she learned more things.

Three gentlemen from other syndicates were waiting for

her at her hotel when she returned, while Mr. Noble was there with yet another and a more generous contract. Mrs. Farley took them all, as well as the cards of their representatives, and retired to her room, saying nothing. On her table was a wire from her husband:

"COMPANY IN FINANCIAL DIFFICULTIES LOST JOB BETTER RETURN IMMEDIATELY—JIM."

Mrs. Farley sat looking out the window while Florence dressed for her first dance, the championship ball at the clubhouse for which as a special favor she was to be allowed to wear her hair up. Carefully the mother spread those four contracts out on the table, carefully she studied them, a look in her eyes that the wives of the commuters in Plainville would never have recognized. Then she slowly took the receiver off the hook. From the bathroom Florence heard her mother's voice, vaguely realizing that it was not the voice of her mother at all.

"Central, 8900 . . . Mr. Townsend, please . . . Mr. Townsend? This is Mrs. Farley; yes, Florence Farley's mother. Mr. Townsend, we expect to leave for home tomorrow at noon. I wonder if you could come round to the hotel for a few minutes before we leave and see me? At ten? That's fine. Ten o'clock. Good-by, Mr. Townsend."

Florence Farley's hair was up on her head when they went south for the National Championships that next summer; but her mother was still the person to be consulted whenever a decision was required.

"My pictures for your magazine? Oooohh, I don't know; you'll have to ask Mother. A dance at the club next week? I'd just adore to go; but I'd better speak about it to Mother first, she rarely lets me go out when I'm in training, you know. The contract for next season? Oooohh, Mr. Townsend, that's entirely up to Mother." Where she played before the

Championships, what homes they would or would not live
at (for wherever the Farleys went now they were honored
and welcome guests)—everything was for her mother to decide. Incidentally, it was Mrs. Farley's idea, when she read
about the benefit concert to be given, that Florence should
put on her best hat and interview the manager. Florence
was surprised at the warmth of the reception she received.
Mrs. Farley was not surprised.

It was her first appearance in public. Florence's voice was
young, fresh, powerful, if unequal and untrained. But the
songs she sang were wisely chosen; they were not beyond
her range, and she had the natural self-possession of one
who had long appeared as a performer before crowds.
Moreover, she was young, pretty, attractive. For weeks before the concert she was advertised and bill-boarded; the
concert hall was jammed with an audience that came out of
curiosity. Of ten newspapers which commented upon the
concert the next morning, nine spoke of Miss Florence Farley, and all used the word "versatile" at least once.

Mrs. Farley had by this time acquired no small share of
business acumen. It was necessary inasmuch as her husband
possessed none whatsoever. Jim Farley was looking for his
third job while his wife and daughter were visiting in Newport or Palm Beach, meeting titled Europeans and the stock-
market nobility of the United States with poise and dis-
crimination. This sort of thing was all very well; but Mrs.
James Farley had her eye on a greater goal. When Florence
went to college that fall she took singing lessons four days
a week with the best instructor the neighboring city provided.

All this was a drain on the Farley family resources. Perhaps one should say upon the family's resources upon the
female side. But the Dean was so helpful; having in some
strange manner heard of Florence's athletic and artistic
record, he succeeded in procuring for her a four-year schol-

arship devoted to "needy and deserving students of the
Baptist faith." Mrs. Farley herself was a Methodist, but
luckily she had no religious intolerance whatsoever. And it
was nice to have Florence in a college where she could get
singing lessons all winter; the way in which that girl neglected her voice culture in summer was really awful!

It was during her freshman year that the question of Wimbledon arose. Mr. Fletcher, now the President of the National Association, telephoned Mrs. Farley that Florence
was expected to sail with the rest of the team in June, a
week before her final examinations. This meant losing the
credit for her whole year's work. Even Mrs. Farley, who
could hardly be said to be indifferent to the many advantages, educational and otherwise, promised by a trip to
Europe, was aghast at the thought of a season in school gone
for nothing. Accordingly she took the next train to consult
the Dean. Once again she found him more than kind—such
a nice man, a real nice man, as she told Jim on her return.
Jim, who was now looking for his fifth job and was getting
to be known as "Florence Farley's father," grunted when he
heard that familiar phrase.

"H'm, why yes, Mrs. Farley," said the Dean in his private
office, "yes, I think we can arrange that difficulty. Here in
the University we have what are called travel credits, credits
granted when a student wishes to spend time doing research
work at the Sorbonne and Oxford or Cambridge. Now of
course, this isn't exactly what Miss Farley is going over for;
but I have no doubt in view of the favorable publicity that
will accrue, and considering the help her name will be to
our new Endowment Drive for the University, that it can be
arranged satisfactorily."

And so it was. The day before they sailed Mrs. Farley interviewed Mr. Townsend. Plans had already been made for
the London correspondent of the *Mail* syndicate to "assist"
Florence while she was in Europe; every day during the

two-months' period a story was to be wired back to New York. For this work Mrs. Farley naturally felt that her daughter should have more than the original contract specified. Mr. Townsend, however, was not impressed with the argument that a trip to Wimbledon had not been foreseen at the time the papers had been signed.

"Well, you know best," sighed Mrs. Farley. "I was only thinking that the MacIntyre Syndicate has been anxious to secure Florence's services for some time, and as her contract with you expires this coming fall—"

"Wait a minute, Mrs. Farley, just wait a minute, please. Now let's talk this over quietly. I didn't say your terms weren't reasonable; I think they are. It's the boss I have to convince, you know. We never paid such a big sum to anyone in sport before. Don't know what he'd say about it. I mean he likes Miss Farley's stuff, and all that, but—well, I'll tell you what to do. You're sailing on the *Luxuria* at midnight? Suite B, A deck. Fine. Now I tell you what. I'll come down to the boat by ten, at the latest, with his answer. And don't you do anything about next year until you hear from me. Understand? Those MacIntyre people—I'd hate to see Miss Farley tied up with a gang of pirates like that, honest I would."

The *Luxuria* sailed at midnight with the Farley family, or at least the female portion of it. The next morning the *Daily Mail* in a large half-page advertisement announced that Miss Florence Farley would write every day for the next two months "a complete, accurate, and lively description of tennis in Europe from the viewpoint of a competitor."

In Mr. Townsend's safe was a new contract running for another two years. It carried a figure in ink, written over a typewritten figure, and was for exactly three times as much as Miss Florence Farley had been receiving previously.

At the moment that the *Luxuria* was being warped out of her pier, the London correspondent of the *Daily Mail* was

sitting in a small office in Fleet Street, waving a long telegram at his assistant.

"Gotta write all the stuff for this girl champion, Farley.
What the hell do they think I am, besides all my regular
work to shove this on me? I'll send 'em what I please, that's
what I'll do, and if they don't like it they can fire me. Sick of
this job; the more work you do the more they give you. Can
you imagine that, Jake, writing stuff for a schoolgirl?"

Neither Florence nor her mother to this day can tell you
how they happened to meet Cynthia Gladesborough in London, who introduced them, or where they were presented.
Somebody at a tea, a dinner dance, somebody after or during Wimbledon brought them together; the meeting proved
mutually beneficial. Lady Gladesborough, who it appeared
had no home, was at home quite as much in Berlin and
Rome as in London. She had a bigger, a broader conception
of sport than even Mrs. Farley; she could look ahead and
visualize the future in a manner that was impossible for the
little lady from Plainville, New York.

Cynthia, Lady Gladesborough, was the sort of woman it
did not help to be seen with in public in London. Long before Mrs. Farley discovered this, the Englishwoman had
proved her indispensability in many ways. Left without
money after the War, with nothing but a title and her wits
to keep her from starvation, the only remaining member of
the Gladesborough family had done rather well by herself
in the years since the Armistice. Did you wish to be presented at Court? See Cynthia Gladesborough. Did you wish
a shooting place for August where you would be in and not
out of society? Cynthia Gladesborough would procure it for
you. Was it your wish to be distinguished during the London season? Anything could be managed provided you knew
Cynthia Gladesborough . . . and had money.

For several days she studied them, wondering how they

could be made profitable, until she heard from the parent of
the daughter's versatility. A singer? Just the thing. That next
afternoon she was back with a proposition so delicately
veiled, so gently insinuated, that one felt it would be cruel
to refuse. In fact, she always made you feel you were doing
her a favor. It appeared that Lady Mountaspen, the wife of
the British Foreign Secretary, had seen Florence at Wimbledon and had been so struck with her charm. Would dear
Mrs. Farley bring her daughter to a small dinner at Eaton
Square, and perhaps she could induce Florence to sing one
or two of those topping Negro spirituals afterward? Just one
or two. Needless to say, dear Mrs. Farley would not refuse,
would understand how Her Ladyship felt, and could accept
this small check. For some pet charity, you know. Once the
thing was done the second time was easier by far.

It was at this party that they met Mary Garden. The great
singer listened with interest and attention to the fresh-faced
girl who had that afternoon jumped from being a Champion
to becoming a World's Champion, and said conventionally
nice things to the mother afterward. From this the story
spread that Florence had "studied under Mary Garden," as
the billboards put it later on at home. What with the singing and the writing, their stay was not unprofitable, and on
the whole enjoyable.

"Have you heard Florence Farley sing?" "Have you seen
Florence Farley play yet?" These were the questions London society asked itself continually during their visit. She
gave a few exhibitions, more than living up to her reputation as a World's Champion, mercilessly beating the English
women pitted against her. Unlike those toughened, tanned,
weather-beaten specimens of British womanhood who op-
posed her on the fields of sport, she was still an eager,
happy, attractive schoolgirl, smiling, frowning, anxious, im-
petuous, joyous, and dismayed in turn. She was a girl, not a
human machine. London, and particularly London society

and that part of London society eager for lions, had almost forgotten that a female champion in sport could flatter the lust of the eye. In ten days Florence Farley had captured the city. Her name was in every newspaper, her picture in every magazine, her songs upon every lip.

She and her mother were fêted and entertained wherever they went. Her fees rose with her popularity. To dine with Florence Farley and her mother was an expensive undertaking; to be asked to dinner when they were present was indeed a testimony to your importance in the great world. Several weeks before they left, a concert manager called upon Mrs. Farley with suggestions for one afternoon appearance. He was sent packing by Cynthia Gladesborough, who returned later in the day with a manager willing to put Florence on for five matinees in succession.

THE ONLY CHANCE TO SEE AND HEAR THE VERSATILE WORLD'S CHAMPION.

HEAR FLORENCE FARLEY SING HER FAMOUS AMERICAN NEGRO SPIRITUALS.

The performance was adequately advertised, and before daybreak on the first afternoon a queue was waiting in a chilling drizzle for the doors to open ten hours later. Seats were obtainable only from Keith, Prowse and Co., at an amazing premium; hundreds were turned away at each matinee.

Meanwhile back in Plainville, Jim Farley was parking his new straight eight in the garage which had just been built under his careful supervision. He had ceased looking for a job.

By the end of Florence's second year as Champion of the World, her relationship to her mother had undergone a subtle change. The change was more real than apparent. Externally they were just the same "good pals" as ever. Outwardly Florence and her mother were inseparable; whatever they did, her mother's opinion was consulted. At any rate in public. But in private, in their twin beds in the hotel room, in the privacy of their suite on A deck of the *Luxuria* (the one occupied by the Prince when he crossed in '22) an astonished world would have learned that the mother of Happy Florence Farley, the Girl with the Laughing Voice, simply did not count in the general scheme of things. Florence was her own manager now.

Nor could one deny that the champion was able to take care of herself in a broken field, either. The years of exacting discipline to master a sport in many ways as complicated as an art or a profession, the constant subjugation of herself to her work, the encounters with the keenest minds in championship matches, minds which had to be mastered and subdued before their possessors were worsted physically—all this had taught her many a stern lesson from which she did not fail to draw profit. Her relations with the press, with the officials of the Association upon whose favors so much depended, with her various business associates, were all nicely adjusted and attuned. She knew the men and policies as well as the politics of the National Association as her mother could never know or hope to know them; she kept a control of affairs that her mother could never keep and, using that lady as a shield, she ran her life upon the' narrow ridge between amateurism and professionalism with a skill and hardihood that even her parent, who was frequently exasperated and always uneasy about her, was forced to admire.

Thus the telephone rang in their private suite. The secretary—Florence's first big dispute with her mother was over the secretary, it was also her first big victory—answered:

"Mr. Fletcher, Miss Farley."

"Oh—I'm too busy. Tell him to call later—no, give me the 'phone, I suppose I'd better talk now. . . . Hello, Duncan. What's that? Not today, my dear. I don't think I can. No, I'm all tied up today, Duncan. Well, let me see. Come up at one and take me to lunch. No, I'll meet you, meet you at the Ritz. Yes, at one. Good-by."

"Florence!" her mother expostulated. "How rude you're getting to be. Asking Mr. Fletcher to take you to lunch at the Ritz. And besides, he is such a prominent man in the Association, you'll get into trouble—"

"Well, if Dunc Fletcher wants to see me he'll have to buy me a meal, that's all. Besides, he isn't prominent any more. Or he won't be after next winter. Mr. Dudley's going in. Yes, they're getting Fletcher out; he's much too old-fashioned for this crowd. They need some new blood, wake 'em up a little."

Her mother gasped at the news. Mr. Fletcher out of the Association? It was as if the President of the United States had suddenly died. As if the country had gone mad. Mr. Fletcher out. She could not foresee their future without his help and assistance, so closely had he been bound up in their lives for years past. Again the telephone tinkled.

"Mr. Dudley," droned the secretary. "Oh, just a minute please, Mr. Dudley." And she handed the instrument to Florence, who indeed had reached for it as his name was spoken.

The voice of the champion was as different from the casual tone she used with Mr. Fletcher as her game was different against different kinds of players. "Ooohh, Mr. Dudley, it's so good of you to bother to call me up. . . . Yes, I want to see you, too. . . . There are just hundreds of things I must ask your advice about. . . . Baltimore? Well, I don't know about Baltimore; but perhaps you—that's one of the things I'm anxious to discuss with you. . . . You don't? . . . Oh, he's a friend of yours. Of course, if he's a friend of yours that makes all the difference in the world. I'd love to play Baltimore. But when can I see you, Mr. Dudley? Today. . . . That'll be delightful. . . . Could you come up and have some tea with me here at five? Yes, at five. . . . Don't send up your name, just come up, 1486. At five. I'll be looking forward to seeing you. Good-by."

The doorbell jingled. On tiptoe the secretary left the room. She returned a few minutes later. "The young lady from the *Times-Despatch*, Miss Farley. That interview, you know. Mr. Smith arranged for it last week."

"A girl? But I thought—I imagined they were sending a man. I just hate girl reporters. Horrid things. Well, I suppose I'll have to see her. Take her into the parlor. And then get that interview out of the file and read it to me while I'm doing my hair."

Ten minutes later the girl reporter, notebook in hand, was getting from the lips of Miss Farley, the World's Champion, an interview which would please any managing editor.

"Yes, I take my sport, you know, just as a game. My music is the principal thing in my life. Of course, I believe a champion has a duty, a great duty to the public who support games. . . . A duty to play fair, to win or lose with a smile. Yes, that's the chief thing about sport, isn't it? A message to the girls of America? Tell them not to take any game too seriously. That's what I always say to my mumsy. Remember it's just a game, win or lose. Now music, that's a thing you can devote your life to, can't you? With me, my sport has always been secondary to my music, even when I was a teeny, weeny child. I remember Mary Garden—oh, yes, I know her very well; you see she gave me the benefit of her knowledge when I was in London two years ago—well, I remember Mary saying to me once that whatever one loves one should make the really big thing in one's life. And I really love my music. Sport—oh, I've played off and on since I was ten, I think. Yes, but I always play in moderation.

"The new President of the Association. Mr. Dudley? Oooohh, are you sure? You heard . . . you did? I just adore Mr. Dudley. But you mustn't put that in the paper, will you? Mr. Fletcher was a lovely man, too. But Mr. Dudley

is—well, he's more dignified, isn't he? I mean he's more conservative. In a way. Not that I don't get along with Mr.
Fletcher, oh, perfectly. We're old friends, very old friends.
But I admire conservative people, don't you? I like all the
officials, though; we never have the slightest difficulty. The
amateur rule? Oh, no, there's never any trouble. I lean backward to observe all the rules of the Association—set an example; a champion should. Don't you think? Yes. Is that all?
So good of you to take the trouble to come way up here on
a hot day like this. Don't forget my message to the American
girls, will you? Play fair. Don't take games too seriously.
Lose or win with a smile. That's the one great lesson sport
teaches us. Thank you so much. Good-by. Good-by. . . .

   "God, what a woman! Miss Jackson! *Miss Jackson!* Get hold
of Mr. Dudley. How do I know where he is? Tell him to
come around at four instead of five. And ask him to bring
his car."

   No girl ever won the championship of the United States
eight times in succession. Miss Florence Farley was getting
ready to do so, and what she set her mind upon doing she
seldom failed in. At the moment she was seated in front of
the same dressing table she had been seated before as a
child with pigtails down her back when she went out for
her first championship. Eight years later she was Champion
of the World, devoting more attention to her countenance
than she did when she appeared upon the concert stage, an
event which happened with greater frequency as the years
rolled by. The only difference in the room was that her
mother, who had occupied the wicker armchair in previous
years, was no longer present. Today it held precariously
Miss Farley's secretary, notebook in hand. Upon the floor
was a pile of opened letters.

   From an array of bottles, tubes, and glass jars with glass
stoppers on the narrow table, she took cold cream out of a

square white receptacle marked "cleansing," spreading it carefully over her face. This, by the way, is the cream you have seen advertised as assisting Miss Florence Farley, Champion of the World, to keep freckles off her face under the hottest sun.

"From Nelson's Stores," droned the secretary. "A concert, on the twenty-ninth, with two stars from the Metropolitan."

"Price?" said the Champion, briskly, between rubs.

"No mention."

"Write 'em and tell 'em our price. No, hold on. . . . They've got lots of money. Write and ask their terms."

Meanwhile she took another kind of cream marked "Tissue," then with the aid of a towel wiped them both off with careful, adept movements. This, by the way, is the cream you may have noticed advertised on the billboards as used by Florence Farley, the World's Champion, to preserve a perfect complexion.

"Gunmetal Soap, testimonial. Five hundred, name, thousand for picture, advertising display, and interview why Gunmetal benefits face pores."

The World's Champion was in the act of grabbing a bottle bearing the magic word "Astringent." A paper label pasted on the bottle bore the words, "As used by Florence Farley." She paused a moment, the container suspended in the air, and dictated a reply.

"Miss Farley directs me to say she would be happy to see you Tuesday at four-thirty at the Ritz to discuss the matter contained in yours of the whatever it is. Next."

"Indianapolis, Lincoln, Nebraska, and Los Angeles want you the same week next month. You have that held open for the Newport party with Mr. Duggan and his family. . . ."

"Never mind that bird. What's the best of the three? Los Angeles? Yes, they know how to spend money out there. All right. Wire them to send reservations on the Sunset Limited from New Orleans the week before the tournament. And we go to New Orleans, tell them, on that fast train of the Pennsy. Next."

With a deft hand she touched the tops of the bottles and boxes on the table and picked out a square cardboard container bearing the entrancing name, "Farley Flower Powder, Spanish Rachel Shade." The white chalk suffused her tortured face. There was a knock at the door.

"Yes." Her voice had the timbre and the sweetness that had made her name famous to music lovers the world over, that had thrilled audiences (and managers) from San Diego to Albany.

"It's me, Florence."

The voice of the champion dulled perceptibly. "Oh. Come in."

Her mother entered. "I just wanted to know, dear . . . I just wondered where we were going next month. Your father telephoned this morning and thought maybe when you were through with the Championships we might all be able to spend a week at the old camp. You know we haven't been there for years."

"Can't, mumsy. Los Angeles." And she continued with earnestness and diligence the application of the lipstick.

"Across the continent in mid-July? Why, Florence! I thought it was all fixed up. . . . I thought you were going to Newport with those Providence people."

"Uhuh. I had it down for Newport, but the Los Angeles crowd have the dough. They put up a proposition that's too good to refuse."

"Florence," said her mother, reprovingly, but also a little timidly. "Florence, you oughtn't to talk that way. It's disgraceful."

"There you go again, mumsy. Cut the Civil War stuff, will you? I'm not in this for my health exclusively, understand? And what's more, I haven't got much more time left as champion, either."

A knock at the door. "Miss Farley. Are you ready? They're waiting outside."

"Com*ming*, com*ming*. All ready," sang out the Champion in the voice that made the newspapers call her Happy Florence Farley, the Girl with the Laughing Voice.

"Come along, mother dear." And the Champion emerged from the dressing room with her arm about her mother's waist. Inseparable, those two!

So You Think
Picking Horses Is Tough

This piece, which is nothing special as literature, gave me a good deal of satisfaction at the time I wrote it for the HERALD TRIBUNE, *because it won me kind words from my farming neighbors.*

The idea came from a conversation I had with Joe Williams and Willard Mullin on a train to Baltimore. We were on our way to the Preakness at Pimlico.

I found myself passionately advocating the poise and gameness of the farmer as a gambler. I rated him high above the largest horse-plunger.

Joe and Willard needled me some, I guess, thus fixing the extravagances I had uttered in my mind. So when I got back to New York I wrote a column and this is it.

STANLEY WOODWARD

There are two major brands of gambling in the United States: (a) betting on horses, (b) farming.

The latter outstrips the former many times over in volume and it involves sums and an amount of sporting spirit that would stagger the heaviest racetrack gambler. The farmer gambles for his living day after day. He hocks his piano, sells liens on his barn and livestock and goes to any extreme when he sees a good thing in the milk market or a three-crop parlay.

He is no small-time operator, sticking a few thousand dollars in surplus cash through a mutuel window. When he plays an entry or a double or a multiple parlay, he goes at it with everything he owns supplemented by all he can raise that he doesn't own.

The farmer decides to improve his dairy herd, so he goes to a cattle sale and buys a bull for a thousand dollars, which he obtained by cashing his wife's insurance. He takes the bull home. It is big and vicious, so he spends another thousand dollars, obtained by selling off the north forty, to build a house and pen for it. The pen has to be made of nine-foot steel pipe sunk three feet in concrete. The house is made of poured concrete and when the farmer gets no higher than the floor he finds he is going to need five hundred dollars more. This he gets by hocking his wheat crop, which looks as if it might be something and which he has planned to use to provide piano study in New York for his daughter, Muriel Mae.

He gets the pen finished and with the aid of three other men and four pitchforks he puts the bull in it. The bull snorts joyously for half an hour while running back and forth in the handsome pen. Then he eats a piece of baling wire with his hay and dies. The farmer persuades a rendering works to come around two days later and haul away two thousand pounds of ex-bull.

It can easily be seen that the farmer is now in a worse position than the greatest race track plunger on his worst day. However, he writes the bull situation off, hocks and mortgages some more of his property and goes about his daily gambling.

Fortunately, the milk, eggs and truck from the place will keep his family alive for a while. To reassure himself, he goes and looks at his oats and wheat. The wheat is part of a two-crop parlay, to be followed next year by a combination of timothy and red clover which he had sowed with the wheat the previous fall.

The wheat is beautiful, but he can't see any clover and timothy. Mentally figuring the cost and feasibility of re-planting, he tries to concentrate on admiring the wheat. It is really beautiful. That night comes a storm which not only takes the roof off the chicken house but flattens the wheat, rendering it virtually null and void.

The next day the farmer concentrates on admiring his oats. They are beginning to show a tendency to curl up and lie down ("lodge" is the term). Something may be saved, however. The farmer goes back to hunt in the chicken house for enough eggs for supper. Mentally he goes over what he gambled on the wheat and oats. It figures up to about $13 an acre, or $230 for twenty "allotted" acres of wheat, and $11 an acre for the oats which is a free crop under govern-ment regulations.

He cheers himself up by thinking that the two hundred dollars he spent for lime will have a good effect on the soil next year. In other words, he has a bare chance of cashing a show ticket.

In order to get started again he sells off his three best dairy cows, or, at least, he contracts to sell them. The next morning he notices that all three are looking ill. The vet-erinarian finds they have chewed lead paint off a fence post and need to be "drenched."

In the middle of the "drenching" operation, which in-volves poking four yards of rubber hose down the throats of the cows and into their quadruple interiors, the customer who contracted to buy them appears with a check. He looks around hurriedly, tears up the check and runs.

Two of the cows get well, the other dies. The customer who retreated was a cattle buyer who had been all over the country looking for animals. He carried on his shoes a little organism known as Brucella Abortis Bang. This was destined to get into the manger and infect the whole herd, necessitating slaughter.

Of course, the farmer didn't know that at the time, so he was chiefly concerned with the loss of one cow and his failure to make the sale.

The next day he cheers up and starts haying. He fears bad weather and puts the hay in a little green. He sprinkles salt on it, a maneuver which he imagines will keep it from heating but which his county agent would tell him was merely a waste of salt.

The hay heats and burns his barn down. It catches his house and burns that down, too. It burns up all his chickens and his corn crib. Fortunately he has kept all his insurance. He collects.

Then a city fellow comes by, likes the maple trees and the brook and buys the farm for $20,000. The farmer charges him $2,500 extra for the bull pen, which did not burn, being made of concrete and steel. For the newly infected cows he gets another $4,000.

After paying his debts he finds he has $22,000. He puts it in war bonds, moves to an apartment in the city and goes to work in an airplane factory.

He has pocketsful of cash, so on Saturdays he goes to the racetrack and bets at the fifty-dollar window. He becomes known as a plunger. Members of his Bible class back home read about him in the paper and say, "Ain't it too bad Henry's turned to gambling!"

The Great Game of Basebrawl

This article first appeared in the New York *Daily News*, June 14, 1957, and is reprinted by permission of Dick Young and that newspaper.

As exciting as fights are on baseball fields, few ever result in blows being struck. This one was different: Drysdale, side-stepping Logan's charge as I recall it, struck two straight blows to the head, opening a cut over Johnny's eye. In the general melee that followed, Gil Hodges, the perennial peace-maker, busily dragged bodies, by the protruding legs, off Drysdale, who was being piled on. Later, when Logan was asked if Don had opened the cut over his eye, Johnny smiled and said: "No, that was from a previous fight."

DICK YOUNG

Don Drysdale, 6-ft.-5-in., 198-pound Dodger pitcher, took on one-third of the Braves' starting lineup yesterday in a chain-reaction brawl that ranks high in the hysterical history of Ebbets Field. It was a furious reaction to a fast ball that had dug into the back of Braves' shortstop John Logan in the second inning of the Dodgers-Braves game.

Quickly and successively, Brooklyn's lanky young pitcher became embroiled with Logan, Ed Mathews and Carl Sawatski of the Braves. Players from both teams milled and clutched—some striving for the restoration of peace, some looking for additional trouble.

Drysdale and Logan, the main-eventers, were thrown out by Umpire Jocko Conlan. Logan suffered a jagged cut and a lump above the left eye, plus a light bruise on the left cheek. Drysdale displayed mottled discoloration around the collar bone. Gil Hodges, the self-appointed referee, sustained a slight spike wound high on the right thigh.

"He knows he's in for a battle when he throws at somebody," said Logan, soaking up his post-fight shower.

Drysdale denied throwing at Logan. "I was just trying to jam him ("jam" is baseball jargon for a pitch off the fists), and the ball tailed in on him."

Logan follows leadoff man Bill Bruton in the Milwaukee batting order. Bruton had banged Drysdale for a homer in the first inning, and again in the second. It is the "code of the hills" that when balls are being hit out of the park in bunches, the batter following the most recent homer hitter had better be prepared to duck.

Logan didn't duck far enough. He twisted, but took the pitch hard in the back. Johnny, writhing as though to shake off the sting, took a few slow steps toward first. As he walked, Johnny held the bat poised over his head as though debating whether to toss it away or use it.

Almost reluctantly, he flung the bat to the ground in the direction of the Dodger dugout, and continued his deliberate steps in the general direction of first base. Actually, Logan, in his blind anger, had drifted out of the base line. He was well onto the grass when he suddenly started to snap angry words at Drysdale. Drysdale answered back, and Logan, who had now reached first, turned and strode toward the mound.

Drysdale dropped his glove and stalked toward Logan. It

looked like a scene from "High Noon," with Drysdale as Gary Cooper.

Logan drew first. He made a wild lunge at Drysdale and the fight was on.

ROUND ONE: Logan led with a left, but was caught coming in by Drysdale's sharp combination to the head. Dodger first-sacker Gil Hodges and Milwaukee first base coach Johnny Riddle, trailing after Logan, grabbed him from behind and dragged him away. (I gave this round to Drysdale.)

ROUND TWO: Ed Mathews, plowing through the crowd of players, jumped Drysdale, wrestled him to the ground and tried to pummel him, but Drysdale covered effectively. Hodges grabbed Mathews by the right leg, pulled him off Drysdale and deposited him on the third base side of the melee. (I gave this round to Mathews.)

ROUND THREE: As Drysdale rose to one knee, Catcher Carl Sawatski, wearing his shin guards and chest protector, jumped Drysdale, and again wrestled him to the ground. Before Hodges could move in, other Dodgers and Braves broke it up. (I called this round even.)

Umpire Conlan ejected Logan and Drysdale, but allowed Mathews and Sawatski to remain in the game. "It's the general practice," the ump explained later, "to throw out the two guys who started it."

In the Brook clubhouse, Drysdale was toweling himself when he related the verbal exchange that had led to the brawl:

Logan: "I'll get you when you come into second base."

Drysdale: "Love second base! If you got a beef, come get it over with right now."

Logan confirmed the tête-à-tête. "I guess he thought I would back off," Johnny announced proudly.

This Logan never backs off. His career is spotted with fights from Forty-second Street to Milwaukee. On May 27, he tangled with Cincy's Hal Jeffcoat. Oddly, Ed Mathews also kibitzed that fight, and in the resultant free-for-all had his right wrist stepped on by Reds' coach Jimmy Dykes. Mathews was out a week, and still wears tape as a memento.

Three years ago, in Cincinnati, Logan battled with Jim Greengrass, won the newspaper decision and, as he left the field, took on Johnny Temple and knocked him down.

When there aren't enough opponents around to fight, Logan keeps in shape by sparring with teammates. In 1953, in a pub on East Forty-second Street, Johnny engaged in a midnight match with Braves' pitcher Vern Bickford. Logan injured his hand in that scrap.

As a youngster, Johnny did some amateur fighting. He is a compact 5-ft.-11 and weighs 185. He is not of the Hibernian Logans. His ancestors came from County Odessa, or thereabouts and, somewhere along the line, the family adopted the name of Logan. But Johnny does not care to be called "The Mad Russian."

The crowd was 8,778, and the gate $19,241.